I0806621

Praise for *How to Succeed in Musical Theatre Without Really Dying*

"Lindsay Mendez and Ryan Scott Oliver run a great class in auditioning and performing for musical theatre, and beyond that, they have a ton of experience, both happy and not-so-happy, in the business of making a career in musical theatre. If I were a performer looking for tips, information, and advice, I'd certainly turn to them!"

—Stephen Schwartz, Tony Award–nominated composer-lyricist (*Wicked*, *Pippin*)

"I can't imagine any better guides than Lindsay Mendez and Ryan Scott Oliver. They have been celebrated professionals and teachers for years and really know how the industry and artistry of musical theatre work."

—Michael Greif, Tony Award–nominated director (*Rent*, *Next to Normal*, *Dear Evan Hansen*)

"In *How to Succeed in Musical Theatre Without Really Dying*, Lindsay Mendez and Ryan Scott Oliver have created an indispensable how-to guide for success in today's industry. If you possess talent, this is destined to be THE owner's manual for developing it into a thriving career. Having worked with Lindsay on Broadway in *Carousel* and admired her intelligence, integrity, and flawless vocal technique, I'm not surprised. *How to Succeed* is honest, passionate, and practical, with granular strategies for everything from time and financial management to cutting the best 32-bar audition selection. Nothing is sugar-coated, but the expert guidance is consistently inspiring, rooted in the writers' understanding that the difference between competence and the excellence that gets you hired hinges on working hard, working smart, and persisting."

—Renée Fleming, internationally acclaimed soprano

"What Ryan and Lindsay have masterfully created is an essential road map for actors. They provide a wealth of knowledge and sage advice pertaining to every facet of the industry. From vocal technique to audition preparation, from self-marketing and proper entertainment industry etiquette, this book is the perfect manual to taking care of one's self as an artist and as a human being, and should be required reading for anyone looking to embark on a professional career in musical theatre."

—Patrick Goodwin, CSA, Broadway casting director

"Lindsay and Ryan are phenomenal teachers who really understand what it takes to prepare for an audition. And their combined knowledge about what to have in your 'book' is truly the best. I wish I had this book when I was starting out!"

—Anne L. Nathan, Broadway actress and educator (*Thoroughly Modern Millie*, *Once*)

"If I were an actor, Lindsay Mendez is pretty much the only person I would ever need to look to for advice and guidance. Not only is she a perfect performer in every way, but she has the mind of a director—and in my experience working with her, her ideas are always right. When Lindsay speaks, I always always wanna hear what she has to say."

—Trip Cullman, Broadway director (*Significant Other, Choir Boy*)

"Simply put, *How to Succeed in Musical Theatre Without Really Dying* is the book I wish I had when I was first coming up in this business. It's the book I *still need* as a theatre educator. It's the book I want all college musical theatre programs to assign as required reading. Compiled from years of hard-won wisdom, this nonprescriptive, many-paths-up-the-mountain guide to—not just success—but *longevity* in business we call 'show' is the balm for any aspiring musical theatre artist's nerves. Read it and sigh a breath of relief."

—Adam Chanler-Berat, Broadway actor and educator (*Next to Normal, Peter and the Starcatchers*)

"I've had the pleasure of teaching alongside Lindsay and Ryan as a guest teacher in their popular Actor Therapy classes in New York City. This book is a powerful extension of the straight-talk, no-nonsense approach they bring to both the craft and business of musical theatre. Knowledge is power—and this book is packed with invaluable insights gained from their collective decades of experience in the industry and the classroom."

—Telly Leung, Broadway actor and educator (*Allegiance, Phantom of the Opera*)

"In a showbiz jungle that can make even the sanest artist spiral, Ryan Scott Oliver and Lindsay Mendez are like your wise, wildly talented theatre friends who actually get it. With a treasure trove of experience and a knack for keeping it real, they offer up guidance that's equal parts heart, humor, and hard-earned truth. This book doesn't just talk at artists—it chats with them, peeling back the mystery of building a meaningful, sustainable life in the arts (with jazz hands and honesty in equal measure). A deeply worthwhile read for any performer."

—Holly Buczek, casting director at HDB Casting

HOW TO SUCCEED IN MUSICAL THEATRE WITHOUT REALLY DYING

HOW TO SUCCEED IN MUSICAL THEATRE WITHOUT REALLY DYING

The Actor's Guide to Booking Work and Building a Career That Lasts

LINDSAY MENDEZ AND RYAN SCOTT OLIVER

BENBELLA

BenBella Books, Inc.
Dallas, TX

BenBella Books, Inc.
8080 N. Central Expressway
Suite 1700
Dallas, TX 75206
benbellabooks.com
Send feedback to feedback@benbellabooks.com

BenBella is a federally registered trademark.

Printed in the United States of America
10 9 8 7 6 5 4 3 2 1

Library of Congress Control Number: 2025040051
ISBN 9781637747995 (trade paperback)
ISBN 9781637748008 (electronic)

Editing by Leah Wilson and Sarah Modlin
Copyediting by Amy Handy
Proofreading by Marissa Wold Uhrina and Lisa Story
Text design and composition by PerfecType, Nashville, TN
Cover design by Morgan Carr
Printed by Lake Book Manufacturing

For Sherry and Beckie,
who nurtured the dream from the beginning,

and Rylee, Ellie, Imogen, Lucille, and Ruby,
who will carry it on. Broadway is waiting for you.

CONTENTS

Foreword xvii

An Introduction 1

The Struggle Is Real 9

PART 1: BUILDING IT

~~Type~~ Defining Who You Are 17

Forget About "Type" 17
The First Quality: Voice 19
The Second Quality: Look 24
The Third Quality: Energy 27
The Fourth Quality: Authenticity 30
Putting It Together: The Branding Statement 31
Branding and Specificity in Practice 33
The Legend of the "Reginacady" 35
Troubleshooting Specificity 36
Your Truth Shall Set You Free 39

Building Your Professional Book 41

Preparing Your Book 42
Your Songs Are First Impressions 43
B-B-B-Ballads!! 44

Genres 47
The Essential Songs in Your Book 49
Comedy Songs: LOL? 53
Other Songs You May Need 56
Troubleshooting Genre 59
Using Your Brand to Select Material 60
Creating a "Pathway" Through Your Book 61
The Overdone Song and Other Myths 61
Coding in Repertoire 63
Other Songs to Avoid 65
Examples of Solid Audition Books 67
Troubleshooting Your Book 71
You Don't Need a New Song for Every Audition 73

The Perfect Audition Cut **75**
The Shape of a Good Cut 78
Shortcuts and Tips for Cutting Music 80
Marking Your Music 85
Troubleshooting Cuts 85

How Working Actors Tell Stories **91**
Storytelling Requires Structure 93
Acting Means Action 93
Acting an Audition Cut Versus Acting Larger Forms 94
Song Interpretation, in Brief 95
Before You Begin: Analysis 96
Context (Story) 99
Actor Versus Character 101
The Moment Before (Inciting Incident) 102
What Do You Want? (Objective) 103

Why Do You Want It? (Stakes) 104
Where Are You? (Location) 105
To Whom Are You Singing? (Scene Partner) 106
What Are You Doing? (Primary Action) 109
How Are You Doing It? (Tactics) 110
In the End, What Happens? (Win/Lose) 112
Example: "Whatever Lola Wants" 113
All Choices Are Positive 115
Example: "I Dreamed a Dream" 115
Example: "I'm Not Afraid of Anything" 117
Interpreting Radio Music 121
Depth and Connection 124
Trust the Process 129

Advanced Audition Techniques. 131

(Almost) Never Lead with a Ballad 132
Walking into the Room 133
Communicating with Your Accompanist 133
Slating and Introducing Your Material 134
Transitioning into Your Story 135
Preparation to Presentation 137
Notes on Vocal Approach by Genre 138
Focus 142
Grounding 145
Radio Songs: Feeling the Music in Your Body 149
Gestures 150
Expression and Energy 157
End with a Fire in Your Eyes and Let the Music Play Out 158
(Extremely) Common Storytelling Problems 159
And That's It 163

PART 2: DOING THE DAMN THING

The Actor's Ultimate Goal 167

The Sad, Sad Tale of the Audition Machine 167

Doing the Damn Thing 169

Getting the Damn Thing Done 170

You the Actor, Inc. 173

The Business Plan 174

Vision Statement 175

Mission Statement 181

Values Statement 183

Using Your Business Plan in Practice 188

Training and Self-Care 189

Training: The Beginning 190

Training II: The Revenge 196

Training III: Resurrection 197

Process-Oriented Perspective 198

Self-Care for the Actor 201

Money and the Hustle 205

No One Teaches You This Stuff 208

Establish a Budget for Your Lifestyle 209

The Artist's Hustle 101 212

Getting an Artist Hustle 216

Growing Your Artist Hustle 219

Artist Hustle FAQ 221

Track Your Finances 223

Save Your Money and Save Yourself 224

Stay Out of (Bad) Debt 225

Don't Live Off Your Savings 226

Websites and Social Media 229
Your Website: Come to My Garden 230
Website Basics Aren't Basic 231
The Very Important Video Page 234
Other Pages 238
Don't Blur Your Brand on Your Website 240
Social Media: Always True to You (In Its Fashion) 241
Post in Four Dimensions 244
Other Unspoken Rules of Social Media 246

Netwerqing 251
Netwerqing Like a Pro 252
The Life of the Parties 254
Survey Your Team 257
Making the Connection: Emails and Messages 260
Let's Go Out Tonight 265
Netwerqing Miscellany 267

Creating Your Own Opportunities 269
Goals, Mediums, and Stories 270
Producing Your Own Cabaret 273
Starting a Theatre Group 282

Time Management 287
Going to the Artist's "Office" 288
Taking Control of Your Time: Planning 290
Taking on the Day: Action 296
Sorting the Day 299
Reviewing the Damn Thing 302

PART 3: BUILDING IT

Congratulations! **305**

Headshots and Résumés **307**

The Shot You Want 308
Finding the Right Photographer 310
After the Shoot 314
A Résumé Is a Picture in Words 317
Résumé Formatting and Sections 318
Strategizing Your Résumé 326

Auditions **331**

Understanding Equity 331
When to Join Equity 334
Audition Basics 336
What You May Be Asked For at an Initial Audition 338
Kinds of Contracts 339
Other Kinds of Contracts 342
Where to Find Auditions 343
Climbing the Audition Ladder 344
Audition Strategy for Nonunion Actors 347
Audition Strategy for Equity Actors 349
What They Want You to Know 351
The Initial Audition Process 352
Troubleshooting What to Sing 354
Do the Assignment, Not Extra Credit 356
Callbacks 357
After the Audition 359
Self-Tapes 361
Managing Your Nerves 363
Every Audition Matters 366

Representation 367

How an Agent Works (for You) 368

College Agent Showcases 370

Pursuing an Agent 370

The Agent Meeting 374

Signing and Beyond 378

Agent Troubleshooting 379

Negotiating Without an Agent 382

Managers 385

Conclusion: Rejecting Rejection 389

Now for the Megamix 397

Acknowledgments 401

Index of Referenced Musicals 403

Credits 411

FOREWORD

Jonathan Groff

Only you can know what is right for you. Take everything with a grain of salt. See this while you read it. Follow your gut. I've gotten great advice from people I do not respect. I've gotten the wrong advice from people I love and admire. Someone's advice will not give you the key to your success—or maybe it will. You won't become successful by following this book to the letter—or maybe you will. Techniques that help you for a while can suddenly become unhelpful. Don't hold on to things that aren't working for you. Take whatever resonates and leave the rest. Being open to new thoughts while also thinking critically is a paradox that I am still trying to live every day.

If you are reading this book, I imagine you have dreams of working on Broadway, or at least of "making it" in the theater in some way. One of my biggest realizations once I "made it" in New York was that, in an essential way, being on Broadway is the exact same thing as being in the school play. For me, that revelation was great news. I love and have always loved doing theater wherever I can—in the middle school play, in a community theater production, in a casino at Christmas while performing on a tour of *The Sound of Music*, or center stage in a Broadway show. The potential for that magical exchange between performer and audience is always there in theater (theatre . . . ?!), no matter the venue.

One of the biggest surprises for me in being on Broadway is that there are a lot of unhappy people there. I think this is a reflection of what can happen when we finally get what we think we want. Many people feel that "once I get on Broadway . . ." or "once I play a lead . . ." or "once I get a great review . . ." or "once I'm in a hit . . ." or "once I win a Tony . . ."—then I will be happy. And achieving our goals often makes us feel great—for a moment.

I became dear friends with the co-author of this book Lindsay Mendez when we got cast in the acclaimed revival of *Merrily We Roll Along*. The experience was a dream come true for many of us, the rediscovery of a Steven Sondheim masterpiece. The material was challenging and rewarding, and many of the artists working on it were at the top of their game.

Playing Frank in *Merrily* also brought me my first Tony Award. I had been in the business at that point for twenty years and in the lead up to the Tonys that year everyone was telling me that it was "my time." I felt gratitude for the love and appreciation from my peers. For them, it was now "my time." For me, I had been living "my time" since the day I stepped off the Amtrak train on October 21, 2004, when I moved to New York from Lancaster, Pennsylvania.

I moved to New York because I was passionately in love with the theater and I wanted to be a part of it in any way I could. My love was pure and I relished every step that got me closer to my passion. There were many wins and losses in those early stages of my career (as there still are), but I came to realize that the temporary thrill of a win or the temporary pain of a loss couldn't shake the essential truth I was learning—the process is the opportunity. Truthfully, getting a job waiting tables on my first day living in New York gave me just as much of a thrill as winning a Tony Award twenty years later. No matter what "stage" you are in, there will be ups and downs. The real reward is a relationship to the process and the personal growth and awakening that can come through both the "good" and "bad" experiences.

For me, experience has always been the greatest teacher. Learning from teachers as experienced as Lindsay and Ryan can be invaluable. May their book be a part of your journey towards your passion. I hope you stay present with yourself as you read. It's your time.

Love,
Groff

AN INTRODUCTION

(Lindsay and RSO are in a rehearsal studio.)

Ryan Scott Oliver: So . . . we're recording our introduction as a conversation.

Lindsay Mendez: *(Singing from* Sideshow) "A private conversation . . ." Yeah, I think it's better.

RSO: Let's tell the people what they've picked up.

Lindsay: Well, people, you're about to learn our secrets. Specifically, the secret to navigating a life as a working musical theatre actor.

RSO: So many people have talent in musical theatre. But the whole picture is so much bigger than talent. This book maps out everything that happens between saying "I want to do this professionally" and *doing it* professionally.

Lindsay: Right. How to make a life for yourself doing it—not just one good year.

RSO: That's right. And we're showing you the way this business can be "businessed" like any other profession. It's something that you can study from all sides.

Lindsay: This book contains the collected, informed strategy of people who have done it, are still doing it, and are working alongside others who are doing it.

RSO: Some of our anxious readers might be wondering who this book is for.

Lindsay: Well, if they're anxious, it's probably for them.

RSO: For starters, it's for all early-career actors. We use "early-career" instead of "young." You don't have to be twenty-one to start a career in musical theatre. Whenever you're ready, this book is for you. It's not just for college students or recent grads, either.

Lindsay: It's also for those who didn't go to school—like me. And it's for working actors who've lost their way—like so many of the students we meet at Actor Therapy. *[Actor Therapy is Lindsay and RSO's acclaimed training program in New York City.]*

RSO: It's also for musical theatre educators. The arts have always been a place for self-discovery, but in many training programs, you have teachers or coaches telling students what their voice type is, what they "should" sing, roles they "should" play, and worst of all, telling them who they are—

Lindsay: But no one can tell you who you are. You *have to* figure that out on your own—by sorting through as much information and feedback as you can find. This book is going to encourage you to take a hard look in the mirror and reflect—on your voice, your energy, your look, and your authenticity.

RSO: Let's not get ahead of ourselves.

Lindsay: All right, all right.

RSO: Is this book just for New Yorkers trying to book Broadway?

Lindsay: Definitely not. These lessons apply to any big market. It's for anyone who is considering or actively pursuing musical theatre as a profession.

RSO: Right, even in major markets that do things differently than New York, this is a blueprint for what musical theatre practice is at the highest level.

Lindsay: That's a bold statement.

RSO: We're bold. Why do you think early-career artists need a book like this? Like, why can't they just skip this book?

Lindsay: For me, this book is partly the two of us sharing our experiences working in the industry, moving here from a faraway place, and saying, "I'm going to stake my claim in this town." It's also sharing what we've learned over the last thirteen years, from the thousands of actors who've come through our doors—the ones who say, "I'm here, trying to do what I love, but I feel totally lost. What do I do now?"

RSO: Right. Or "I was told that I'm XYZ, but I believe I'm something else. How do I realize myself fully, and present that effectively?"

Lindsay: There are lots of ways to break into this business, and we're going to explore that from all angles. Most busy actors we know have their head down, focusing on "doing the thing." There are individual books on acting, or on auditioning, on repertoire, on business—but most are written by academics and outsiders.

RSO: No shade to the scholars.

Lindsay: No, nothing but props to my smarties. But there isn't a comprehensive guide that collects all of those subjects *and* is written by working artists who are doing it. I think high school and college education helps you learn about yourself and what you can do, but then you're dropped on your ass in Midtown, and it's like, "Good luck to you. Figure it out."

RSO: Well, speaking of that, you mentioned you didn't go to college. You came all the way from Los Angeles to New York City. If you had this book on the day you got here, how would that have changed your experience at the start?

Lindsay: So many of my insecurities would have been alleviated. And I wouldn't have been lying awake at night, thinking, "Did I sing the right thing?" or "Is what I'm trying to show coming across?" A lot of the questions I had early on were about who I was and where I fit inside the industry. A book like this would have given me confidence—which could have opened doors sooner for me, no pun intended.

RSO: I don't get it.

Lindsay: It's a *Merrily* ref—

RSO: I also think that so much of this book is about dispelling myths and offering answers for today's musical theatre—a post–social media, post-pandemic, post–self-tape world. So many incredible artists we coach have star power hidden beneath misinformation, misdirection, and unhelpful feedback . . . but everything they *really* need to know—and what working actors and everyone behind the table knows—most people never get that information.

Lindsay: Right. That's the information you get by *doing* it, living it. Even in expensive BFA programs, you're still hearing about it at a distance, in a vacuum.

RSO: It's not about gatekeeping the information. It's about the reality that there are a billion actors and only a few jobs available at any one time—the kind of scarcity you'll find in any competitive profession. There's no single quick-fix secret that works for everyone, but there is a map to guide your private artistic journey. A lot of actors think this is a "pick me" sport like dodgeball, but it's much closer to training for the Olympics.

Lindsay: Sports . . . really?

RSO: It's what I had.

Lindsay: You're on your own path—which is why you need a survival guide like this one. People aren't just standing out on 8th Avenue, trying to help you. Everyone's trying to make it here, you know?

RSO: We should talk about how we've structured this book.

Lindsay: Go.

RSO: This book is in three parts. The first is called "Building It." We cover everything from understanding your audition book, to the songs that should be in it, to making a perfect cut, interpreting a song, and audition techniques. Nailing this part is the key to separating yourself from other people on the line—

Lindsay: Because the sad fact is that most actors come here thinking they've mastered it—

RSO: And maybe they *did* master it for high school, for college, for their community theatre. But in New York and other major markets, reaching mastery is on a whole new level—the highest level. So, part one is a soup-to-nuts manual to show actors how to get into casting's "yes pile"—

Lindsay: To be seen as somebody serious and ready to work. Not just a fan with a dream.

RSO: The second part of the book is called "Doing the Damn Thing," and it's an eight-part deep dive into the business *and the life* of the working artist. We're talking about finance and business plans and creating your own opportunities and networking and a lot more—all the subjects that, for so many people, might seem tedious and beside the point.

Lindsay: Like me. I was one of those people.

RSO: I was gonna ask if you were asleep.

Lindsay: Not anymore. Honestly, for me, the second part of this book—the business and life focus—it's paramount. I think most of us dream about success in musical theatre because we like to wear costumes, and get on stage, and share our feelings. And I think that that's great. But at the end of the day, you have to *live*. Pay your bills. Have health insurance. Exist beyond Broadway.

And I remember that hitting me really hard after my first Broadway show closed. Being like, "Oh shit, I don't have a job again. I won the prize and now it's over." And it was at that point I thought, "This isn't about one season. It's about every season for the rest of your life."

RSO: And you figure it out when you realize that show business has more to do with "business" than with "show." In fact, every artist is a small business. In a sense, we're all selling vacuum cleaners.

Lindsay: Which I think troubles young artists. But it shouldn't—if you want to buy a home, support a family, and (god forbid!) retire one day, at some point you have to think in dollars and cents.

RSO: S-E-N-S-E, right?

Lindsay: Of course.

RSO: Then the third part of this book is "Booking It." Headshots, résumés, representation, and the great, wide world of auditions. Most of our readers probably have a head start on all of that, but our focus is strategy: what makes a *useful* headshot, how to make your résumé speak compellingly, and how to (and when to) get representation—plus, how to navigate the relationship once you're in it.

Lindsay: Understanding the union and, if you're non-Equity, planning the right time to join. And finally, knowing which auditions to go to, which ones not to go to, how to prioritize your time, and how to build rapport with casting.

RSO: It's a lot of information, but we've been very intentional in the way we've organized it. There's a reason why we save "Auditions" for the end.

Lindsay: To say it again: it's a lot of information. When you start to think, "Why didn't anyone tell me about this?" or "I hadn't thought about this that way," you'll know you're stepping from the "outside" of the industry to the "inside"—

RSO: Regardless of what you've accomplished so far. For some readers, there might be a couple of chapters you won't totally grasp how to put into practice because of where you're at in your life. But that's why we hope this book will stay with you for a while—so that you can come back to those sections as you grow. When it's time to get that agent, or it's time to start supporting yourself financially, or you're ready to put on a solo cabaret—

Lindsay: Or you're totally lost, and you need to reset.

RSO: Yup. You, reading this book, you're receiving the collected answers to the many questions we've been asked over these years.

Lindsay: *(As Old Rose in* Titanic*)* "It's been eighty-four years . . ."

RSO: This book will solve a problem you've had, you're having, or you will have. In a way, we hope that when you finish this book, you'll feel both panic (at how much work there is to do—the work that most never realize they still have to do) and inspiration (at all you can accomplish, that's both in your control and easily in reach).

Lindsay: Absolutely. We'll affirm some of what you know and dispel many more myths you need to forget . . . and if you start to see the work ahead *and* feel empowered to do it, we've done our job—and so have you.

RSO: We're not fucking around. And we don't think you, reader, are fucking around, either. You're serious about this. You're completely aware of how hard it is to be in this business and do the thing. This is a blueprint for how to do the thing, strategically and successfully.

Lindsay: "Without really dying." While *thriving*, in fact. We're not promising you that this book is going to get you on Broadway in six months. We are promising you that you will find out more about who you are. The best of who you are, the "most you" that you can be—

RSO: Which is really the first mile on the rainbow brick road to Broadway. You can't get there without it, which is why so many lose their way.

Lindsay: And we're going to show you how to find stability.

RSO: How to look in the mirror and say, "I know what I'm doing."

Lindsay: "This is what I'm supposed to be doing."

RSO: And so long as you can enjoy that journey, you're going to be just fine. We promise.

(There is a long, heavy pause.)

Lindsay: . . . And scene.

RSO: And scene. Curtain.

Lindsay: Whew. Spilling all your secrets really takes it out of you.

RSO: Yeah, I feel like I was just on the stand.

Lindsay: That's what we get for recording the introduction last. For us, it's the end.

RSO: But for our reader, it's just the beginning.

Lindsay: Ooh, chills. Yeah. It's just the beginning.

THE STRUGGLE IS REAL

Meet Gabby. She's a few days away from twenty-nine, and tonight she's worried that her career as a musical theatre actress may be at its end.

Gabby arrived in New York City with a BFA in musical theatre, a killer voice, a decent knowledge of theatre history and the industry, and an expensive headshot. Though these are all things she was told would set her up for success on Broadway, she's been regularly disappointed that most of her auditions have come to nothing. Sure, she's freelanced with a few agents, landed a few paid gigs, and had a bunch of close callbacks . . . but so many years have passed without dependable momentum. While a few of her equally unhappy actor friends speculate that "the industry is against us," lately Gabby has decided, "I don't think I have what it takes."

Gabby's been thinking a lot about destiny. Specifically, hers. Maybe unconsciously, she's always believed the performing arts were a mystical business where a glorious few are preselected for greatness—and, she guesses, "sucks to suck" for the rest. At twelve years old, she wasn't wondering *if* she'd win a Tony, she was only trying to decide how many. Back then, Gabby carried with her a private guarantee that *she was special.* It was written in the stars that she would be chosen.

But suddenly she's practically thirty, dejected and bitter, and still considered early-career. Her life schedule has been revised too many times, and tonight she's found solace at the bottom of a bottle of six-dollar merlot.

She's decided that the business she once viewed as shrouded in mysticism is actually cursed by randomness. Her number was never called, the hour's too late, and she has no choice but to face the music—or lack thereof. And so Gabby abandons her lifelong love of musical theatre and resolves that tomorrow, she'll start figuring out a new career path.

> ***Most early-career musical theatre actors confuse competence with excellence.***

Gabby isn't a real person, exactly, but we've known hundreds and hundreds of actors whose stories mirror hers. We suspect you do, too.

Her story breaks our hearts because her crappy finale could have been rewritten. And if *your* story feels at all like Gabby's—regardless of how old you are, where you trained, or what credits you've accrued—we're confident we can help you write yourself a better ending.

The myth of the "It Factor"

Beyond excellence in acting is the falsehood of the "*It* Factor," the idea that says a lucky few are born with *it*, while most are not. "Some people got it and make it pay / Some people can't even give it away," Stephen Sondheim says through Mama Rose. Stars like Bernadette Peters, Hugh Jackman, and Audra McDonald have all been said to have *it*: bankable talent and a magnetic stage presence that leaves audiences talking long after the curtain falls.

But there's a reason Mama Rose has a breakdown spurred by this way of thinking. This is really a question of belief: fate versus free will.

Has some cosmic force predetermined the limitations of our talent and already decided how far we'll go? Are some of us inherently "good enough" to succeed, while the rest are just wasting time? Or is our future ultimately in our own hands? Can we shape it through the choices we make and the experiences we undergo?

Finding success in the performing arts is more in your control than not.

We believe that there is no *It* Factor (fate), and that what leads artists to rewarding careers is persistence and hard work (free will). After all, some actors dance in the back of five Broadway shows, mostly unnoticed by the public, only to win a Tony in their fifties, seemingly out of nowhere. Does that mean that suddenly they found *it*? Why wasn't *it* seen before? Others make a splash right out of college, leading a star-studded production to tremendous reviews, but then find themselves unable to maintain the spark. Did they turn twenty-five and suddenly lose *it*?

We believe *it* means expertise of the craft, industry savvy, business acumen, a collaborative mindset, tolerance of rejection, and above all, perseverance. When our experience and preparation relaxes our anxieties ("I know what I'm doing"), when our knowledge of the craft saturates our work ("I am ready"), when confidence intersects with an acute awareness of one's body, mind, and skill in the given moment ("I am worthy"), when our voice is free and our determination to tell a story is precisely focused ("I have something valuable to share"), we are empowered to create an experience for our audience that wows. The casual theatre-going fan on a vacation might think we've demonstrated God-given star power, but we leave that hot take to the out-of-towners, because we know we've *worked* to achieve this moment. This is what *it* is.

This achievement is reachable by anyone who commits to the work. Sure, some are born with enough raw gifts that they make the journey look easy. And yes, others must work a little harder. But there are no preselected few. There are only those who do the work, who recognize that competence isn't enough to succeed in the arts and persevere unrelentingly toward greater *excellence.*

The path from competent to excellent is clearly paved, but it's much longer than most actors prepare for.

Your Roaring Twenties . . . or the Great Depression?

The developing actor cultivates their love for musical theatre through high school. The best of them pursue a BFA in musical theatre, assured that their streak will continue. Too often, however, this journey turns into a grueling gauntlet of disillusionment, personal upheaval, and miseducation on what it takes to build a career in musical theatre today.

The basic skills they achieve over these four years are clouded by the illusory vacuum of the BFA experience far, far away from Broadway. Once they arrive on planet Earth, they're stumped by this alien Broadway culture that they've mostly only heard about. They audition relentlessly (still burdened by confusing messages from peers and mentors back home on the mother ship) without realizing that—much like a Martian or an unpolished, naive thing—they look green. As they leave their auditions, those behind the table decide they are ill-prepared, disorganized, or, worse, "a little cuckoo."

At its core, performing is about the gift we give an audience, not the gratification we gain for ourselves. When actors ignore this truth, the struggle persists. Some eventually run out of gas, while others come to suspect they got into this for the wrong reasons (like making Dad proud, or proving their classmates wrong). Their focus has been on becoming a star rather than a contributing member in an industry of artists. They haven't considered that their primary job as an entertainer is to *entertain*.

For one or more of the reasons mentioned above, too many competent actors decide they are not good enough, and they quit. This is unnecessary, and a disservice to us all.

The solution

The journey from being "skilled enough" to expertly prepared is taken one step at a time. One foot carries the weight of the past, and the other pushes forward into the future, while the body feels each footfall in the present moment. The expert actor has developed a deep understanding of their craft and the history of their art, appreciates where the industry stands today, rises to the expectations of the field, and strategically positions the sale of their most precious product: themselves. They've discovered their own singular voice and they amplify it, using their artistry to break new ground, expand the industry itself, and show it—and themselves—what they're capable of.

The journey to excellence must be twofold:
honoring the industry *(its past and present)*
and revolutionizing the industry
(pushing it into the future).

We're here to show you the way. Let's get started.

PART 1

BUILDING IT

~~TYPE~~
Defining Who You Are

Your professional journey begins when you fully identify and embrace who you are today.

Every person involved in a production has the same job: to tell the story. For you, the actor, the components of your individual self—all the things that make you *you*—help shape the narrative. Combined with your talent, these qualities are part of what the creative team considers when casting. Amateur actors assume that measurable aspects (like singing the highest note or nailing the most turns) matter most, but in reality, it's *specificity* that matches the right performer to the right role.

Specificity is the set of traits that makes you singular: *your voice, look, energy, and authenticity.*

FORGET ABOUT "TYPE"

Along the way, the concept of an actor's specificity has been reduced to one frustrating little word: "type." Its meaning has been twisted over the years in an unfortunate game of telephone, rendering it into a dangerous label that hinders an actor's understanding of who they are.

For decades, actors have referred to themselves using a few subjective words like "leading man" or "belty best friend," as though all leading men look or sound the same (they don't) or all supporting female roles are belters (they aren't). For some, their understanding of "type" is really about billing: Their type of soprano is Mary Poppins, Julie Jordan, and Christine Daae—aka the leads. But those three roles, despite how similar they seem, are separated by character-based elements such as, say, comedic chops, vocal timbre, or a natural sense of innocence.

Others find that their physical type relegates them to an earlier curtain call, as characters like Marcellus Washburn or Motormouth Maybelle. This stereotyping bleeds into tricky tropes about what protagonists are "supposed" to look like: namely, conventionally attractive, skinny, and white.

Yet since the dawn of musical theatre, writers have consistently rejected these clichés, creating roles for actors of all appearances and identities. This antiquated notion of "type" is not only unhelpful, it's inaccurate.

"Type" aims to be objective, but it isn't. That's why the term has fallen out of favor. Today, many casting directors prefer the phrase "how an actor fits into the story." While this shift is an improvement, it's still too vague for you, the actor-strategist.

"Specificity," on the other hand, is both objective and strategic. It allows you to self-define key qualities that are consistently demonstrable (your voice), clearly observable (your look), emotionally perceptible (your energy), and fundamentally immutable (your authenticity). From there you can identify the traits that are the strongest—both within yourself and relative to your competition—and ultimately establish an artistic brand that sets you apart.

Best of all, specificity isn't determined by chasing industry trends, limiting ourselves to outdated casting tropes, or stewing over an offhanded, soul-shaking comment your voice teacher made sophomore year. The only person who decides it is you, today.

Your specificity, or brand, is how you choose to present yourself in the world of storytelling.

(We'll use "specificity" and "brand" interchangeably here, but the word "type" may creep in—like a subway rat—when it's necessary.)

THE FIRST QUALITY: VOICE

Your singing voice is often the first thing you consider when defining your type.

Most musical theatre actors get into the artform through singing. As they develop their voice, they're likely to explore a wide range of styles and work to push their vocal range both higher and lower. This leaves some singers at sea in discussing their instrument, sure that as a professional vocalist, they can (and should) be able to do everything. But here we face one of the most important principles in determining our specificity, especially as it relates to the voice.

Casting is less interested in knowing everything you can do and more focused on what you do best—both within your own skillset and compared to other actors.

Defining your voice can be approached a variety of ways, but most begin with voice type.

Voice type identifies your singing range and the kind of roles that align with it.

Common voice types are alto, soprano, tenor, baritone, and bass. Other categories like baritenor, contralto, or mezzo-soprano* are also frequently used.

While precise note ranges can be debated, we provide the following as a reference, which reflects the expectations of Broadway today. Keep in mind that these ranges indicate where a singer is most comfortable, even if they *can* sing higher or lower.

SOPRANO *Singing mostly in head voice or mix*	A3—A5 (Down to G3, up to "high C," or C6)	Bess (*Porgy and Bess*), Maria (*West Side Story*), Anne (*A Little Night Music*), Luisa (*The Fantasticks*), Christine (*Phantom of the Opera*), Leslie (*Giant*), Jerusha (*Daddy Long Legs*), Sibella (*A Gentleman's Guide to Love and Murder*)
ALTO *Singing mostly in belt or chest voice*	F#3—C5 (Down to E3, up to E♭5)	Ado Annie (*Oklahoma!*), Mary (*Merrily We Roll Along*), Mary Magdalene (*Jesus Christ Superstar*), Eponine (*Les Misérables*), Effie (*Dreamgirls*), Elphaba (*Wicked*), Natalie (*Next to Normal*)
TENOR	B♭2—A4 (Down to A2, up to B4)	Enoch Snow (*Carousel*), Henrik (*A Little Night Music*), Pippin (*Pippin*), Zangara (*Assassins*), Sonny (*Xanadu*), Fabrizio (*The Light in the Piazza*), Orpheus (*Hadestown*), Burrs (*The Wild Party*)

---

* We find that most misuse the term "mezzo-soprano" when they really mean "belter"—and thereby "alto," not soprano. The offenders tend to be afraid that if they say "alto" it will imply they have no upper range. Mezzo-sopranos are sopranos with a slightly lower tessitura and relatively darker sound—but that doesn't necessarily mean they are belters. In theatre, altos are inherently belters, so if that's how you sing most of the time, say "alto."

BARITONE	G2—G4 (Down to F2, up to A♭4)	Emile or Lt. Cable (*South Pacific*), Capt. Von Trapp (*The Sound of Music*), Anthony (*Sweeney Todd*), Coalhouse Walker (*Ragtime*), Leo Frank (*Parade*)
BASS	F2—F4 (Down to E♭2, up to G4)	Sergeant of Police (*Pirates of Penzance*), Judd (*Oklahoma!*), Fred/Petruchio (*Kiss Me, Kate*), Joe (*Showboat*), Sweeney Todd and Judge Turpin (*Sweeney Todd*), Caiaphas (*Jesus Christ Superstar*), Hades (*Hadestown*)

Vocal character indicates timbre, power, and vocal approach.

Words like "belt," "mix," "falsetto," and "head voice" clarify vocal quality and technique. For those coming from the classical world, terms such as "lyrical," "dramatic," or "coloratura" can be borrowed.

The word "legit" is often misunderstood to mean soprano head voice exclusively, but altos—even belters—can sing in a legit style, too. The difference between belters Annie Oakley and Elphaba, for example, is that the former belts in a legit style and the latter a contemporary one—and never the twain shall meet (just imagine Ethel Merman singing "Defying Gravity"). Legit singing is rooted in classical training with healthy vibrato, open vowels, and a warmer sound compared to contemporary or pop singing. In classic musical theatre, regardless of voice type or placement, the preferred sound will almost always be legit. Legit singing is the opposite of contemporary singing and, as we'll soon discover, "contemporary legit" singing (for shows like *Les Misérables* and *Beauty and the Beast*) blends the two.

To illustrate how vocal approach can differentiate similar ranges, consider these two examples of the same tessitura (a singer's most comfortable note range), each defined by a distinct style or technique.

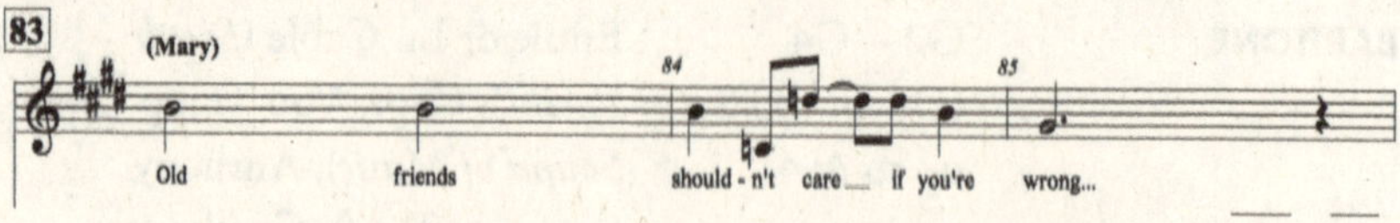

Mary singing "Old Friends" in *Merrily We Roll Along*

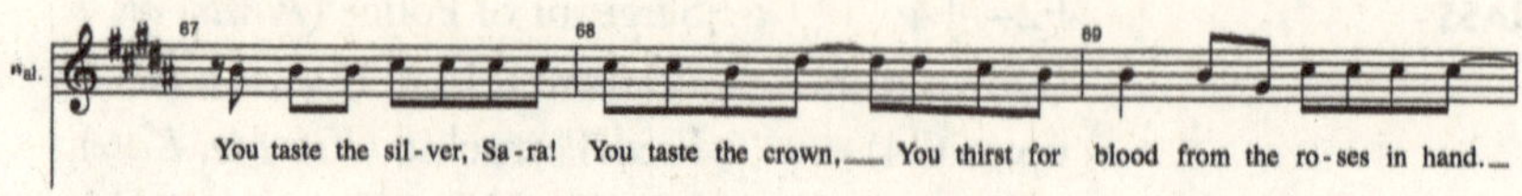

The Balladeer singing "The Ballad of Sara Berry"
from *35mm: A Musical Exhibition*

A quick listen to these moments on original cast recordings reveals that the first is consistently performed with a mezzo-soprano mix, while the second employs a vibrant belt. If either approach were swapped for the other, it would transform both the song and the character.

Vocal genre *(optional)* suggests a musical style *intrinsic to your voice.*

Designations like "rock," "folk," "jazz," "R&B," or "pop" can highlight a specialized style ingrained in your musical approach. While this can be advantageous, it also implies a potential challenge escaping that style. However, if your voice naturally aligns with a specific musical genre, clarifying it as part of your voice type places you at the top of the list for the projects that suit you and saves time for those that don't.

Additional indicators include secondary voice descriptors, which can point out high and low points of your range or other notable qualities. Always lead with your strongest (and favorite) descriptors and keep any additional information concise—if it's necessary at all. The human voice is a flexible and varied thing.

Defining your voice

Combining these descriptions we get voices like "alto belter," "rock tenor with vibrant falsetto," and "dramatic mezzo-soprano with strong belt to C4." In the last example, the singer highlights both their legit sound and belt, while suggesting their legit work might have a slight edge.

Use the chart below to create a combination that best describes your instrument. Beyond the basic voice types, everything is optional—add only what is authentic to you and avoid adding modifiers just for the sake of it.

Coloratura*	Soprano	Bright	Head voice
Lyric	Mezzo-soprano	Warm	Mix
Dramatic	Alto	Mellow	Mix-belt
Legit	Contralto	Smoky	Belt
Rock	Tenor	Dark	Falsetto
Pop	Baritenor		
Folk/Country	Baritone		
Gospel	Bass-baritone		
Jazz	Bass		

Optionally, you can add your exact range using the image below.

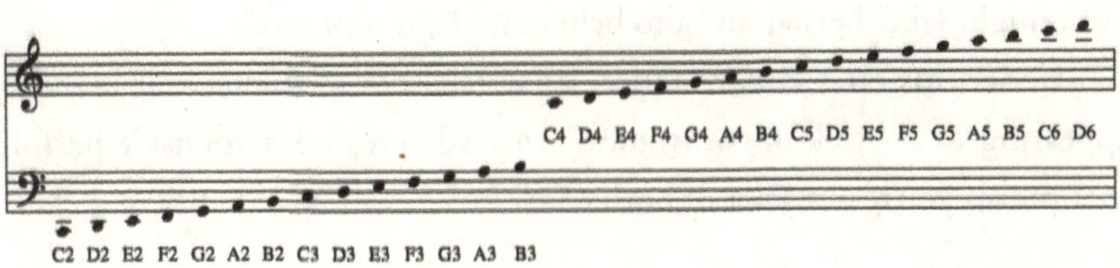

As with selling a car or an apartment, lead with your strongest qualities and avoid vague or suspicious phrases like "folk alto with mix." The phrase "with mix" detracts from clarity—if you're positioning yourself as a

* This descriptor applies to sopranos only.

potential soprano, chances are someone else is marketing it better. Instead, focus on what you want to be known for—in this case, as a folk alto.

It's okay to be creative ("a sparkling soprano") as long as it doesn't sound cutesy ("a voice like bubbles in a bath"), and don't be afraid to be exact ("soprano to high D6").

Too flexible: Choosing between soprano and alto

Many female performers struggle to choose between alto and soprano because they have experience singing in both ranges and fear limiting their opportunities if casting comes a-calling for the one they haven't picked. While men have bridging terms like baritenor and baritone-bass, these categories represent subtler distinctions compared to the stark contrast between a woman's belt and head voice.

In our experience, most women who claim to "do both" actually excel in one—and deep down, prefer it over the other. To stand out in Broadway's hypercompetitive landscape, choose the range where you feel strongest and most confident.

That said, there are exceptions. Consider Jessie Mueller, who earned acclaim as both Julie Jordan (a lyric soprano) in *Carousel* and Jenna (an alto belter) in *Waitress*. An actress who feels professionally equipped to pursue both might label herself an "alto belter and legit soprano."

Under this rarer circumstance, it's crucial not to dilute your brand by appearing as a "jack-of-two-trades." Instead, prepare a robust repertoire that proves you're a master of both.

THE SECOND QUALITY: LOOK

In days past, physical appearance wasn't always explicitly stated for many roles on a breakdown because it was implied through outdated tropes. Casting a "leading lady" implied someone skinny, young, and conventionally pretty; "dancer" suggested someone tall, long-legged, and visibly muscular; "comedian" roles were reserved for funny-looking or superlatively tall, short, skinny, or heavy actors. This problematic history may make actors hesitant to describe themselves physically, assuming that headshots and auditions will let the creative team judge for themselves.

But we encourage actors to take command of this narrative.

Describing your look as part of your specificity is both a declaration of pride and a tactical play.

Recognize that all shapes, sizes, and styles deserve their shot at ingenues, villains, dancers, and beyond. Like your voice, your physical appearance is another unique quality that helps tell your story.

Your look is how you proudly describe your physical appearance.

This includes:

- Playable age (using a phrase like "high school," or a range like "18–22" or "mid-thirties")
- Height (tall, short, towering, petite, pint-sized)
- Body shape (athletic, curvy, skinny, "dad bod")

By offering this information confidently, you clarify for the creative team that they should see you the way *you* see you.

Playable age

Though no one can ask your official age during a casting process, having a clear understanding of the age you appear as—both in person and onstage—helps you zero in on the roles you're perfect for and leave the rest to the rest. Whatever you decide, you can sing it from the mezzanine, or more shrewdly, demonstrate your understanding through the characters you pursue.

If you feel you look your age, then your playable age is typically a few years on both sides. For recent college graduates, this might mean a range of two or three years (a twenty-one-year-old might say eighteen to twenty-four), while older actors might play four or five years in either direction. If not, own the age that works for you at this stage in your life and career, whether that's significantly younger or older than your actual age.

But problems arise that stem from our early training. In high school and college, far too many actors are told they will "work when they're older," implying that a nineteen-year-old who could pass for twenty-three is cursed to lose a decade of her career (not to mention the fact that this is told most often to curvier or taller women). As a result, actors in their early twenties too often prepare material for forty-year-old characters, because that's what they worked on in school—a misguided disruption to their momentum.

High schools and colleges license musicals with cast lists requiring teenagers and old folks, leading to situations like this: A seventeen-year-old boy (who is giving "maybe could buy beer") ends up playing roles like the Mysterious Man, Mayor Shinn, and Uncle Arvide at school, and thinks that's where he fits in a professional ensemble. Martin may look older than his peers by a little, but no casting director in a major market will mistake him for being older than twenty-three. Students in this position are best advised to focus on roles their own age as soon as they can.

You, of course, have a level of control to push your playable age slightly up, down, or expanded on both sides, based on how you style yourself. A twenty-five-year-old, for example, might opt to play a little older by styling herself in a short heel and a dress, or younger by arriving in sneakers, jeans, and a T-shirt.

While it's true that some will continue to grow into their bodies over time, nothing should keep you from booking professional work based on your body *today.* When in doubt, remember that most of us look our actual age (give or take), so lean on the facts to set yourself up for success.

Additional physical qualifiers

Physical traits that can't be easily altered by costuming increase your specificity. For instance, facial features deemed "nerdy looking" (whatever those are) could be useful, but being bald gets a dismissive wave from the wig department.

You're empowered to boldly brag about your body, whether you're buff, chubby, lanky, statuesque, androgynous, hunky, ultra-femme, or voluptuous. If you're proud of a particular qualifier, neither modesty nor shame need apply.

Be front-footed about your appearance to establish an edge, especially for roles where such a look supports the storytelling. For example, an actor who enthusiastically embraces his "femme/androgynous" appearance may be thought of more readily for a role like Mary Sunshine in *Chicago* than a peer with a similar look who hasn't owned it.

Finally, in the quest for precision, beware of words like "average" when talking about height or shape—or, worse, descriptors that tell us what you *aren't*, like "not too thin," "not too tall." Better to find a phrase that evokes an iconic image, like "the boy or girl next door."

THE THIRD QUALITY: ENERGY

The most elusive of the first three qualities to describe is your energy.

Your energy describes natural personality traits that define your essence.

Whether bright-eyed, macabre, kind-hearted, cerebral, intimidating, ferocious, enigmatic, strait-laced, neurotic, zany, or seductive, your energy reflects the infusion of your personality into your work.

Many well-respected artists who have embraced their innate energy have enjoyed long, successful careers as go-to actors in their niche: character actors like Josh Gad, seductive comedians like Jane Krakowski, or dark-hearted villains like Patrick Page. Later in their careers many such actors often *break through* their reputed energy and deliver transformative, legendary performance.

While this approach may make some bristle ("I'm an actor; shouldn't my *energy* be as versatile as the characters I want to play?!"), consider how a friend might describe you to someone else. Whether at a party or in a professional situation, your personality is likely to come into play to provide relevant context, underscoring the truth that the way we engage with our world is as much a part of how we tell stories as our voice and our appearance.

And as always, only you get to decide which aspects of your energy are essential and which are irrelevant.

Determining the energy you "bring to the party" won't box you in, but it will allow you to set yourself apart. While others might fabricate these traits on stage, they're intrinsic to who you are. It's true that an actor's job is to inhabit characters who are not themselves, but an actor's personality acts as a prism through which the narrative comes to life. Frequently, a specific energy is exactly the quality a director is looking for.

Take the demon barber Sweeney Todd. Three directors, each with their own vision, might cast three entirely different Sweeneys, while keeping his voice and look unaltered (baritone or bass, male, late thirties to forties).

- In Director A's rather traditional production, she's looking for a "brooding, macabre" presence to prep us for all that throat-slitting. Secretly, she is looking for that "inherent sadness" in the actors who audition.
- But Director B is looking for a "bad boy" energy, suggesting the killer streak was already inside Sweeney and Judge Turpin merely unleashed it. Anyone who seems "too nice" won't make it to callbacks.
- Director C, meanwhile, envisions a "sunny and warm everyman." By presenting a relatable, guileless character, this director aims to emphasize the tragedy of a sweetheart driven to psychopathy.

This is how we end up with three energetically different Sweeneys . . . like Len Cariou, Johnny Depp, and Josh Groban, respectively. By embracing your natural energy, you position yourself as a perfect fit for the roles you're most suited to play—while leaving room for transformation later in your career.

FYI: Everyone's "quirky"

"Quirky" is about as useless as saying you're "different." As drama kids, weren't we all just a bit odd? What actor would identify as a regular, everyday, not-strange-at-all "normie"? If we dig deeper, we harness our inner kook by amplifying it through a "sub-quirk."

A "sub-quirk" describes a "quirky" brand more precisely.

Are you perhaps . . .

- **A silly little ninny noodle?** Hey, why's everyone so gosh-darn serious? Everything's a game if you play hard enough. You're always goofin' and cheesin', and there's nothing wrong with that, sunshine.
- **Charmingly neurotic?** Your nervous energy is panic for our amusement. Never unhinged, you know that misery loves company, and your suffering is spellbinding.
- **Especially spooky?** You're mired in the macabre, a little witchy, and pulled toward all things grisly and dark-sided. On a beautiful day you're dreaming about horror movies.
- **Queerky?** Being in the alphabet mafia is *literally* 99 percent of your personality. Why walk when you can sashay? You'll play straight, but your character probably has a secret gay agenda.

The list goes on, and sub-quirks are best when you create one all your own. Find the curious gold beneath your peculiar surface and prove why "quirk" rhymes with "work."

THE FOURTH QUALITY: AUTHENTICITY

"We're casting *people*, not *actors*" is an oft-sung refrain in casting circles.

The immutable elements of who you are offstage can profoundly shape the stories you tell, especially when they magnify the truth of the characters you portray.

Authenticity refers to aspects of your identity, history, or lived experience that informs the stories you tell.

In some cases, your authenticity transcends the story itself, contributing to a larger social narrative. Authentic casting has become particularly important in addressing issues of appropriation, underrepresentation, and giving voice to perspectives that haven't been given their due stage time.

As with other qualities, be clear about which elements of your life define your identity *and* the art you want to make. These might include:

- Your ethnicity (e.g., Black, Filipino American)
- Nationality (e.g., Cuban, Canadian)
- Gender (e.g., transmasc, nonbinary)
- Sexuality (e.g., aromantic, queer)
- Relationship structure (e.g., polyamorous)
- Religion or religious experience (e.g., Jewish, ex-Mormon)
- Where you're from (e.g., Texan, Los Angeleno)
- Disability (e.g., neurodivergence, uses a wheelchair, actor with cerebral palsy)

Other, less fixed aspects can be worth considering. Imagine for a moment a character who is a reclusive gamer who spends most of her waking hours playing *Call of Duty.* One actor who auditions is herself a lifelong gamer, while another hasn't played a video game since she was six. The former wields a controller like an extension of a limb, understands the mechanics of competitive gameplay, and can ferociously spout gamer-speak. For the latter, all of that must be researched, explained, or taught—and the writers (likely also gamers) are keener to work with someone they share a shorthand with rather than starting from scratch with a newb.

This could be true for other self-assessed, powerful life experiences, like being a singer-songwriter, a band geek, a marathon runner, or a burlesque dancer.

When thoughtfully incorporated, authenticity adds depth to your specificity. We're not suggesting you expose your entire personal life for your artistic brand. It should never feel exploitative or calculated only for the sake of casting. Most importantly, the decision to share these elements must be yours alone—not dictated by agents, teachers, or even family.

As an example, Lindsay's mom was born Russian-Jewish, raised Mormon, and converted to Catholicism—but Lindsay doesn't strongly identify with any of those. Conversely, her father is Mexican American, and that identity is deeply important to her. When one of her first agents suggested she blanch her Mexican last name to "Matthews," said she to that agent, "Bye Felicia."

PUTTING IT TOGETHER: THE BRANDING STATEMENT

With these four components defined, the clever actor can paint a fully dimensional portrait of a singular artist.

Branding *harnesses your specificity as a strategy.*

For anyone put off by the idea of artistic branding, first know that every artist with a "voice" has, by definition, established a brand.* The trouble creeps in when someone fabricates a brand that misleads or deceives, or is otherwise inauthentic to them.

---

* Even the rebellious and anti-commercial artist Banksy has a brand: anonymous, exclusive, hype-driven, and socially critical. We think Banksy would be proud of that description—if only anyone knew their identity to ask them.

When you're in control of your own branding, the descriptions of your voice, look, energy, and authenticity combine to illustrate how you fit inside a story. This concise sentence or short paragraph, far more than the sum of its parts, should brilliantly define you and you alone. In short, it's a masterpiece of self-description.

> SAMUEL RICKETTS is a punk-pop crooner from the cornfields of Iowa, a geeky boy-next-door who answers the question "What do you get when you combine Curly from *Oklahoma!* and Brendan Urie from Panic! At The Disco?"

Samuel's statement clarifies that his voice is suited to popular styles from rock to jazz, implying he can bring grunge and edge or soften it to smooth and lyrical (from *Spring Awakening* and *American Idiot* to *Jersey Boys* and *Bandstand*). His description subtly signals that he's going to bring something extra to legit and classic musicals. Without even seeing his headshot, he's pitching a mix of nerd and hick, perfectly suited for roles in *Hair* or *Be More Chill.*

> PATRICE SENECA is a spunky neurodivergent queen from a loud, Greek-Jewish family. This 5'3" but mighty comedic actress has the fiercest of belts that exists in both the pop/rock and musical theatre worlds.

Patrice's branding statement leads with authenticity and boldness, reframing her disability as a superpower. She emphasizes her sense of humor and petite stature and showcases her belt as a defining vocal quality. Though she probably sings soprano, she omits it strategically to keep the focus on her strongest skill, which perfectly positions her for roles like Adelaide in *Guys and Dolls*, Ado Annie in *Oklahoma!*, Fanny in *Funny Girl*, Paulette in *Legally Blonde*, Janis in *Mean Girls*, a Fate in *Hadestown*, or one of the queens in *Six.*

`HANNAH PEPPER is a sweet and bubbly 5'1" dancer and mezzo-belter full of sunshine and spirit. Your girl Friday on the outside, this dumb blonde ain't nobody's fool!`

Hannah puts her identity as a dancer first (including, notably, her height), which signals her suitability for dance-heavy shows like *Cats*, *A Chorus Line*, *An American in Paris*, and *MJ*. Energy courses throughout, and in her clever finish she subverts a trope. The Hannah she presents is a perfect Lorelai Lee in *Gentlemen Prefer Blondes*, Olive Neil in *Bullets Over Broadway*, Patti Simcox in *Grease*, Lois Lane in *Kiss Me, Kate*, Doralee in *9 to 5*, or Lucy Grant in *Bright Star*.

BRANDING AND SPECIFICITY IN PRACTICE

Once you put together your branding statement, it's time to put it to work.

The first place to feature your branding statement is on the front page of your website, replacing any long-winded "About Me" section (more on websites later). Your statement, paired with a professional photograph, establishes what you offer as a performer and sets useful expectations while your visitor explores the rest of your site.

Branding statements can also feature in social media bios, and they might even begin a program bio—especially if you don't have a big list of credits yet.

Some actors like to put a one-sentence branding statement on their résumé in place of other stats (especially those who want to put certain authenticity front and center), but that's up to each actor.

You might share your branding statement with teachers, mentors, or representation to discuss how your work aligns with your vision of yourself. It's vital to avoid advice telling you what you should or shouldn't be and ignore anyone who suggests that a core part of your identity isn't "in" right now. A brand is not a costume—it's a proclamation.

The most helpful feedback on a branding statement reflects on how effectively you're putting your self-description into practice. Useful critical feedback might include:

- You describe yourself as a legit soprano but only have alto belter songs in your book. Time to determine whether your vocal assessment or your rep application is truer to who you are.
- You mention being nonbinary as a part of your professional identity but only sing material from the gender you were assigned at birth. Is that aspect something you want to honor more?

Analyzing why you've prioritized certain elements and set others aside provides valuable insight—but as always, it's your life and you have the final say.

Your branding statement is also a helpful guide as you explore casting breakdowns, reducing guesswork while prioritizing which auditions to attend.

Make no mistake: A significant part of the casting process happens outside the audition room in conversations and emails between the creative team and their contacts. A clear brand makes it easier for your colleagues and mentors to discuss you with others in the industry. When they can effectively and accurately articulate who you are, they're better equipped to put your name in the ring—and know exactly which role to call you in for.

We understand that many actors find the process of identifying their type confusing and stressful. Sometimes they'll decide to play it safe, keeping all their options open. They make their brand so broad that they claim to be equally right for both Laurie *and* Ado Annie, both Gabe *and* Henry, both Fantine *and* Cosette—effectively spreading their brand so thin that it falls completely apart.

When an actor says they fit two completely opposite characters in a story, it creates a problem for both casting *and* the actor.

THE LEGEND OF THE "REGINACADY"

Somewhere in the concrete jungle lies a strange creature called a Reginacady *(ruh-JEE-nuh-KAY-dee)*. She has stumped experts for years, because describing her is an exercise in contradiction. All at once, the Reginacady is a leader—but she's also a follower. She is brutal, but somehow equally good-natured. She is cruel yet merciful, stunning yet plain, predatory yet harmless. Some say she disguises herself in packs of Karens and Gretchens, yet others claim she hunts near Janises and Damiens. Peculiarly, Reginacadys are quite a pervasive species—yet are, by their very nature, almost impossible to spot. In fact, the Reginacady has rarely ever been seen . . .

Because she can't seem to get an appointment.

We hear it all the time. "When it comes to *Mean Girls*, I look like a Cady, but my personality is much more Regina." "Inside I'm a Rizzo, but people always see me as Sandy at *Grease* calls." "I think I look like a Gabe in *Next to Normal*, but my voice is better suited for Henry." "Natasha or Sonya in *Great Comet*? I could do either!" Maybe the actor *could*, but this mindset makes them less competitive for either.

Every role in a show is defined by characteristics relating to age, gender, voice type, energy, and authenticity—including the various ensemble members who are "tracked" to understudy them. Even in rotating casts where gender and age are shifted around (like in *Hadestown*), casting balances the company as a whole. If an actor decides to live in the cracks of a cast list—whether their strategy is to go after multiple roles at once, or because they don't know where they fit—they're likely to be overlooked in favor of the savvier actor helping casting do their job.

It's true that swings (who cover many different roles) are a vital part of a cast, regularly saving performances by going on for absent actors. While there are lifelong swings who genuinely enjoy the pace of this work, most actors appreciate their time as a swing but look forward to playing non-swinging tracks. (And if the swing life *is* your passion, you're likely well-known for it and coming to the call specifically to grab that track.)

In a group of characters of similar age, gender, and voice type—like say, the Pink Ladies in *Grease* or the students in *Les Misérables*—interchangeable though they seem, their characters are far more unique than you might realize. Be judicious and determine precisely where you best fit today. Casting may have other ideas, but at least you came prepared.

TROUBLESHOOTING SPECIFICITY

Here are some other common challenges actors face when identifying their specificity, and strategies to address them:

The actor is confused about who they are

Confusion about type stems from confusion about oneself. Yes, human beings contain multitudes, but your task is to remain objective and ruthless with the facts. Vocal inconsistency ("I can usually hit that note"), body dysmorphia ("I could bulk up for that role"), or a sense of being lost in your life path can all make self-knowledge and personal branding difficult. This journey may also spark tough conversations about your heritage, sexuality, or gender.

It's okay to still be figuring things out—especially if you're young (though we know some very wise seventeen-year-olds and some very clueless thirtysomethings). Be active in the hunt for your singular identity, but don't feel the need to rush somewhere you're not ready to be.

Begin with what you're sure about and build from there.

The actor can do a lot of things and doesn't want to label or limit themselves

In the highly competitive world of casting, casting directors can usually find a "12 out of 10" in exactly the criteria they're seeking. Someone who is more of an "8 out of 10" in the same area isn't likely to stand out, no matter how many other things they can do. Additional talents are irrelevant if they don't meet the team's immediate needs.

Focus on your greatest strengths at the start and make yourself a name for them. You'll become the go-to choice for roles that align seamlessly with your brand, and at that point you can begin to expand your reputation in any direction you wish.

The actor wishes something about themselves were different

It's human to want to be a better dancer, a higher belter, thinner, shorter, or younger—even to cling to a younger version of ourselves. While everyone should pursue self-improvement, remember that there's nothing about your look or identity that should prevent you from working professionally today. Ironically, the traits actors often dislike about themselves the most—"too curvy," "too short"—are often the very same qualities that set them apart and get them hired. The real obstacle isn't your appearance or ability, but the self-loathing that hinders your progress.

The actor is too concerned with what other people think, instead of focusing on what they think

It's tempting to poll all your friends over questions of specificity, relying on the words of others instead of cultivating your own beliefs about yourself. Anyone you ask to fill in these blanks for you—whether they're a fellow actor, a teacher, or even an industry pro—is sure to load their response with their own baggage, about themselves *and* about you. While it's useful to get feedback and remain open to others' perceptions of you, this information should complement or clarify your thoughts, not reformat them. Do the work on your own first.

The actor is afraid their brand will change

Good news: it *will* change!

Your brand is not a static label, but a reflection of who you are at one point in time. As you grow older, you will evolve physically, emotionally, and artistically. Life experiences will shape who you are and how you present yourself. Identifying your specificity today is simply a statement for the present.

The actor is fixated on playing their favorite star role

Obsessing over roles like Ariel, Cathy, Ponyboy, or whoever Jeremy Jordan last played ensures you will always be "behind" in the industry, chasing a role from seasons ago rather than refining your individual power.

Many actors stall their momentum trying to mold themselves into an image of a character (or actor) they idolize, while not building up the necessary résumé to get them taken seriously for those star tracks. While it's possible to upend a creative team's vision in the audition room, this "from stan-to-star" mindset ignores what it takes to build a viable, long-term career.

Characters are not brands. Jenna, Anastasia, and Christian aren't comprehensive identities. And what's funny is that the actors who land these roles are always the ones who show the creative team how they will apply their own brand to the character.

Lindsay never considered Elphaba a likely part of her career trajectory, primarily because of the physical type typically cast in the role. Instead, she committed to going after roles that she connected with authentically, like Rose Fenny in *Dogfight*. It was this performance—deeply rooted in her vulnerability, vocal flexibility, and the ability to tap into being an outsider—that caught the attention of *Wicked* director Joe Mantello and ultimately led to her casting. The creative team wasn't looking for a replacement; they wanted the Lindsay Mendez version of Elphaba.

Finally, once you achieve the role you've always dreamed of, what then? If your identity is so wrapped up in booking just one big role, you may find yourself at sea afterward. By investing in a more holistic strategy, you create a plan for the long haul.

YOUR TRUTH SHALL SET YOU FREE

The industry isn't trying to push you to become something you're not. The components that make a human being an individual are never "in" or "out," and there are no trends you must follow in casting. Be yourself. In fact, be *the most* of who you are, and never let someone else tell you who you should be. Who you are today is more than enough for today. Tomorrow, you'll change a little, and who you become will be enough for tomorrow.

Once we harness the powerful components that make us who we are, we see that standing out in a competitive business is as simple as introducing ourselves. No part of defining your specificity should feel like putting yourself into a box. Though you are perpetually growing and changing as an artist, every opportunity to advance involves describing what makes you unique and what *you alone* have to offer.

What makes you different is what gets you hired. From a business standpoint, your specificity offers clarity to those who want to work with you—and tells them why they should.

Building Your Professional Book

Your audition book (hereafter referred to simply as your "book") is a curated collection of audition-ready songs that showcase your personality, vocal range, and proficiency *singing different genres*. The songs in your book create a singular identification card that represents you—and you alone. The exact combination of songs should be so distinctively yours that if a peer who is even vaguely familiar with you were to pick up your misplaced binder, they'd instantly recognize it as yours.

It's useful to think of your book like the ideal collection of clothes in your wardrobe. You have something for every situation and reliable options for everyday use. Each item is carefully selected over time, demonstrates personal taste, responds to trends, and always ensures a perfect fit. There are a few "go-to" favorites and a few standout choices reserved for special occasions. There are favorite colors, perhaps an inclination toward a certain style, and even when your collection feels complete, you always keep an eye out for something new to replace a piece that's overstayed its welcome.

Or, if fashion isn't your thing, imagine your book as a box of tools. You keep only what's most useful and functional while staying ready for key emergencies, because too many tools would be too heavy to carry. Or it's a painter's palette, where you invest in your favorite colors and leave a little space for inspiration, since having too many colors on the board would blur them together and leave nothing of real use.

Your book is a complete expression of your brand at this moment in time. As you grow and change, so too will your book.

Your book *is not* a memory box meant for sentimental items you can't let go of or a file cabinet of everything on record. It's also not a clutch purse with only your phone, keys, and a credit card—just what you need for tonight—because you can't be totally sure you won't need your driver's license, cash, or hey, maybe even your toothbrush!

PREPARING YOUR BOOK

Your book should be contained in a no-frills ring binder. You can keep the cover clear for a sleek, no-fuss look, with résumés and headshots tucked neatly into an inside pocket. Alternatively, you can use the binder as a canvas for self-expression, decorating or personalizing it as you wish.

When it comes to storing your sheet music, we recommend avoiding plastic protective sheets because the glare from fluorescent lights can be distracting for accompanists. If you prefer to use them, opt for "no glare" plastic sleeves. It should go without saying that bringing loose-leaf music (often called "toilet paper music"), bound vocal selections, or published scores to an audition is unprofessional. Your sheet music should always be clean, well-formatted, and easy to read.

Type-A artists (RSO is one, *plus* a Virgo: a terrifying combination) might be tempted to tab their book by song title—or, more chillingly, print a table of contents. Don't. Either choice sends an unsettling message: The book never changes, or it was completed one dark and stormy night and "It's *done* now, okay???" It could even send a message about the actor, like perhaps they also had a nervous breakdown about whether to organize their home library by author, title, or color, and have yet to recover.

Instead, tab your book by primary musical genres (which we'll outline in a moment). Most auditions will request a specific style (or "the style of the show"), so this way you keep relevant options together. This approach organizes your book without micromanaging it.

YOUR SONGS ARE FIRST IMPRESSIONS

At its heart, a first audition is an initial job interview. You've brought your résumé, and now you're telling a prospective employer why they should pay *you* to do the job for which they're hiring.

Most of the time the songs in your book serve as your introduction to casting directors. Once they're familiar with you and believe your specificity aligns with a particular role, they'll call you back with sides from the show. Later in your career they may skip the initial audition and call you in directly for an appointment.

Your book's primary purpose is to offer a warm welcome into your world, introducing you in all the dimensions we've discussed so far. Many of the songs in your book should function as a charming showcase of your personality. We call these "Peggy Sawyer" songs (named after the girl just off the bus in *42nd Street,* trying to make it big in the Big Apple), a "first date" song, or our favorite, a "nice-to-meet-you" song.

A nice-to-meet-you song is *(usually)* an up-tempo, bright, and charming introduction to your brand.

On a first date with a prospective beau or a hang with a potential new pal, your goal is to charm, delight, and leave a positive impression. You want to put a smile on their face, make them curious about you, and leave them eager for a second meeting (a callback), when you might go deeper so that they learn more about you. If you instead bring unhinged intensity, darkness, negativity, or private misery to the first date, there's no point in thinking about a later moment, because they're already flagging down the waiter. ("Next!")

What makes a "nice-to-meet-you" song

To find the material that will perfectly introduce you, consider whether you could sing the song while hanging out with someone for the first time. Using wide suspension of disbelief, think about how the lyrics and tone introduce you. You might:

- Tell them about yourself ("I Can Cook, Too" from *On the Town*)
- Offer something you're super into ("Beethoven Day" from *You're a Good Man, Charlie Brown*)
- Bring a little sass (Gretchen Wilson's "Redneck Woman")
- Share some inspiration ("Go the Distance" from Disney's *Hercules*)
- Outline some hopes and dreams ("My White Knight" from *The Music Man*)
- Celebrate something ("Let's Hear It for the Boy" from *Footloose*)
- Tell a funny anecdote ("The Love of My Life" from *Brigadoon*)
- Flirt a little (Ingrid Michaelson's "You and I")
- Express love at first sight ("I've Never Been in Love Before" from *Guys and Dolls*)
- Crack a dirty joke (Rachel Bloom's "Jazz Fever")

Pretty straightforward, right? And yet many, many, *many* actors struggle with this concept—long after they know better. Some claim they "don't connect" with spirited, entertaining, or joyous material, believing that presenting a sunny demeanor feels "fake." Unless the actor is a real-life incarnation of Wednesday Addams, this resistance signals a narrow-minded perception of musical theatre. And anyway, have they heard Wednesday's song from *The Addams Family*, "Pulled"? It's pretty darn spunky.

B-B-B-BALLADS!!

Ah, ballads . . . we meet again.

> ***A painfully commonplace problem among actors is their obsession with ballads.***

Your book *will* contain a few slower-tempo songs of greater depth, but too many young actors confuse ballads with "acting pieces." They misunderstand "real" acting as grasping at tragic heights and wailing lamentations, but don't realize how such pieces read as distancing and, ultimately, unimpressive.

Consider the emotional landscape of an early-career actor: the constant prospect of rejection, the unforgiving fluorescent lights beaming down, the sight of their ex–best friend at the same call. The nearest emotions they have available are too often discomfort and fear.

But making someone laugh in spite of it all? Bringing our self-confidence into the terrifying audition room and pushing past our nerves to get comfortable, finally charming and *entertaining* them? These are demonstrations of truly impressive talent. In the end, any piece of music expertly prepared can be a showcase of great acting.

When a ballad *is* warranted is when it's requested as a second song ("Do you have anything else today?") or as a showcase of dramatic range, contrasting with an up-tempo first selection.

Select ballads with care, because in an audition room some are more useful than others. For example, "How Glory Goes" (*Floyd Collins*) and "Pretty Funny" (*Dogfight*) are beautiful compositions, beloved by performers and casting directors alike, but they're tricky tunes to bring to a first meeting. Most of us remember the way our hearts broke the first time we heard them. When an unknown actor brings these powerful numbers into the room, at best they're asking the casting director—who may be wolfing down a salad or texting her wife about the dry cleaning—to journey with them to that 11 o'clock moment of darkness and despair in . . . oh, about thirty seconds. At best, the actor is admitting they have little idea of the song's expectations, and at worst, their performance comes off in bad taste.

But ballads like "People Will Say We're in Love" (*Oklahoma!*), "Not While I'm Around" (*Sweeney Todd*), "Unusual Way" (*Nine*), Joni Mitchell's "A Case of You," "Lost and Found" (*City of Angels*), Alicia Keyes's "If I Ain't Got You," "Everything I Know" (*In the Heights*), or Beyoncé's "Halo" are positive ballads, because they demonstrate depth without sinking into hopelessness.

Positive ballads are slower-tempo songs that express joy and hope, or work through a moment of darkness to arrive in light.

Negative ballads, meanwhile, are slower-tempo songs meditating on anger or misery, punctuating a character's low point, and ending in the very darkness where they began. Examples of negative ballads include "Still Hurting" (*The Last Five Years*), "She Used to Be Mine" (*Waitress*), "Empty Chairs at Empty Tables" (*Les Misérables*), "Burn" (*Hamilton*), Eric Carmen's "All by Myself," and Natalie Imbruglia's "Torn." This second category is full of amazing, heartbreaking songs—but can you imagine sharing any of these stories hanging with someone for the first time?

We should also note that the way we're using the term "ballad" is as much about tempo as it is about tone. While most ballads are slow and somber, there are many (especially in contemporary musical theatre) that feature a driving accompaniment, like "I'm Not Afraid of Anything" (*Songs for a New World*), "I Miss the Mountains" (*Next to Normal*), "Safer" (*First Date*), "There Are Worse Things I Could Do" (*Grease*), and "Always Starting Over" (*If/Then*). While these songs' tempos course with energy and power, we consider them ballads because they fight through inner turmoil and hinge on moments of great emotional struggle. They don't pass the "first date test" (ironically, not even the song from *First Date*), so we classify them as ballads.

For your book, we recommend including three to four ballads in different genres—mostly positive, with maybe one negative for rare occasions (but no more). Nobody should "specialize in ballads." When an actor overloads their book with too many depressing songs, we affectionately call it a "funmergency"—it's time to breathe some joy back into their repertoire!

GENRES

Most early-career actors should aim for about twelve contrasting songs in a variety of genres.

For mid-career, highly specialized, or niche performers, fewer songs may suffice, while wider-ranging utility players or artists showcasing different vocal approaches may require more. Greater than fifteen songs in a book will lead to back problems from lugging around that heavy binder—and may also spread your preparation thin. On the other hand, fewer than seven songs may leave you lacking for the many requests you'll encounter.

Casting specifies genres in the breakdown to see how you handle the style's musical conventions. Each requires its own interpretation, technique, and energy. The following is an overview of the many genres prevalent on Broadway today.

Opera	*Porgy and Bess, Sweeney Todd**
Operetta	*Pirates of Penzance, A Gentleman's Guide to Love and Murder*
Vaudeville/Roaring '20s	*Chicago, 42nd Street, Thoroughly Modern Millie, Ragtime, The Producers,* LaChiusa's *The Wild Party, The Drowsy Chaperone*
Standards	*Crazy for You, An American in Paris, Anything Goes*
Legit/Golden Age	*Oklahoma!; Carousel; Brigadoon; Camelot; Kiss Me, Kate; Oliver; My Fair Lady; West Side Story*
Classic Broadway/Showtune	*Hello, Dolly!; Mame; Annie; Gypsy*
Cabaret	*Cabaret, Jacques Brel Is Alive and Well and Living in Paris, Working, Ordinary Days*

* Yes, we know it's also a musical, but give us this one, okay?

Sondheim	*Company, A Little Night Music, Merrily We Roll Along, Into the Woods*
Jazz	*City of Angels, Ain't Misbehavin'*
Folk	*Girl from the North Country, Bright Star, Violet, The Notebook*
Country	*Shucked, The Spitfire Grill, Best Little Whorehouse in Texas*
'50s–'60s	*Grease, Little Shop of Horrors, The Marvelous Wonderettes, Hairspray, Crybaby, All Shook Up, Beautiful*
Motown	*Memphis, Motown, Ain't Too Proud*
Rock	*Hair, Jesus Christ Superstar, Evita, Cats, Aida, Spring Awakening, American Idiot, Murder Ballad*
Pop	*The Wiz, Carrie, Mamma Mia!, Legally Blonde, Everybody's Talking About Jamie, Six*
"Poperetta"/Megamusical	*Joseph and the Amazing Technicolor Dreamcoat, Les Misérables, The Phantom of the Opera, Miss Saigon, Titanic*
Disney	*Beauty and the Beast, Anastasia, Newsies*
Latin/Hip-Hop/R&B	*On Your Feet, In the Heights, Holler If Ya Hear Me, Freestyle Love Supreme, Hamilton, Hell's Kitchen*
Electronic/Dance	*Here Lies Love, American Psycho*
Contemporary Legit	*The Mystery of Edwin Drood, Parade, Marie Christine, A Light in the Piazza, Grey Gardens, The Bridges of Madison County*
"Contemporary Musical Theatre"	*Children of Eden, The Full Monty, The Last Five Years, Dirty Rotten Scoundrels, Wicked, The Book of Mormon, Suffs, Lysistrata Jones, Matilda, Dear Evan Hansen*

If you are auditioning for the rock musical *American Idiot*, delivering "I Have Confidence" from a score of Golden Age showtunes like *The Sound of Music* will not help the creative team see how you'll handle performing Green Day—and vice versa. The competitive actor is prepared for these genres while acknowledging their own strengths and weaknesses. While this can seem like a daunting proposition, we've simplified this wide array to the essential categories.

THE ESSENTIAL SONGS IN YOUR BOOK

Most books should include the following categories.

Two contrasting "classic" songs

You need at least one up-tempo and one ballad from a score of operetta, showtunes, vaudeville, standards, or cabaret. You may have as many as four contrasting songs, especially if you are particularly proficient at singing legit or if you have a wide vocal range and, say, need to showcase your alto and your soprano voices for different auditions.

Some refer to this as Golden Age, setting a composition cutoff (pre-1957, pre-1965, etc.), but in the twenty-first century this can be confusing when we consider pastiche scores (songs imitating styles from earlier periods) like *Thoroughly Modern Millie* and *A Gentleman's Guide to Love and Murder*. "Classic" suffices.

Note that "legit" doesn't necessarily mean soprano head voice. It speaks to unrestricted vibrato and a more classic sound, as we'll explore later.

Two (or more) contrasting "radio" songs*

Choose at least one up-tempo and one ballad hitting pop, rock, Latin, hip-hop, electronic, or R&B—anything with a radio-friendly sound from the

---

* Some actors resist having non–musical theatre songs in their book. Sometimes they're very young and learned from older teachers that radio music is unnecessary,

1970s to today. Considering how many subgenres this encompasses, you could have up to five songs in this category if several styles or decades are your jam. At least one of your songs should be a "Top 40" hit from the last ten to fifteen years.

(Folk, country, and songs from the 1950s–60s are their own category.)

One (or two) contemporary musical theatre song(s)

The "contemporary musical theatre" genre refers to musicals written in a popular style after 2000, but earlier musicals dating as far back as the 1970s (*Jesus Christ Superstar,* some of *Pippin,* and Maltby and Shire song cycles, for example) may qualify. The key here is "written in a popular style," where the music draws from musical idioms off the radio of the day, and the lyrics relate to modern issues.

You might have a contrasting up-tempo and ballad, but if you have only one, it should be up-tempo and tell a story.

The right contemporary musical theatre songs for you should feel like they were written for *You: The Musical.* The music vibes like your personal soundtrack and the lyrics feel straight out of a scene from your life. Above all other songs in your book, your up-tempo should be something you could naturally express as yourself.

Too many early-career performers overload their book with contemporary musical theatre ballads, because these are their "favorites." We understand how self-gratifying it is to belt out all that angst, but the rule continues: If a defeated, furious, or miserable song is from the playlist of your personal life, you're telling the casting team something they wish they didn't know (save these for your cabaret).

---

or they themselves are of an older generation. It's true that before 2000, musicals with rock, pop, country, or folk scores were rarer on Broadway and could be avoided easily. But today, radio music dominates musical theatre—no two ways about it. That's why having radio music is a must for any working actor today—and it may even be what you're asked to sing most often.

You need one positive contemporary musical theatre ballad at most, and if you have none, a radio ballad would be a fine substitute.

One "contemporary legit" song

"Contemporary legit" is a term we've coined to bridge genres like "spectacle musical," "megamusical," "poperetta," and "Disney."* These scores live somewhere between a classic and a popular sound. They also require tremendous vocal power, as heard in *The Phantom of the Opera*, *The Light in the Piazza*, *Titanic*, *The Secret Garden*, *Beauty and the Beast*, *Ragtime*, *Anastasia*, and most of the Frank Wildhorn canon. This genre is not to be confused with operetta (which is lighter, comedic, and classic) or rock opera (which is contemporary musical theatre).

Chances are this song will be one of your ballads (see, we don't hate all ballads!).

Because this genre can be tricky to identify, here's a useful test. Virtually any show written after 1980 that is set in the past *and* has a score meant to sound abstractly "old"—while not being 100 percent authentic to the time and place—is a contemporary legit show (the same way that in most period films, a vaguely British accent stands in for whatever language the characters should be speaking in).

For example, consider these musicals written after 1980. *Les Misérables* takes place in nineteenth-century France but doesn't sound particularly French or like the popular music of the time (chansons, café music, and opera). *Floyd Collins* takes place in the 1920s but mixes modern country with a folk-contemporary score. *Ragtime* takes place at the turn of the

* We mean "Disney" here in the sense of their contemporary legit musicals from the Disney Renaissance: *Little Mermaid*, *Aladdin*, *Hunchback of Notre Dame*, and the like, and their counterparts from other studios, like *The Prince of Egypt*. Nonetheless, we think "Disney" is a highly confusing genre to request, because Disney can technically mean classic (*Snow White*, *Pinocchio*, *Pete's Dragon*), gospel (*Hercules*), contemporary musical theatre (*High School Musical*, *Descendants*), or even '50s–'60s (*Teen Beach Movie*). Yet you wouldn't sing "Once Upon a Dream" if you're going in for Sharpay . . . making having a "Disney" song in your book problematic.

twentieth century and, while it has its share of ragtime influence, most of the score lives somewhere else (consider "Back to Before," "Gliding," and "Wheels of a Dream"). All of these are contemporary legit.

Contrast these using our test with the score of *A Gentleman's Guide to Love and Murder*, set in the same period as *Ragtime,* but which authentically and consistently imitates operetta (classic). *Thoroughly Modern Millie* is set at the same time as *Floyd Collins* but has a roaring '20s feel throughout (also classic). Meanwhile, *Spring Awakening* is set in 1800s Germany but features a notably anachronistic rock score (contemporary musical theatre).

Make sense?

One song from 1950s–1960s radio

Covering Motown, '50s–'60s pop-rock, and some very groovy jazz, this category is ideal for an up-tempo—but could feature the right ballad.

The point is that the song represents the sound of those decades. To be safe, it should probably come from off the radio, though some musicals written during or in the style of this time can qualify. There are casting directors who don't think that musicals with a '50s–'60s score (like *Little Shop of Horrors* or *Hairspray*) apply here, but we note the difference between "Somewhere That's Green" (a song that doesn't sound like the time at all) and "Grow for Me" (a song meant to sound pulled from the FM dial).

One (or more) folk or country song(s)

Musicals written in a folk or country style make it to Broadway every season, so even if the styles aren't on your gym playlist, they're vital to your audition book. Whether it's Johnny Cash, Joni Mitchell, Reba McEntire, early Taylor Swift, Mumford and Sons, or Noah Kahan, there's a place for everyone somewhere in this genre.

Your book could have an up-tempo or ballad—or both if this is your wheelhouse. If you love this genre, you could have a folk *and* a country song, or something that bridges the genre like country-rock or folk-pop.

One Sondheim song

Honoring the grandmaster of the art form, this category demonstrates your skill in handling challenging lyrics and complex music. Since Sondheim's passing, revivals of his musicals are filling seasons more than ever, and breakdowns frequently request a song written by him. Yours can be a ballad or up-tempo.

Given how much of his material leans older, make sure it's age-appropriate (no twenty-year-olds singing "Ladies Who Lunch," please). Your Sondheim song might also work as one of your classic songs.

The rest: Extra material and wild cards

To arrive at twelve total songs, your book might still have available spots. Consider these options:

- An additional contrasting piece in one of the genres above
- A song in a specialty genre that highlights unique skills (e.g., opera, art song, pop songs in foreign languages like Spanish, K-pop, rap)
- A "wild card," a song you'll rarely bring out, but that you have just in case
- Or simply your favorite song (It's your book, after all!)

COMEDY SONGS: LOL?

A comedy song—the kind that casting may request in an audition breakdown—isn't just "kinda funny." It's really fucking funny. The reviews for the latest Broadway sidesplitter aren't "My nephew laughed a couple of times!" or "I smiled knowingly at the irony!" They're "Sorry, at the ER—still laughing!" and "I shat myself!"

A comedy song demonstrates your ability to make us actually laugh.

Don't mix up "charm" or "character" songs with comedy songs. Whether it's a classic tune featuring clever lyrics, or a well-known song from a recent smash, just because people laughed the first time doesn't mean they'll bust up on the hundredth.

George Carlin simplified the mechanics of successful humor. Paraphrased:

Comedy lives at the intersection of expectation and surprise.

Funny lyrics are great, but when the audience has the lyrics memorized there's little surprise—so there are little laughs. A truly great comedy song takes time to find and careful execution to nail. This is why when you're asked specifically for one, better to leave *Something Rotten's* "Right Hand Man" out of it (but do bring it in when asked for a contemporary musical theatre song).

Do you need a comedy song?

Not necessarily. RSO once hosted a master class with a multi–Tony Award–winning writer where a student delivered a ho-hum performance of a sort-of-silly song. "Why do you have this song?" the writer asked. The student replied that it was in her book because she thought she needed a comedy song. The writers asked, "Do you consider yourself funny?"

"My friends tell me I'm funny," she offered weakly, knowing where this was headed.

"But as a performer?"

"Comedy isn't really my thing."

And the writer said that was all the reason she needed to let go of her comedy song.

Comedy is a raw talent and practiced skill, like singing soprano or shining at Shakespeare. Some embrace a gift for gaffe, instinctively drawn to comedic roles, while others are drawn elsewhere—and that's a beautiful thing. Put another way, if you've tried and worked at it and have decided you're not a very strong tap dancer, why buy new tap shoes?

Every comedy song won't work for every comedian. Jennifer Simard, Annaleigh Ashford, and Leslie Margherita have very different comedic brands. When looking for funny additions to our book, we use our strengths to get them rolling in the aisles.

What's *your* sense of humor? Silly with a goof? Slapstick with a pratfall? Raunchy with a sex joke? Dark as hell?

The most important part of choosing a comedy song is finding one that makes YOU laugh.

Where comedians find great comedy songs

Scope out songs from lesser-known musicals. If the material is outrageous on its own, it could work for you. Examples include "All About Ruprecht" (*Dirty Rotten Scoundrels*), "Model Behavior" (*Women on the Verge of a Nervous Breakdown*), and "I Just Wanna Dance" (*Jerry Springer: The Opera*).

If that leaves you empty-handed, dig deeper. Musical television shows like *Crazy Ex-Girlfriend* and *Girls5Eva* have been all the rage, but people don't mine them enough for the terrific audition material they contain. Similarly, you'll find wonderfully insane musical numbers tossed into films and shows, and you can pull one-off numbers like "Stu's Song" (*The Hangover*), "Muffin Top" (*30 Rock*), and "A Little Bit Alexis" (*Schitt's Creek*).

Stand-up comics write funny songs, too: Garfunkel and Oates, Bo Burnham, Tenacious D. Some more "serious" bands have made names for themselves as jokester rockstars, like Wolves of Glendale and Jazz Emu. For better or worse, AI-generated songs* can be wildly funny, and sometimes even for the right reasons—Obscurest Vinyl is one of our favorites. You'll probably need the songs transcribed, but the cost is well worth it when yours is the only book that has the song.

* RSO notes that he, as a human, is likely to be replaced by the artificial intelligence he is recommending.

Or imagine someone coming into a theatre audition singing a nostalgic, ridiculous television theme song, like the ones from *The Mary Tyler Moore Show*, *Step by Step*, *Duck Tales*, or even *Pokémon*. Somewhere between the feeling that "this shouldn't be an audition song" and "I can't believe this is happening right now" is a hilarious sweet spot.

But the most successful comedy songs aren't necessarily born as comedy songs. They're funny because an actor *makes* them funny. Consider a seven-foot-tall "queerdo" singing the Cranberries' "Zombie" like an unhinged sociopath, or an exceptionally stunning, statuesque blonde singing Randy Newman's "Short People (Got No Reason to Live)."

Subverting original intention can bring humor to a merely charming song: "Good Mornin'" (*Singing in the Rain*) sung with a hangover, "I Know Things Now" (*Into the Wood*) but it's about an awful hookup, or "I Got No Strings" (*Pinocchio*), but you keep falling down and sing half the song crumpled on the floor. Just don't let anyone steal your idea!

OTHER SONGS YOU MAY NEED

Your book should function like a Swiss army knife, with songs that are multipurpose and adaptable to virtually any audition need. As you build your book with the suggested genres, consider songs that could kill two birds (or three, even) with one song you've already found, or a "wild card" (a song you'll rarely pull out but will be glad you had for the times you do) or two.

Three "go-to" songs

These are your workhorse pieces—songs you'll sing at 90 percent of your auditions. As we've said, ballads should never be your go-tos. These three are almost always:

- Your classic up-tempo
- Your radio up-tempo
- Your contemporary musical theatre up-tempo

A song from a show currently on Broadway

Including a song from a show currently running (or recently closed) helps casting directors and agents understand where you see yourself in today's commercial landscape. This selection can be in any genre or tempo. Avoid Broadway megahits, or songs associated with popular characters that everyone thinks they're right for. If one of your standard rep doesn't qualify, then this would be a wild card.

A patter song

A song with a quick-paced, tongue-twisting lyric. Any genre will do, and this could double as your comedy song if you need one.

An "easy sing"

You wake up for your audition, and your voice isn't at its best. This song is still useful, but it doesn't require an extensive amount of power or range. If you frequently find yourself vocally compromised, include one in both classic and contemporary.

Something you could potentially sing a cappella if you had to

Have a song prepared—almost certainly a radio song—you could easily bring out a cappella if the casting team isn't providing an accompanist (though, if they're not, make sure the audition is legit!).

A powerhouse number or power ballad

This wild card song is there to demonstrate outrageous vocal power for singers who have an extremely high, impressive, and *consistent* upper register. We're thinking of Vivienne's section of the "Legally Blonde Remix,"

Sia's "Chandelier," and Bon Jovi's "Living on a Prayer" as examples—but these *only* come out when the breakdown specifically asks for a song "showing range" or that is "super belty."

Similarly, you may also get use out of a power ballad, a slower-tempo song with enormous vocal force. These don't have to be particularly high, and you'll find them in every genre, from early radio ("You Don't Own Me," "Alone") to contemporary musical theatre ("Burn," "She Used to Be Mine"), and as virtually every major song in a contemporary legit show.

A "high drama" piece

We know, we know, we told you to avoid songs like this. But actors who feel particularly mature may be ready for a piece of greater emotional scope, like a crushing 11 o'clock number or total meltdown (the end of "Soliloquy" from *Carousel*, Seymour's bit of "Meek Shall Inherit" from *Little Shop of Horrors*, "Your Daddy's Son" from *Ragtime*). You should never sing this first (and probably not second), but you might if they ask, "Do you have . . . I dunno . . . something super dramatic?" or even just, "What else ya got?"

A song you can play on an instrument

Many shows are looking for actor-musicians. If you play an instrument (piano, guitar, ukelele, etc.), have a piece you can play and sing at the ready—but don't accompany yourself unless they ask you to.

A song celebrating your authenticity

Songs for queer characters, gender-bending or gender-fluid expressions, songs in a foreign language you speak, or pieces sung by characters of your nationality or ethnicity are encouraged, especially if you love them and want to make sure this part of your specificity is represented in your book.

TROUBLESHOOTING GENRE

When creative teams request a certain genre, they're assessing how well a performer handles the style and conventions of that type of music—regardless of when it was written. This can raise questions, so let's clarify some common scenarios.

Pastiche

Songs written today that authentically imitate an older style are called "pastiche"—such as *A Gentleman's Guide to Love and Murder* (operetta) and *Hairspray* ('50s–'60s style)—and should be categorized by the genre they emulate, not as contemporary musical theatre. We know there are some sticklers out there who believe Golden Age must be from the actual Golden Age of musical theatre, but generally these attitudes have relaxed.

Jukebox musicals

Radio songs later placed into jukebox musicals (*Mamma Mia!*, *Jersey Boys*, *Jagged Little Pill*) are still radio songs from their era, not musical theatre—at least as far as audition material is concerned.

For example, most songs in *Jersey Boys* would be '50s–'60s, while *Mamma Mia* and *Jagged Little Pill* would fall under radio (though if your book specializes in radio music, you could delineate them as '70s pop and '90s rock).

Be mindful that singing major songs from jukebox musicals could center you around that show's main character. So if you have "Beautiful" in your book, it might suggest a role like Carole King is part of your brand—whereas something else from King's *Tapestry* might not have the same effect.

Where theatrical arrangements exist for a song that began on the radio, use the original, not the update. A great example is Tom Kitt's superb redo of "You Oughtta Know" in *Jagged Little Pill*. Thrilling as it is, when they're asking for pop-rock they're looking to see you take on Alanis, not the character of Jo.

Rock/pop songs in contemporary musical theatre

When a creative team asks for pop-rock, they're not looking for contemporary musical theatre—no matter how pop- or rock-influenced it is.

Interestingly, the reverse can *sometimes* be true for material written by narrative-driven singer-songwriters like Joni Mitchell, Taylor Swift, or John Mayer. For instance, singing "My Stupid Mouth" by John Mayer for a contemporary musical theatre audition can work, even though it's a radio song.

USING YOUR BRAND TO SELECT MATERIAL

There are hundreds of options in every category listed above, and a good place to start is with material you love. Once you've separated out a long list of strong contenders (about fifteen to twenty ideas per spot), judiciously compare your specificity to each song.

> *The songs in your book should be a direct extension of who you are and the unique brand you're selling.*

Like your wardrobe (a metaphor we'll continue to lean on), everything in your book should:

- Fit you perfectly.
- Make you feel good about who you are.
- Express your personal taste, style, and individuality.

Yes, you want to *like* everything that you sing, but liking a song isn't enough if it ultimately doesn't serve you by showcasing your strengths.

Characters in musical theatre are imbued with detailed specificity, just like you are. When your specificity aligns with a character (it's a role you feel you are perfect to play right now), songs written for that character are ideal choices. They provide clarity to casting about the kind of work you're ready to take on.

Radio music is more flexible, because recording artists cover other singers' songs all the time. Unlike in theatre, the story is the music itself, instead of the musical's narrative. Regardless of who or how it was recorded originally, search for radio material that suits your voice (remembering keys can change—more on that in a second) and matches the energy you bring into the room.

CREATING A "PATHWAY" THROUGH YOUR BOOK

While your book should demonstrate variety, your goal is to cut a clear "pathway" to the dream roles you want to play today, straight through the center of it. That is, this pathway is dotted with major characters who feel similar and are connected to your specificity. We might think of their relationship to one another as familial, as though the characters are all part of one family tree (yours). From contemporary legit, to classics, to '50s–'60s, to the later radio decades, to contemporary musical theatre, we find roles that are rooted in a sort of archetypal framework.

Consider the road between Eponine (*Les Misérables*), Meg (*Brigadoon*), Violet (*Violet*), Sandy (*Grease*), Shelly (*Batboy*), and Cady (*Mean Girls*). All these women are powerful belters with access to some mix; they're young, headstrong, and determined, with an "everygirl" quality. We see these traits passed down between them, and they create a clear, collective impression. Importantly, there's still variation: Sandy is an innocent, Meg is flirtatious, Shelly is an angsty teen, and Cady is straight-edged and down to earth.

These characters' songs would make an excellent and cohesive set for the right actor's book. But if this same actor had Christine from *Phantom of the Opera* or Heather Chandler from *Heathers* (both of whom feel disconnected from the others), this could—as we say—"blur the brand."

THE OVERDONE SONG AND OTHER MYTHS

Musical theatre actors hear dozens of dos and don'ts about what to sing, but much of what they hear isn't true. Partly this comes from that same bad game of telephone that ruined "type": a drama teacher who knows a vocal coach who knew someone who once took the Q train to Times Square is doling out advice. The worst of these rumors is "Oh, don't sing that song! It's overdone."

In New York City and other major theatre markets, virtually every song is "overdone" . . .

Casting directors hear hundreds of songs every day of the week. They've probably heard your selection three times before you come in—and if they haven't, there could be a reason.

. . . but don't sing the big hits of the last few seasons this season.

Some frequently sung pieces *should* be avoided altogether—but not necessarily because of how often they're sung. Some songs are so popular that it's hard for the creative team to see the performer's specificity behind the song's reputation in the zeitgeist.

These songs tend to be the stan-approved, standout hits from a season's dominating musicals, both new works and revivals. In recent years, songs like *Anastasia*'s "Journey to the Past" or *Waitress*'s "She Used to Be Mine" fulfill that definition, but in 2011 when *On the Town* returned triumphantly to Broadway, "I Can Cook, Too" once again became the order of the day. Eventually these moments pass, and the song becomes fair game again (*Carousel*'s "Mr. Snow" supplanted "I Can Cook, Too" after the 2018 revival), but some songs stand the test of time. "Defying Gravity" will be an unsafe bet for years to come, and "On My Own" is only beginning to recover.

Despite attempts, there is no official list of songs that are off-limits, and when one is made it's quickly rendered out-of-date. Use your instincts for what songs to avoid, while remembering that the list is much shorter than you think, and ever-changing.

It's totally okay to sing Sondheim, Adam Guettel, and Jason Robert Brown at a New York City audition.

Some have it in their heads that certain composers' works are too hard for a pianist to play at an audition. At least in New York City, where accompanists are well-versed in standard rep, even the most challenging sheet music is fair game. Occasionally, you'll run into an audition accompanist who struggles, but that's on the casting directors who hired them (and the team is probably well aware of the struggle).

Outside of NYC, it could be fifty-fifty. Once you've got the feel for your area, make an informed call about your book's range of difficulty.

CODING IN REPERTOIRE

Though every useful song is technically overdone, one of the most important things we consider when choosing one piece over another is its potential "coding."

The "coding" of a musical theatre song is the significant connection between actor specificity and the song's original context.

You're already familiar with this concept. You know, for example, that a white woman should never sing "Your Daddy's Son" (*Ragtime*). It's a song written for and illustrating the unique experience of a Black woman. Among the song's coding is the race and gender of the character it was written for.

You also know that a legit soprano with no belt or strong chest-mix shouldn't try for Elphaba (Glinda is more her track). Elphaba and Glinda's polar voice types are an integral part of the musical storytelling: Initially showing how opposite they are, there is a poignant reversal in "For Good," when Elphaba takes the higher harmony. Were their voice types to be ignored, we would lose an arrival of powerful understanding between the two characters.

Coding occurs when a work reaches such cultural relevance that it absorbs the character-driven context from which it is drawn. You can't hear "Your Daddy's Son" or "Defying Gravity" without thinking of Sarah and Elphaba, respectively, and an actor will be hard-pressed to divorce the songs from their singers and stories. The more well-known and beloved a musical work is, the more our society perceives it as exclusive—or, said another way, we instinctively recognize who is "qualified" to play Tracy Turnblad (*Hairpsray*), Bess (*Porgy and Bess*), or Francesca (*The Bridges of Madison County*)—and conversely, who is not. These criteria become ingrained in the character's identity—their appearance, voice, energy, and authenticity—embedding them into the fabric of the work itself. Tracy is a plus-sized white girl, Bess is a Black mezzo-soprano, and Francesca is a mother of two teenagers. These roles are betrayed when a skinny girl takes on Tracy, a belter with no legit looks at Bess, or a woman too young to have two children tries for Francesca.

But the most deceptively coded pieces tend to be standout songs from iconic musicals, Top 40 radio hits from the last month, or timeless works whose original performances still echo through today.

Take "Waving Through a Window" from *Dear Evan Hansen*, one of the most highly coded songs in recent years. The actors who've taken on Evan fit a narrow description: a teenage-looking "boy next door" with a bright tenor pop voice and introverted energy. If an actor matches these traits, "Waving" might be a strong choice for their book. However, the performance is bound to disappoint if they fit the look and feel but lack the right voice type—like, say, a baritone who can't hit the notes—or vice versa.

Or take the case of a forty-year-old man attempting the youthful "I'm Alive" from *Next to Normal*—a scenario sure to leave casting flabbergasted. (If this actor sees himself as Gabe, casting better start looking in the old folks' home for his parents, Dan and Diana.)

Meanwhile, works that were once significant but have been twisted a hundred ways over the years can *lose* their coding. A song like the Gershwins' "Someone to Watch Over Me" has lived so long in the public consciousness as to be performed by all genders, young and old, and in every key, style, and tempo imaginable. Madonna's "Like a Virgin" has been parodied and rearranged over and over again, ripping it from its kinky roots and allowing an actor to bring their unique specificity to the material. The more a work is manipulated culturally—either because it has lost all connection to its origins or because it loses its relevance—the more it becomes fair game.

The bad news is that
early-career actors tend to gravitate
to the songs with the most coding
like a moth to a flame—to their own detriment.

The good news is that
the vast majority of songs available
have no coding or very little at all.

Actors who don't align with the demands of a highly coded song are better off choosing material that matches their own specificity—or selecting a piece with minimal coding, where they can bring something new to their performance.

OTHER SONGS TO AVOID

Avoid "doubles" in your book

You want something representative of yourself in each genre, but you don't need two songs that serve the same purpose, or a "double." One will likely do more for you than the other.

A legit soprano doesn't need "Somebody Somewhere" from *Most Happy Fella* and also "My White Knight" from *The Music Man*. Both are classic soprano ballads and not wildly different enough to justify why you'd need both. If difficulty were the deciding factor, "Somebody" proves the slightly more impressive song with its extended high tessitura.

Remember, your book is not a book of different characters. It's a book of different musical genres and feels.

Don't let hyper-specific characters stand in front of you

Your audition material tells the table who *you* are, not how well you cosplay as an extreme character. A song like "I'm Not That Smart" (*The 25th Annual Putnam County Spelling Bee*) is so connected to the oddball (man-)child Leaf Coneybear that the actor is forced to choose between ignoring the well-known idiosyncrasies designed into the song or impersonating what's already been done—and both options are disappointing. The actor should ask themselves what they're trying to convey. Whether it's comedy, quirk, or high singing, a different song will help us see the actor.

Beware brand-new contemporary musical theatre songs

Doing hot-off-the-presses material that you're 99 percent sure the people behind the table have never heard before isn't a great idea, because they will be distracted by the song itself ("Who wrote this?" and "Is it any good?"). They won't be focused on what they should be focused on, which is you.

However, if the song is from a brand-new musical with traction (a major regional premiere, a production Off-Broadway), it might be all right—but you sing it at your own risk.

While we're here: Don't worry about singing songs from unpublished scores. Unless you broke into the theatre and stole the music off the keyboard-conductor's stand, you're probably not the only one who has it, and no one is going to blame you. (Plus, RSO thinks that when a composer clicks "save as PDF," the fight against illegal sharing of the music is already over.)

EXAMPLES OF SOLID AUDITION BOOKS

Book example #1: Sandy

Sandy is a physically fit, five-foot-six Black woman. She's twenty-seven but feels she can still play eighteen to mid-twenties. Her dream roles include Julie in *Carousel*, Juliet in *& Juliet*, Dawn in *Waitress*, and Natasha in *. . . Great Comet*. She has a powerful belt coupled with a strong legit soprano, and has been cast professionally in both voice types to prove it.

Classic Up-tempo	"A Lovely Night" *(Cinderella)* "Blow, Gabriel, Blow!" *(Anything Goes)*
Classic Ballad	"What's the Use of Wondrin'?" *(Carousel)*
Contemporary Up-tempo	"Ready to Be Loved" *(Edges)* "Zero to Hero" *(Hercules)*
Contemporary Ballad	"Sal Tlay Ka Siti" *(Book of Mormon)* "I Hate the Bus" *(Caroline or Change)*
Radio Up-tempo	"I Wanna Dance with Somebody" (Whitney Houston)
Radio Ballad	"Gravity" (Sara Bareilles)
Folk/Country	"Follow Your Arrow" (Kacey Musgraves)
'50s–'60s	"White Boys" *(Hair)*
Contemporary Legit	"Just Around the Riverbend" *(Pocahontas)*
Sondheim	"On the Steps of the Palace" *(Into the Woods)*
Other	"Keepin' Out of Mischief Now" (Fats Waller)

Sandy has fourteen songs in her book to show off both her alto and soprano ranges, but not in every category. She has a standard contemporary musical theatre up-tempo in "Ready to Be Loved," but offers a higher-energy, gospel-tinged option in "Zero to Hero." She acknowledges a dream role with the sweet and silly "Sal Tlay Ka Siti," but is prepped to break hearts with "I Hate the Bus" should it be necessary. Her contemporary legit choice is a safe bet by showing off both a little chest and head voice, and though she could have opted for an alto song in her Sondheim category, she thinks the Sondheim sopranos Philia, Cinderella, and Anne are more her speed.

Book example #2: Frankie

Frankie is a five-foot-five, heavyset man who identifies as queer and half-Cuban. He's thirty-seven years old and feels he plays late twenties to late thirties. He self-describes as "a powerful tenor, silly, sassy, and *thicc*," is an excellent mover, and taps well. His dream roles include the Baker in *Into the Woods* and Barry in *The Prom*.

Classic Up-tempo	"I Really Like Him" *(Man of La Mancha)*
Classic Ballad	"Mr. Snow (Reprise)" *(Carousel)*
Contemporary Up-tempo	"Barry's Going to Prom" *(The Prom)* "There's Life Outside Your Apartment" *(Avenue Q)*
Contemporary Ballad	*Does not have one*
Radio Up-tempo	"The Lazy Song" (Bruno Mars) "I'm Still Standing" (Elton John)
Radio Ballad	"Who Says?" (John Mayer); *also doubles for folk/country*
Folk/Country	"I Hate Love Songs" (Kelsea Ballerini)
'50s–'60s	"Build Me Up, Buttercup" (The Foundations)
Contemporary Legit	"Out There" *(The Hunchback of Notre Dame)*
Sondheim	"It Takes Two" *(Into the Woods)*
Other	"Piragua" *(In the Heights)*

This book hits all the important categories and demonstrates versatility and excellent taste. Because of his type, Frankie thinks having an older and younger contemporary up-tempo will help him point toward two sides of his age and doesn't think he needs a contemporary ballad. His two radio up-tempos offer different energy, and he knows he can show off his voice with "Out There" and "I'm Still Standing." While his book is full of comedy—even his ballads have an edge to them—he can access his sincere side with either "Mr. Snow (Reprise)" (also a clever and unexpected choice) or "It Takes Two." Finally, he really loves "Piragua" to show off his connection to Latin material.

Book example #3: Jake

Jake is a twenty-two-year-old, five-foot-eight white guy with an athletic build who describes himself as "the lovechild of Aaron Tveit and Gavin Creel." He's an intermediate mover and has so far been cast in strapping young man roles and love interests. His dream roles include Gabe in *Next to Normal*, Claude in *Hair*, Whizzer in *Falsettos*, and Fabrizio in *The Light in the Piazza*.

Classic Up-tempo	"I Met a Girl" *(Bells Are Ringing)*
Classic Ballad	"Ilona" *(She Loves Me)*
Contemporary Up-tempo	"Can't Stand Still" *(Footloose)*
Contemporary Ballad	"When She Smiles" *(Lysistrata Jones)*
Radio Up-tempo	"Animal" (Neon Trees) "Crocodile Rock" (Elton John)
Radio Ballad	*Uses his folk/country ballad*
Folk/Country	"Bless the Broken Road" (Rascal Flatts)
'50s-'60s	"Ladies Choice" *(Hairspray* film*)*
Contemporary Legit	"The Streets of Dublin" *(A Man of No Importance)* "Santa Fe" *(Newsies)*
Sondheim	"Talent" *(Road Show)*
Other	"The Flesh Failures" *(Hair)*

Jake's book hugs his specificity tightly and suggests he's confident pursuing the tracks he's been seen for. There is a throughline of physical appeal in the roles he's taken from, and "Ilona" also signifies that even though the Link Larkins and Jack Kellys will make up most of his early career, he knows the smarmy Kodaly is a better fit for him than Georg in *She Loves Me.* His "Streets of Dublin" will be multiuse in both contemporary legit and contemporary up-tempo, and he's elected for his Sondheim tune a role Gavin Creel performed. The dramatic "Flesh Failures" is a great wild card for him as a role he's right for (Claude), plus a chance to show a more intense side (should it be called for).

Book example #4: Sara

Sara is a five-foot-nine, twenty-four-year-old white woman who plays her age. Her dream roles are familiar but suited to her: Carole King in *Beautiful*, Jenna in *Waitress*, and Elphaba in *Wicked*. She's aware that she belongs to the largest demographic of actors and has worked extensively to make her book hyper-unique to her.

Classic Up-tempo	"You Can't Get a Man with a Gun" *(Annie Get Your Gun)*
Classic Ballad	"Time Heals Everything" *(Mack and Mabel)*
Contemporary Up-tempo	"Legally Blonde (Vivienne's Reprise)" *(Legally Blonde)* "This Is How a Dream Comes to Me" *(Shrek)*
Contemporary Ballad	"Infinite Joy" *(Elegies)*
Radio Up-tempo	"Barracuda" (Heart)
Radio Ballad	"Rise Up" (Andra Day)
Folk/Country	"Whoa, Mama" *(Bright Star)*
'50s-'60s	"Natural Woman" (Carole King)
Contemporary Legit	"Woman" *(Pirate Queen)*
Sondheim	"So Many People" *(Saturday Night)*
Other	"The Nanny Named Fran" (theme song from *The Nanny*) "The Wizard and I" *(Wicked)*

Sara has a big voice and knows that vocal power will be an asset to her, so she's carefully selected many songs that feature an impressive belt without being too screamy (she threw "Get Out and Stay Out" . . . out). "You Can't Get a Man with a Gun" is a deceptively challenging big-belt song that's less done than "I Cain't Say No" or "I Can Cook, Too." She's very interested in contemporary musicals and has two different options: the pyrotechnic "Legally Blonde (Vivienne's Reprise)" for when she has limited time and needs to show range, and a comic cut of "This Is How a Dream Comes to Me" when she wants to focus more on her charm and sense of humor. While "Barracuda" and "Woman" are also impressive displays of vocal chops, all her ballads showcase easy intimacy that tells the creative team she is much more than "just a big voice." For kicks, she has a delightful gem in *The Nanny* theme song, and should it ever be called for, she said "fuck it" and added Elphaba's first big song in there . . . just in case.

TROUBLESHOOTING YOUR BOOK

"I think I'm just going to skip a '50s–'60s song in my book."

Some wonder why they have to hit all our listed musical genres. They consider leaving one or more out, especially if they never plan to go in for a show in a particular genre, but we think this is a big mistake.

> **Preparing material in every genre maximizes what you can audition for and increases your chances of regularly booking work.**

It's normal to prefer one genre over another, but ignoring one means ignoring hundreds of auditions. You won't be able to bring in a song in the style of that specified genre, and even if *you* don't think you're right for a folk-country musical, if a creative team loves your outside perspective, any one of them could be your next big contract.

Like making sure you're safely prepared with all the necessary gear for a weekend in the wilderness (pack that flare just in case it could save your life!), the amount of effort it takes to add that last genre into your book is tiny compared to what windfall it could bring you.

"Nah, you don't understand. Classic musical theatre sucks."

We hear this a lot, and we understand. For some actors, classic musical theatre feels antiquated and out of touch with their experience, full of tired and seemingly irrelevant stories. Yet we've seen many powerful revivals update and reinvent older musicals, breathing fresh life into the past and casting new shadows on the present.

Other actors acknowledge that, until about the last decade, classic musical theatre has too frequently marginalized and tokenized people of color and people of size, and this frustration pushes them away. Lindsay certainly felt that way early in her career, but it was the role of Carrie Pipperidge in *Carousel* that won her a Tony Award. This and many, many other examples offer hope that the industry's handling of the genre is evolving for the better. And above all, we must be the change we want to see in the world.

> *An actor working today should remember that finding themselves in the theatre of the past will allow them to be part of the future.*

"I can't sing pop. Why bother?"

Still other actors feel that most radio music is for the cool kids and their cool sound, and it's not their bag as an uncool drama nerd with a big Broadway voice. But with so many shows asking for radio material, it's vital to take the time to overcome this self-limiting misconception.

Most people who enjoy singing radio genres arrived there by listening, singing along, and imitating the sounds they heard. No one comes out of the womb singing jazz; it's something they learn to do through exposure and experience. The near century of popular music is as widely varied as the scores of musicals are, and with a little research anyone can find themselves somewhere in the genre. Not every pop singer belts like Demi Lovato and not every country singer twangs like Billy Ray Cyrus; think of innovative sounds like Joni Mitchell, Amy Winehouse, Florence and the Machine, Billie Eilish, Chappell Roan, and Orville Peck.

And though we might not know you yet, we think you're pretty cool.

YOU DON'T NEED A NEW SONG FOR EVERY AUDITION

You don't need a specific song for a specific show—aka, your *Heathers* song.

While you will be casually asked by an agent or a casting director in a master class, "Do you have a song for *Heathers*?" (etc.), what they're really asking is, "Do you have an up-tempo go-to song in the genre of the show I'm bringing up?" Your go-to contemporary musical theatre song, if it's truly perfect for you, will automatically point to where you fit in the show.

> **When you start picking out songs exclusively for dream shows and roles, you will soon find your book overstuffed and underprepared.**

For instance, if an actor identifies as a bubbly girl with a silly sense of humor and she sings "Positive" from *Legally Blonde* as her up-tempo go-to contemporary musical theatre song, this may suggest she's a good fit for Heather Duke. "But wait!" she says, "My friends tell me I'm a Heather Chandler!" Then why isn't her go-to contemporary musical theatre song "Till Someone Gets Hurt" from *Mean Girls* or "Special" from *Avenue Q*?

Constantly trying to bend ourselves like pretzels into our dream roles will leave us looking desperate and unfocused. In NYC and other professional markets, creative teams don't have to compromise on someone who, on Thursdays, *could* be the role. Instead, they're looking for someone who intrinsically *embodies* that role and has built their career (and to some extent, their adulthood) around that archetype.

It's better to focus on less material that you've mastered and can manipulate toward characters than more material you've worked on less, that's just there to show you in a certain light.

Let yourself, the actor, do that work—not a new song. And while we're here:

It is 100 percent okay to sing the same few songs at most of your auditions (and you probably should).

If you ask a working actor what they sing when asked for something from their book, they'll likely say, "Oh, I sing X for pretty much everything." That's not laziness. They simply realize that hyper-focusing on individual shows and getting a "perfect" song for each is a waste of time. They're better served singing something they've mastered that shows casting exactly who they are.

The Perfect Audition Cut

Just as important as selecting the right song is choosing the right cut, or the section of the song you're going to audition with. Because casting directors hear hundreds of cuts in a day, they're accustomed to a particular structure. Just like a headshot, résumé, and the audition itself, a well-crafted cut distinguishes the professional actor from the amateurs.

> **An *excellent audition cut* starts powerfully, builds to a climax, *and* wastes no time.**

Length

The first thing to determine when building a cut is its length. Though we tend to think of them as thirty-two bars, sixteen bars, and even eight bars (agh!), don't get bogged down by counting bars. We can't rely on the number of measures alone because time signatures and tempos can make two pieces with an identical bar count completely different lengths. In the end, thirty-two bars really means "about one minute," and sixteen means "about thirty seconds."

Because a full song is almost never requested, begin by preparing your audition piece as a thirty-two-bar cut. Then, when a sixtten-bar cut is called for, simply start about halfway through and go to the end—as the end of your cut is where the "meat" should be anyway. Similarly, an eight-bar cut (about fifteen seconds) focuses on the last quarter of your planned cut.

First page of a cut for "I'm Not" *(Little by Little)*

Start of the cut

The ideal start of your cut features one or two bars to establish the key and tempo. This introduction also gives you time to fully enter your story. More than two bars will waste time, because the accompanist isn't the one auditioning.

For these reasons, we strongly urge against beginning with just a bell tone (a single pitch played out of tempo) before a song, and it goes without saying that starting with an a cappella pickup note or phrase into the accompaniment risks a total disaster.

In this excerpt from "It Takes Two" (*Into the Woods*), the Baker's Wife begins after a bell tone. To be safe and smart, we cut the bell tone and have the accompanist vamp her opening bar until she's ready, marking it "vocal last time."

You have the right of way when it comes to changing or reshaping your music. If the bar before your entrance is problematic (because it's in a different key or tempo, for example), get creative, just as before.

"Wait" *(Sweeney Todd)*

In this example, the bar that precedes the start of the cut is harmonically vague and technically includes a *poco ritard* before you come in: a doubly dicey setup. By asking the accompanist to repeat the entrance bar, the singer has both the tempo and key provided, and like jumping into a game of double Dutch, they maintain control.

We can't overstate the importance of beginning your song with a bar or two of introduction, however creative you must be to make that happen.

THE SHAPE OF A GOOD CUT

***A good cut begins in the* middle part of your voice,**
***ascends through* nonrepetitive musical material,**
***climaxes on a powerful* "money note,"**
***and concludes* quickly.**

The journey of the cut should be something like this:

Dynamic shape of a cut

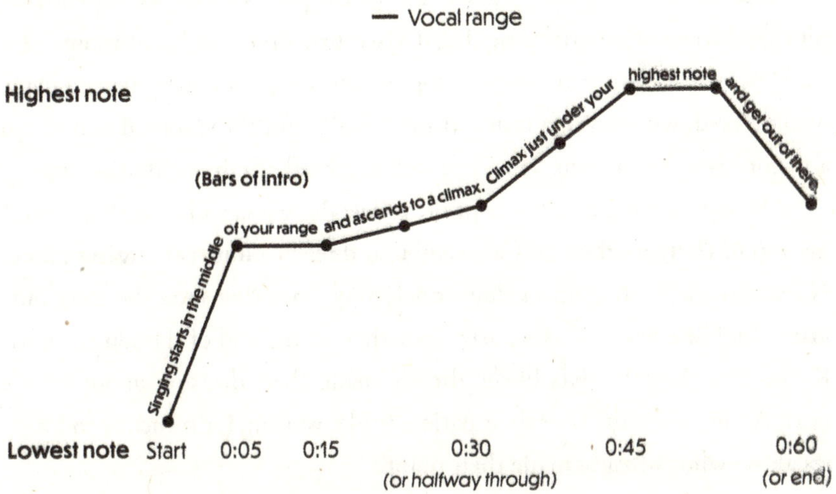

Start your cut in the **middle part of your voice** to capture our attention from the start, while still having somewhere to go. This means not beginning on notes so low you're hard to hear or so high that you startle the table. Carrying forward the "auditions are first dates" metaphor, you'd be bored by someone who showed up mumbling and turned off by someone who arrived screaming.

From there your cut **builds in excitement,** meaning that the energy increases and your vocal performance climbs in intensity (likely through higher pitches). If your cut enters measures that dissipate its energy (like the pre-chorus of many radio songs, or bars of suspended tension between two sections), try cutting them out, so long as it works musically and doesn't distract the listener.

Skip over repetitive, identical material—which you'll find mostly in radio material, which is designed to be catchy through repetition. If the verse has four lines that are the exact same, do the first two and skip forward, or start at the last two. Make sure to maintain the integrity of the song. If making the cut snags our ear in a bad way, leave it alone.

This all leads to your cut's **musical climax** with a "money note." This term refers to a pitch that is both thrilling and consistently manageable, for *you* specifically. Avoid your highest-conceivable notes (we call them "shower" or "voice lesson notes," as those seem to be the places where we dependably hit them) so you don't risk cracking disastrously under audition-room pressure.* Whatever you perceive your top note to be, your climax should live a whole step down or even a minor third. It's all right if the song doesn't have a major high note as long as we've reached a kind of climax another way.

Once your song reaches its peak, you've done your job and you should **get out of there** as gracefully as possible and reach a **natural ending place**. No additional verses, no mellow concluding lines that fade the song out, just a final line that *feels* conclusive (whether it's the end of the song or not). Know that the table has likely already made their decision about what's next. Additional time tries their patience, like waiting for someone to finish speaking who's already made their point.

SHORTCUTS AND TIPS FOR CUTTING MUSIC

While every song is different, there are some common shortcuts to start with as you begin making your cut.

AABA songs

Slightly more than half of all classic musical theatre songs (and many radio songs written before 1970) are written in an AABA structure. This form features two nearly identical A-sections with a "hook"—usually the song title—that give way to a contrasting B-section before returning to a final A-section.

* Further, after botching the note in an audition or class, many actors insist, "I can usually hit it at home." But you're not auditioning at home; you're in person and under additional pressure that you have to account for. If you miss the note once, it's likely to happen again. Even if you're almost sure it won't, is that a risk you're willing to take? Consider changing the key if it's appropriate, or reconsider the entire song.

"SO IN LOVE" (*KISS ME, KATE*)

A1 Strange dear, but true, dear,
When I'm close to you, dear,
The stars fill the sky,
So in love with you am I. **←Hook**

[Potential cut: A2 through end of A3]

A2 *(Nearly identical to A1 except for final note)*
Even without you
My arms fold about you.
You know, darling, why:
So in love with you am I. **←Hook**

B *(New musical material)*
In love with the night mysterious,
The night when you first were there.
In love with my joy delirious,
When I knew that you could care.

A3 *(Nearly identical to A1 except with a larger finish)*
So taunt me, and hurt me.
Deceive me, desert me.
I'm yours till I die,
So in love, **←Hook**
So in love, **←Hook**
So in love with you, **←Hook**
My love, am I.

Potential cut

A good place to start to look for a cut would be beginning at the second A-section and singing to the end (A2, B, A3). (This cleverly skips repeating two sections with virtually the same musical information.) If that feels too long, look at the B-section to the end (B→A3).

"LOSING MY MIND" (*FOLLIES*)

A1 The sun comes up,
I think about you.
The coffee cup,
I think about you.
I want you so,
It's like I'm losing my mind. **←Hook**

A2	The morning ends,	
Identical to A1	I think about you.	
	I talk to friends,	
	I think about you.	
	And do they know?	
	It's like I'm losing my mind. ←**Hook**	
B	All afternoon,	
New musical	Doing every little chore,	
material	The thought of you stays bright.	
	Sometimes I stand	**Potential cut**
	In the middle of the floor,	
	Not going left,	
	Not going right.	
A3	I dim the lights	
Nearly identical	And think about you,	
to A1 except with	Spend sleepless nights	
a larger finish	To think about you.	
	You said you loved me,	
	Or were you just being kind?	
	Or am I losing my mind? ←**Hook**	

AABA songs can vary in form, like AABABA (which "Losing My Mind" becomes when performed in full) or AABACA. Use good judgment to find your best sixty seconds. When in doubt, start at the end and work backward from there.

Verse-Chorus songs

Nearly all radio hits after 1970 (and slightly less than half of musical theatre songs) follow a verse-chorus structure, in which narrative-driven verses give way to catchy, repeated choruses. In contemporary pop and rock, choruses are often preceded by a pre-chorus, a section that builds tension and leads into the chorus. Longer verse-chorus songs frequently incorporate a bridge in the middle, introducing a contrasting section before returning to the final chorus. Conventions of more recent verse-chorus radio songs include starting with two verses and doubling choruses.

Start looking for a cut with the first verse and first chorus, which will usually be sufficient. If not, look at the bridge into the final chorus. If there's a pre-chorus, you can probably skip right over it if it pulls back the driving energy of the building verse (as it's often designed to do).

If you're uncertain if the song is an AABA or a verse-chorus song, look for a repetitive chorus. If you can't find one, it's probably an AABA.

Cutting "Where Is the Life That Late I Led?" (Kiss Me, Kate)

This song has a pretty straightforward cut with one verse (the first) and one chorus, but we can cleverly jump all the way to the end for the big finish. We skip the introductory section (not useful), and there's no need to repeat a verse or a chorus, as that's all repetitive material (and would make the cut far too long at any rate.)

"WHERE IS THE LIFE THAT LATE I LED?" *(KISS ME, KATE) (SUGGESTED CUT)*

First Verse In dear Milano, where are you Momo?
Still selling those pictures
Of the Scriptures
In the Duomo?
And Carolina, where are you, 'lina?
Still peddling your pizza
In the streets-a Taormina?
And in Firenze, where are you, Alice?
Still there in your pretty itty-bitty pity Palace?
And sweet Lucretia, so young and gay
What scandalous doin's in the ruins of Pompeii.

Final chorus Where is the life that late I led?
Where is it now? Totally dead!
Where is the fun I used to find?
Where has it gone? Gone with the wind!
I've oft been told of nuptial bliss
But what do you do
At quarter to two
With only a shrew to kiss?
So I repeat what first I said
Where is the life that late I . . . *(cadenza)*
Led!

As a trickier example, there is no obvious cut of "Agony." Worse, it's a duet for two princes and an actor could feel schizophrenic if he attempted to sing both parts. One option would be to sing Cinderella's Prince's verse and chorus and then *cut to* the final chorus (which luckily is in the same key) to give the song a finish.

"Agony" (Into the Woods) (suggested cut)

Verse 1 [CINDERELLA'S PRINCE]
Did I abuse her
Or show her disdain?
Why does she run from me?
If I should lose her
How shall I regain
The heart she has won from me?

Chorus 1 Agony—!
Beyond power of speech
When the one thing you want
Is the only thing out of your reach

Chorus 5 Agony
That can cut like a knife!
I must have her to wife.

MARKING YOUR MUSIC

Once you've determined your cut, mark it clearly for the accompanist.

First, **make sure the title of the song is clear**. If you aren't starting at the beginning where the title is printed, handwrite it in at the top of the page you are starting on. Seeing the title helps knowledgeable accompanists instantly recall the song's general tempo and feel, even if you want to adjust it to be faster or slower.

Mark "START" and "END" where the accompanist should begin and finish playing, keeping in mind that you probably want one or two bars before and after you sing.

It should go without saying, but **make sure your photocopied or printed music has all the information on the page,** especially if the copied pages are slightly askew (as with a scan or a bound book pressed against a copier). Commonly missing or obscured items include chord markings on the top of the page and bass lines on the bottom of the page.

Draw attention to any important tempo, time signature, or key signature changes with a highlighter (or penciled circle)—especially those you've had botched in the past. Accompanists are doing their best to sight-read accurately, but better to be safe than sorry.

TROUBLESHOOTING CUTS

Skip introductory sections

It's almost never advisable to sing a song's introduction (e.g., "Whenever I see someone less fortunate than I . . ." in "Popular" from *Wicked*) as part of your cut, because they inherently set up the main part of the song—which is what your audition should be. This is like showing up to a date and before you ask them a single question about how they are, you launch into a story about what happened yesterday at work. Everyone is ready for the actual date to begin.

Introductory sections of much older songs may be marked as a "verse" before a "refrain" on the sheet music. In common parlance we think of such old songs as having an "introduction" (e.g., "When I worked in the mill weavin' at the loom," in "If I Loved You" from *Carousel*) and a "song proper" ("If I loved you . . .").

Skip the introduction section and start with the main part—but don't confuse this advice and skip your vital one to two bars of intro, which are always recommended.

Stick to better-known verses rather than picking obscure ones

Some actors choose to do less-familiar verses because they think it will make them stand out, but that's more of a distraction than a good idea—the equivalent of greeting someone with "Salutations!" instead of "Hey!" Choose the better-known verse for its familiarity.

Optional: Avoid starting on "And," "But," or "So"

You might find that the best musical place to start in your cut begins with a conjunction or preposition. Some people frown upon this as a grammatical no-no, but it's easily solved by simply omitting the word.

In "Hold On" from *The Secret Garden*, many actors wisely start at "And it doesn't even matter if the danger and the doom come from up above," and continue to the end. To avoid starting with "and," cut the word out and begin with "It doesn't even matter . . ."

They're not casting high notes

Some actors feel compelled to choose songs around their ability to belt stratospheric pitches at casting directors—but what they hope will be an extraordinary display of pyrotechnics ends up setting the stage on fire (in a bad way). You want to be *impressive*, not *oppressive*.

Whether it's a "screlted"* F5, a beautifully spun D6, a rock tenor's wailed B♭4, or a falsettoed C5, all of these exceptional high notes are, at best, party tricks. At worst, in the first-date metaphor, they're like casually mentioning how much money you make or name-dropping your famous relative. It might be pertinent later, but for now it feels obnoxious and beside the point. The point of an initial audition is to get a strong sense of your talent and personality while keeping space to show them (a little) more.

Unless they specifically ask in the breakdown to sing "a song showing range," the assignment is simply to sing a song in the genre and show some personality. Should the role they have you in mind for require higher, brasher, beltier, screltier material, they'll give you the callback sides or vocalize† you.

"But the lyrical arc?"

Don't anguish over telling a complete lyrical story from once upon a time to happily ever after in a cut. That's overthinking it. In the same way that an excerpted scene in a play can be effective without seeing what comes before or after, reshape the story around the shortened material. The creative team is probably familiar with the full song as well as the show it's from, so they'll be with you wherever you drop the needle.

---

* In case you missed it, "screlt" is a delightful portmanteau combining "scream" and "belt."

† To "vocalize" an actor means to test their vocal range through scales or warmup-like patterns, ascending or descending by half step until the team is satisfied by a highest or lowest note. This happens usually before callbacks (where the given sides would test these notes) and in rare circumstances. Savvy singers may practice vocalizing themselves and negotiating between various registers (for example, switching from belt to head voice earlier or later in their range).

Transpositions for cisgender actors

Can you transpose the key of your audition cut? The answer is sometimes a rousing "yes" and other times a foreboding "no," but usually the right answer is subjective.

Nearly all radio songs, and most showtunes that have been performed in multiple keys from the many artists who've taken them on, are acceptable to transpose to your heart's desire.

Songs written for the theatre, meanwhile, get dicier. The composer wrote them for a specific character, and the song's range and key may be a part of the storytelling. By changing the key, we might be changing the story.

Similarly, songs notable for their high or low range are coded with their difficulty ("Chandelier" by Sia, "Rainbow High" from *Evita*, "Glitter and Be Gay" from *Candide*). Making the key easier can feel like cheating.

Calling back to our previous tip about ensuring you're not overblowing your voice with a brutally high note: It's one thing to raise a key so that it sits more comfortably in your voice, but it's another thing to raise it for the sole purpose of showcasing a range that wasn't asked for.

Transpositions for trans, nonbinary, or queer actors

If you identify as any of the above, transpose at will if it will bring life to your book and present yourself as you wish to be seen.

Some gender-bent songs are more effective than others. We find they work best when they make an impactful statement about gender or romance, like "Maria" from *West Side Story*, "She Loves Me" from *She Loves Me*, and "Material Girl" by Madonna.

When that's missing, it feels more like the actor just really loves a song without considering how it could confuse the creative team about who they are. If a female-identifying actor sings "The Night That Goldman Spoke at Union Square" from *Ragtime*—a song written for a male character that has nothing to do with gender or romance—the table is left with more questions than answers.

New arrangements

If you or someone you know has experience arranging music, spice up all or part of your audition cut to keep things fresh.

Bear in mind, though, that you don't want to surprise your accompanist *so much* that they're distracted by an unintuitive version they've never seen, of a song they intimately know. If you have time, have a vocal coach play through the song to make sure the arrangement is clear.

If the song has a well-known ending with an exciting high note . . .

. . . and you don't sing that part of the cut, the creative team may assume it's because it's out of your range. Don't hide behind curious cuts that imply more about what you *can't* do than what you *can*.

But remember that it's okay to leave them wanting (a little) more

Intrigue your potential collaborators, but don't take on the pressure of telling them everything about yourself on the first go. Some actors sing material that is too long, too high, or too complex because they're insecure that a more conservative approach won't be enough. You want to show a lot, just not everything you've got—and when deciding between adding or subtracting bars, the latter is usually the safer bet.

Don't end on a "staircase to nowhere"

Make sure the musical end of your cut feels like the end of *something*. Don't stop in the middle of a section (regardless of bar count) or at a place that leaves us going, "YES? AND?" Be wary of finishing at the end of a verse or bridge that is musically designed to overflow into the next section.

For example, imagine singing "On My Own" at your audition this way: *"A world that's full of happiness that I have never KNOOOOOWN!"* Pause.

"Thank you." This would be, as we say, a hate crime against musical theatre. Finish the cut!

Finally, do the assignment, not extra credit

The assignment of a first audition is to sing a song in the requested genre at the requested length. The cut begins in the middle part of your voice, proceeds to an exciting climax, flashes your awesome personality, and demonstrates your incredible specificity. Also:

- Well-known songs are okay.
- Don't lead with a ballad if you can help it.
- The most common version of the cut is usually best.
- Don't make a choice just to be different or work too hard because you're afraid you won't stand out.
- Trust that being highly personable and extremely skilled is all you need to book the job you're right and ready for.

How Working Actors Tell Stories

When a singer is off-pitch or misses a rhythm, they hear it (and so do we). When a dancer is out of step, they feel it (and so do we). But when an actor's performance is general, confusing, or altogether undercooked, they often have no idea.

The unaware actor thinks that acting is a matter of taste, as opposed to the more objective fields of singing and dancing. If they *feel* the emotions of a song enough, they believe, it'll be good storytelling. But the craft of acting is more like pitch, rhythm, and dance technique than they realize, and for this reason their auditions regularly fall flat.

Art is subjective, *but* craft is not.

Artists defy rules, necessarily, but they thrive through the conventions of their craft. We understand that an orchestra out of tune or a starkly visible wig line is categorically *wrong.* While watching a performance, we're familiar with our companion's knee grab when the lead actress nails a glorious high C or when the center-left dancer falls out of their turn. Accuracy in singing and dancing feels, in many ways, definable.

But whether it's due to lack of training or insufficient experience, the craft of acting often eludes musical theatre performers. Many talented performers start as big fish in tiny high school ponds, where their voice and charisma earn them annual leads, and their raw, natural acting instincts are heralded in comparison to their peers. But as they go upstream into college and beyond, the bar of their acting skill raises . . . and largely goes unchecked. They continue taking voice lessons and dance classes where their progress is easier to measure, until one day they get the dreaded note that their storytelling is "general" or "unspecific," and they have no idea where the note is coming from. Put very bluntly:

The sad truth is that most actors don't know how to tell a story in an audition —but think they do— which is why most actors don't get callbacks.

The working actor, meanwhile, has understood that the extensive demands of the acting craft don't begin after the audition, and know where to focus their time in preparation.

Working actors spend most of their time on their song's story rather than their vocal performance.

They begin with a series of essential questions to answer, a problem to solve, and a world to build. And like any craft, thankfully, the skill can be taught—and with practice, mastered.

STORYTELLING REQUIRES STRUCTURE

In storytelling, our job is to avoid delivering a performance that merely scratches the emotional surface ("unspecific") by demonstrating only the song's most basic information ("general").

When we're in the audience, we search for meaning from what we're watching. Scene by scene, our brains ask questions to relate what we see to our understanding of the world. Above all, we seek one essential thing: truth.

Who is the character and what do they really want? Where is their suffering coming from, and what drives them forward? Who or what is stopping them, and why? What will happen if they don't accomplish their goal? The consummate storyteller knows these answers and more, ready to create an entire world of story through a well-crafted performance.

ACTING MEANS ACTION

You'd be shocked at how often coaches stump their students mid-song with a simple question: "What are you doing?"

The student *knows* the coach doesn't want to hear "I'm, uh, singing a song?" but they've nonetheless succeeded at doing only that: singing with no other task at hand. Like driving a car without a destination, this is a waste of gas (and gas, like time, is expensive).

Acting means "to act" (and set story in motion).
Acting means "to do something" (and accomplish a goal).
Acting means "to take action" (and create change).

Acting is not *feeling*, it's *doing*. When you watch a play or film or read a work of fiction, you're always checking in with your characters, asking them, "What are you doing?" Feelings are by-products of character action for both the actor and the audience. It isn't enough to simply know the character's situation—essential as that is to the setup—and of course, the "act of singing" is really . . . well, just singing.

Drama means conflict.

Whether we're talking about the artform or that thing that's currently blowing up your friends' group chat, "drama" requires a problem to solve. In the song you're singing, you the character have (or create) some challenge you are working through, moment by moment, leading to a positive or negative outcome.

Story doesn't begin until a problem does.

For writers, exposition is vital to preparing a story. Like putting out the ingredients for a recipe, you aren't cooking until you turn on the heat.

Imagine if, at the start of a play, you watch two characters talking about seemingly nothing at a café. As the minutes tick by, you'll eventually ask (like your Aunt Pam watching freshmen do devised theatre for the first time), "What is happening?" When you decide, "I guess they're just talking about what they did this morning," the inactivity onstage loses you, and you get really bored, really fast. But the second one of the characters reveals they've come to the café in order to carry out a hit on the other—but they don't wanna ("Cuz I love you, Miyumi, and always have")—*now* a story has officially begun.

You the character have the same task as the scene above. Quickly grab your audience with, well, a task at hand. Through your clear context, you enter an intriguing conflict and—in the confines of 16 or 32 bars—work to solve it.

ACTING AN AUDITION CUT VERSUS ACTING LARGER FORMS

This book focuses on acting through song—and really, through *excerpts* of songs in the form of cuts. Telling a story in just thirty to ninety seconds may sound like insufficient time to show the full extent of your skill, but that isn't the goal—just as a job interview isn't a challenge to demonstrate every single thing you could possibly bring to the company. The ability to show how you tell a story in a short moment, made-to-order, is equally as important as demonstrating it in a full two-hour performance, just as the power to nail a job interview is vital to presenting your ability to do the job itself. First impressions promise what you're capable of, and if your auditor is indeed interested, they'll ask for more (a callback).

Audition cuts require the same process of thoughtful consideration that larger forms do, because both are stories in their own regard. Like two-page works of fiction, they're just *short* stories. The songwriters create tiny tales inside larger scenes that add up to a larger narrative: arcs within arcs within arcs.

SONG INTERPRETATION, IN BRIEF

All audition cuts essentially follow the same outline:

Something just happened.

Suddenly, you have a problem to solve, and if you don't, all will be lost.

You enter the scene as the music begins.

Someone (or something) holds the key to what you want, and immediately you take action to get it.

Your first effort fails, so you try something else. Tension rises.

Again, failure, so you try something even riskier, until at last, you win.

Or you lose. The point is that by end of the song something has *changed.* You the character have concluded your *mission* in success or failure. Combined, you've *told a story.* Story creates *feeling* for the actor—and, for your audience, *meaning.*

BEFORE YOU BEGIN: ANALYSIS

As you put your audition cut in front of you and start the detailed process of fleshing out your story, you begin by examining the song information you've been given.

Learn the song correctly

In our younger days, we learned songs by listening to cast albums. This was fun and effective, but in the professional sphere this should only be a last resort.

The best way to learn a song is by plunking out the pitches as written on the sheet music (or have them plunked for you). This way you're sure you're starting with exactly what's written and not absorbing another actor's choices—even the original Broadway performance. It also promises that the pitches are correct, as many recordings feature performances where notes have been altered by an actor—or not sung correctly at all, as you'll find on some older cast albums.

Music

Your song's melody and accompaniment offer a buffet of information that may feel obvious on first blush: up-tempo major-key songs are fun and slow minor-key ballads are sad. But a closer look reveals more.

Music, like its lyric, is never arbitrary; every decision the composer makes is intentional. You don't have to be a music theory expert to appreciate the details a composer has tucked into the song. The key is to listen, evaluate, and discover meaning within the music and apply it to the story.

What is the shape of the melody? Is the melody roughly same-note throughout, indicating emotional meditation (Fantine's "I Dreamed a Dream" introduction)? Is it a scalar ascent reaching upward ("There's no denying times is hard, sir," in *Sweeney Todd*'s "The Worst Pies in London")? Is it rhapsodic, sprawling a wide range ("Gethsemane" from *Jesus Christ*

Superstar)? Operatic, with sustained notes soaring in the upper register (the refrain of "Where I Want to Be" from *Chess*)? Chromatic, moving in half-steps out of the key ("Got my tweed pressed/Got my best vest," etc. in *Gyspy*'s "All I Need Is the Girl")? Pattery, tightly packed in rapid succession ("Poison in My Pocket" from *A Gentleman's Guide to Love and Murder*)? Composers make a choice to write catchy tunes—that is, ones that are simple, repetitive, easy to absorb, and echo. If your song's melody isn't, why not?

What is the range of the melody, and what does it say about character? For the character and their established range (soprano, baritone, etc.), where does their melody sit? Where does it reach its highest and lowest points in the song? If a soprano's song features a held note at the tip-top of her range (the ending of *The Sound of Music*'s "Climb Every Mountain"), it may mean something noteworthy is happening. If a note plummets so low that it stretches the bottom of a character's voice ("Artists are *bizarre*," in the title song from *Sunday in the Park with George*), why has the composer set it that way? Songs that live in the character's higher, more challenging tessitura may indicate passion, desperation, or urgency; those living in the middle may indicate lower stakes, comfort, or security; and those at the bottom may support quietude, reflection, or even bitterness (Sweeney's grumbling, "There's a hole in the world like a great black pit . . .").

How does the accompaniment relate to the melody? Does the accompaniment dance around the melody? Does it provide texture or rhythm? Is the bass rhythm a consistent beat—or is there no bass at all, leaving the melody feeling more like a freeform recitative? Does the piano's right hand double the vocal line, adding weight to the melody, or does it work against it harmonically, letting it feel more suggestive than tuneful? Not all melodies are of equal importance to a composer. Identifying which should be brought out and more fully sung, versus those that are more elusive and spoken-sung, may help influence your vocal approach.

When and why does the music change? When we sense a shift in the music, there is usually a shift in the story. If a song lives in one musical place for several sections and then changes feel, time signature, or tempo, what has caused the change? If there is a key change, why? What does the direction of the key change mean to you? Not all of them go up a step! "The Wizard and I," interestingly, actually goes *down* for its climax.

Collect the information you learn from the music and note your observations. If you impress yourself with your discoveries, you're likely uncovering details others haven't.

Lyrics (monologue)

The lyrics of a solo song are, effectively, a monologue set to music. Still, many actors dread the exercise of reciting the text of their song, because without music to support them, they're left unmoored, uncertain, and uncomfortable. Just as you mine music for story information, you must also pull the lyric apart. You'd easily sing your tune without the words ("la, la la"), but by focusing on *only* the words, you can better understand what a character is trying to *say* rather than just what the they *feel.*

Underline key conjunctions and prepositions. Words such as "but," "and," "so," "or," and the like guide the direction of thoughts in your character's journey. "But" turns to a new thought, "and" affirms or amends it, "or" considers an alternative, and "so" sums it all up. Each has many uses, so (So! So!) decide what each means to you in context of your lyric.

Note punctuation. Which thoughts end in periods (statements) and which in questions? Where are commas placed, and what might they tell you? Does the lyricist use ellipses (. . .) to indicate an unfinished thought (what has distracted it), or the em dash (—) for an interrupted thought (what has interrupted it)?

Make sense of utterances and nonsense words. What does your character mean when they sing, "Ooh," "Ahh," or "Doo-doo-doo"? These nondescript syllables *do* in fact have meaning, and you must identify why the writing team has opted for sounds rather than words. What is not being said and why (because it can't be), or what has been said so much that we explode into noises?

In this tiny example from "Everybody Loves Louis" (*Sunday in the Park with George*), Sondheim's punctuation marks and prepositions reveal a tremendous amount about his long-suffering leading lady Dot.

We lose things.

(Complete thought. A simple fact for Dot.)

And then we choose things.

(She adds to this another simple fact, a related thought care of "and.")

And there are Louis's

(No punctuation indicates she already knows the second half of this sentence)

And there are Georges–

(The em dash interrupts her thought with a surprise.)

Well, Louis's

And George.

(The "well" deflates her and the plural "Louis's" and singular "George" define Dot's show conflict in just four words.)

But George has George,

("But" starts a counterargument, and the comma carries the thought.)

And I need–

(The em dash tells us she doesn't know the next word and finds it.)

Someone–

(Again, she doesn't know who "someone" is—until she remembers . . .)

Louis–!

Examining the text offers insight into how a character thinks, laying a path for the psychological journey ahead of you.

CONTEXT (STORY)

The context surrounding the song details your character's world with color and nuance. Most of this information is right there in the script.

Many musical theatre teachers tell their actors to *personalize* their story in an audition—in other words, forget about the show it's from and "make it their own." This means substituting a moment of lived experience or imagined, relatable circumstance in place of given show context. Suddenly, "Don't Do Sadness" (*Spring Awakening*) isn't about a troubled young student contemplating suicide; it's about getting fired from your retail job.

Boooooo!

While there's merit to this way of thinking, it's ultimately misguided. It's true that the people behind the table are looking to meet you and not Moritz, but by ignoring the established information provided by the script we create more problems than we solve. Show context is inherently high stakes, structured around the most momentous events in a character's life—and likely, more dramatic than the selected life event in yours (at least, we hope).

In musical theatre songs, you should almost always use the context directly from the show.

When you begin the song in your audition, the table is instantly transported to that moment in the story. Most pros in the business know their musical theatre history and will fill in your backstory by instinct, flash-forwarding the scenes before your song to the second you've started your cut—all in the blink between recognizing the tune and hearing you start to sing. They then watch you play out your version of the scene, absorbing your performance alongside the story as they know it. This is an incredible advantage for you, because it puts the entire room on the same page.

But if you come in with your own personalized context, you're telling a story that's different from the one your interviewers are anticipating. To make matters worse, you don't get a chance to explain, "Oh, P.S., I'm not doing this in show context. It's actually about this one time at science camp . . ." So they watch, increasingly confused by what they're seeing until, if you're lucky, they figure out you aren't doing it in show context and—whoops, your cut is over.

ACTOR VERSUS CHARACTER

Context also provides character information, with all their accompanying quirks, history, and destiny. But when singing a character's song for an audition, the question arises: Are you yourself, or are you the character?

In an audition setting, you're actually someone in between. (This is further evidence that the approach to an audition cut from your book is related to, but not the same as, singing callback sides or digging into the role once you've been cast.) They aren't looking for your fully realized take on Dot from *Sunday in the Park with George* to see how you might fit into their production of *Light in the Piazza*, but Dot's "Everybody Loves Louis" *combined* with your storytelling choices may help them see you as Franca.

Just as in a job interview, where you're showing your prospective employer your "warm, professional self at a glance," here you're applying a genuine version of yourself to a special environment through the song you've specifically chosen to sing.

When we examined how best to choose material for your book, we focused on finding cuts that fit your specificity and allow you to showcase various aspects of who you are.

**With the right material,
your audition allows you to present yourself
through a character in a story.**

Your song's character becomes a filter through which you showcase yourself. It tells the table how you want to be seen, heard, and understood—akin to choosing outfits, restaurants, and discussion topics for a first date. These choices don't completely define you, but they inform the experience you want someone to have with you.

Let's break down the story essentials of an audition cut. We'll use three very different examples: "Luck Be a Lady" (*Guys and Dolls*), "I Know Things Now" (*Into the Woods*), and "I Miss the Mountains" (*Next to Normal*).

THE MOMENT BEFORE (INCITING INCIDENT)

Something just happened . . .

In the moment before you start singing, you experience a life-shaking event. It's because of this event, in fact, that you must sing: You've just won the lottery or learned someone has died. Instantly, you're filled with emotion and an urgent need to express yourself.

After you've slated your name and your song title, you should next take a beat for yourself. This isn't purely to separate real you from character you. More importantly, it gives you time to recall what just happened. Take the time you need (and probably a second or two more than you think).

In "Luck Be a Lady," Sky Masterson has just bet a throng of hungry gamblers $1,000 each on a game of craps in the hopes he'll win and force them all to attend a prayer meeting (thereby saving Sarah Brown's mission and winning back her love). But can he do it?

In "I Know Things Now," Little Red Riding Hood has just emerged from the belly of the wolf and come face to face with the harsh reality of the world. Can she make sense of this terrible trauma?

In "I Miss the Mountains," the pill-numbed, grieving mother, Diana, has reached a breaking point, determined to flush her medication down the toilet to regain both her sense of joy and of pain—even at the cost of her sanity. But will she do it?

Your moment before breaks your life open, forcing you to pull it back together again through action.

In these moments before, each of these characters has found their circumstances no longer acceptable, understandable, or sustainable, and *they alone* must change it—through pursuit of an objective.

WHAT DO YOU WANT? (OBJECTIVE)

Suddenly you have a problem to solve . . .

Your objective is the precise thing you're after in the song. By the end, you'll either win it or lose it. It could be obtaining a special object, taking a physical action, getting a response from another person, or undergoing an abstract experience—but no matter what it is, it must be clear.

Your objective is the clearly
defined thing, person, or event
you win or lose by the end of the song.

To win, you hold the magic lamp in your hands, you finally take that step out the door, you receive the apology, you hear the "click" of comprehension . . . or in losing you drop the lamp, relock yourself inside, watch them walk away, or you accept a painful realization. The objective may be stated directly in the lyric, implied indirectly, or staged in such a way that we get it.

Your objective must be definable
in both a positive and negative sense
(you know what winning or losing looks like).

For Sky Masterson, it's his belief that he can gain power over luck (personified as a woman in his own mind) and win the dice roll. Sky's belief that he can control the outcome is key to his character. Another gambler might believe in the odds, making their action "to hope." This is dramatically weak, because the character has succeeded in "hoping" the second the song starts, giving them no further reason to sing. For Sky, the song is a battle he fights actively with Lady Luck, like a knight with a dragon.

Meanwhile, for Little Red, she "should have heeded her [mother's] advice / but he seemed so nice." She sees an emotional gap between common sense and her adolescent desire, discovering that, to grow up, she must bridge the gap. Sure, the little caped kiddo would probably say she's just trying to figure out what the hell she just went through, but the actor understands more.

For Diana, relief is as simple as flushing away her medication. Her lyrics are entirely in metaphor ("mountains" are the peaks and valleys of her emotions) and nowhere in it does she mention medications or toilets, but the staging makes it clear.

WHY DO YOU WANT IT? (STAKES)

. . . and if you don't, all will be lost.

Your stakes create emotional intensity and heighten your scene. They communicate the value of your objective and justify the urgency of your actions.

Stakes are why you (and we) care about your story.

Stakes are relative to the character at hand. In "Some People" (*Gypsy*), the $88 that Mama Rose needs to get her kids started on the Orpheum Circuit is everything to her . . . but it's chump change to the wealthy Miss Dorothy in *Thoroughly Modern Millie*.

Stakes are also relative to the present moment in a character's life. For Jean Valjean (*Les Misérables*), choosing between his freedom and his sense of morality is the ultimate crisis in Act I's "Who Am I?" but by Act II his world has expanded so exponentially that in "Bring Him Home," the life of his daughter's lover, Marius, is now of greater importance than his own.

Absolutely anything can be of high stakes in the right situation. Consider the act of eating a delicious chocolate chip cookie. To the average person, this is a delightful treat on an inconsequential day, but to the morbidly obese man in a struggling marriage who's promised his partner he'll lose weight, eating a cookie is an earthshaking decision.

Stakes are not the same as seriousness.
Stakes indicate importance and value to a person.

"A Little Fall of Rain" (*Les Misérables*) is high stakes because Eponine is dying in the arms of the man who never loved her, but stakes are no less high in "Small World" (*Gypsy*) because Rose's winking flirtation with Herbie will secure a booking agent for her two daughters (and, thereby, their futures). The former is gut-wrenching while the latter is charming, but both moments are of crucial value to those involved.

For Sky Masterson, if he doesn't win, he will lose the love of his life. For Little Red, if she doesn't make sense of her experience, she'll never learn and may repeat her mistake . . . only then she might not be so lucky. For Diana, if she doesn't make this decision, she will never feel again.

WHERE ARE YOU? (LOCATION)

. . . *You enter the scene as the music begins.*

Yes, you're in a terribly lit room standing in front of strangers who are determining if your dreams will come true today—but once the piano starts playing, you're transported somewhere else entirely.

> *Location governs the width of your focus and what grabs your attention.*

Your location can be:

- **Fully closed** (Benny's dispatch office, Judd's shack) and you keep your focus intimate, near to yourself, and totally centered on your scene partner
- **Fully open** (the town square in River City, the island of the clambake), where you have a wide and far-reaching view, full of people, places, and things in the distance that might distract you
- **Somewhere in between** (Motormouth's record store, the stage of Velma's club)

Existing in this place you've arrived to, you communicate your location by how far left, right, up, or down you look; what catches your eye in front of or around you; and the comfortable or dangerous feeling you have being there. Let your eyes outline the set around you.

Location is your private playset and fills your world with truth. In "It Won't Be Long Now" from *In the Heights*, the ambitious-but-stuck Vanessa is on the street, and the actor must see the full boulevard before her: the elevated train above, the boys around the way just behind, the neighborhood salon to her left, and finally, the imaginary airplane that will take her away from the Heights soaring across the sky. These are just what's indicated in the lyric—to say nothing of what the creative actress might see in her mind's eye.

By contrast, in "Pretty Funny" (*Dogfight*), the betrayed Rose Fenny sits in her modest bedroom. Close by she sees the window and the curtain, the dress just a little to her right. This auditioning actress sees a teddy bear on her bed that reminds her of the innocence she's lost. She sees the vanity that now feels absurd. She shakes her head at the invisible door through which her mother, asleep, won't enter to comfort her.

Sky Masterson is in a dank sewer surrounded by gamblers who desperately want him to fail. Little Red has stepped away while the Baker consults with Granny a ways off—and considering the devouring she's barely survived, she may be looking over her shoulder for other cross-dressing wolves. Diana is completely alone in the privacy of her bathroom.

TO WHOM ARE YOU SINGING? (SCENE PARTNER)

Someone (or something) holds the key to what you want . . .

Identifying your song's scene partner is not only one of the most crucial questions to answer, but it's also one of the trickiest. The heart of the answer always lies in the central conflict: "Someone holds the key to what you want."

You are singing either to one person, multiple people, or yourself.

Characters can make pivotal decisions singing to one person (Raoul to Christine in "All I Ask of You," Hildy to Chip in "I Can Cook, Too") or to a group of people (Lois Lane to the audience in "Always True to You in My Fashion," Anita to the other Sharks in "America"), each of these situations clearly laid out in the story. Their scene partners hold the key to their success so that *they must sing the song* to get it. Raoul wants Christine to accept his love, Hildy wants Chip to know she's much more than a great lay, Lois wants the audience to understand the benefits of her sexual strategy, and Anita wants to win the argument.

But when we are singing to ourselves, things get thornier.

When we sing to ourselves, we visualize two or more sides of our mind having an argument, and only one side can win.

It might be a debate between two facets of our personality, like the "brave" and the "fearful" sides, as in "The Life I Never Led" (*Sister Act*), where Sister Mary Roberts faces the chance to become the outspoken woman trapped inside her (brave wins). Or it could be the "uncertain/insecure" side and the "delighted/worthy" side as in "A Quiet Thing" (*Flora the Red Menace*), where Flora processes what it feels like when all her dreams come true (her delighted side wins). It could be more than two sides, as in "On the Steps of the Palace" (*Into the Woods*), where Cinderella must decide to stay and be caught by the prince who could reject her, or escape and return to her miserable home life with the devil she knows—but option C wins, and she decides to leave him a clue ("for example, a shoe").

Some songs are deceptive. In "Changing My Major" (*Fun Home*), Medium Allison *seems* to be singing to Joan—but Joan is asleep, and therefore cannot participate in keeping something from Allison. This leaves Allison singing to herself in a conversation between the Allison who doesn't believe what's happened and the Allison who is stepping into her sexuality. The latter wins.

Similarly, Fredrik and Carl-Magnus ostensibly sing the duet "It Would Have Been Wonderful" (*A Little Night Music*) to each other, addressing each other from the top: "Sir." "Sir." But the song then makes it clear they're only working through the same situation: to reconcile *within themselves* their troublesome passion for Desiree. They aren't asking for anything from the other as they plan their next action: Fredrik realizes he can't hurt his wife, Anne, and Carl-Magnus doubles down on his quest to attain Desiree. The song doesn't explicitly state this, but now the actors individually know what they're doing during the song.

Can your scene partner change, such as starting with your scene partner and then ending alone—just as they change in both "Get Out and Stay Out" (*9 to 5*) and "Send in the Clowns" (*A Little Night Music*)? In these, Judy and Desiree, respectively, begin singing their songs to their exes, but finish alone. While this happens in staged productions all the time, it's tricky without another body onstage to show someone entering or leaving a scene—and watching someone's eyes trail an imaginary person to the door, open it, and leave, could feel at best silly, and at worst spooky.

In an audition, it's best to choose one scene partner and stick to them.

Of course, this doesn't mean you can't sing to one person *and* have moments of self-reflection—as Maria does in "I Have a Love" (*West Side Story*). The point is that your external scene partner holds the key to what you want, and only through them can you win or lose. Though Maria's primary goal is to convince Anita to bring her message to Tony at the drugstore, there's no doubt she's also reassuring herself that, despite all the bloodshed, she's in it to win it with her man.

Returning to our trio of characters and their songs, all three are singing to themselves. Sky Masterson is singing to himself because Lady Luck is not a real person onstage and ultimately the power lies with him (he's not singing to the gamblers since they cannot help him—and really, he's trying to ignore them). Both Little Red and Diana are attempting to solve an internal problem.

WHAT ARE YOU DOING? (PRIMARY ACTION)

. . . So you immediately take action to get it.

Based on the person you're singing to and what you want, you define your primary action. Not just any action: *interesting* action, because the story you're sharing is only as interesting as the action that drives it.

The more exciting and unique the action is, the more exciting and unique the performance will be.

We express action with an infinitive verb (for example "to confess," "to threaten," "to celebrate") or verb phrase (to confess remorselessly, to give an ultimatum, to explode with joy). But it's right at this point where many amateur actors dampen their otherwise excellent preparation with a weak, unspecific verb phrase that causes those watching them to remark that their acting felt "general."

Weak action = weak choices.
Weak choices = "general" performances.

Examples of weak verb phrases include "to decide," "to tell," "to explain," "to show," "to understand," and "to convince," because these phrases could be applied to almost any song. To make our performance singular and one of a kind, we must dig deeper.

Instead of "to tell," we find more exciting options like "to proclaim," "to caution gravely," or "to leak a secret." All of these are richer versions of "to tell," and each promises a performance unique to the others.

This is also the beginning of how we make a song our own. Whereas the given show context offers story elements like "moment before," location, scene partner, and objective, choosing your action provides your performance with a singular perspective.

Testing your action phrase

We have a test to help you determine if your action is strong enough. Imagine you're in a rehearsal studio, and someone comes rushing in screaming, "Come quick! Someone is ________ in the other room!" If you would be tempted to check it out, it's likely a strong verb phrase.

If they arrived screaming, "Someone's telling someone something in the other room!" or "Someone's making a decision!", you might respond, "Okay . . . cool?" But if they came shouting, "Someone's confessing to a crime in the other room!" or "Someone's seducing someone in the other room!" you might go, "Seriously? Can we watch?" Now you are an *interested* audience.

Often your verb phrase will require a few drafts as you plumb your performance to greater depths, but the further you dig, the richer it's likely to be. Don't be afraid of using a thesaurus, because research will help you clear away surface-level ideas and brainstorm something more inspired. Your verb phrase can include an adverb if it isn't already implied in the original verb and modifies it with greater consequence. For example, in "to propose marriage lovingly," the adverb "lovingly" feels redundant, but "to propose marriage *dangerously*" would be something to see.

We realize some actors get turned off by the academic nature of determining their action phrase, but we can't overstate how vital this step is. We don't blame them for glazing over at the word "infinitive," but while no one may learn what your chosen verb phrase is, the process of discovering it is also part of the process of going deeper with your story.

Sky Masterson's action might be "to conjure his power over luck" (something he believes is tangible), Little Red's could be "to dissect a near-death experience," and Diana's "to rip apart her safety net at the risk of falling."

HOW ARE YOU DOING IT? (TACTICS)

Your first effort fails, so you try something else. Tension rises. Again, failure, so you try something even riskier . . .

Using your exciting primary action, you now break it down into tactics. These supporting actions roadmap your song from start to song finish, and define the choices you make in real time. Tactics keep action alive. If a person were "to proclaim" for three minutes straight, all that barking gets old.

> **Breaking primary action into smaller tactics creates living, growing performances that mirror the way we behave in real life.**

A well-told story launches a protagonist after what they want. They begin cautiously, with safe, conservative choices, and build to larger, more dangerous ones (*tension rises*)—because, if they asked nicely and got what they wanted, the story would be over as soon as it began. Instead they try one idea but their opponent (who holds the key to what they want) resists them, so they get braver. They ask firmly this time, but *still* their opponent refuses. Finally, they blackmail, threaten, pummel, or manipulate them until their opponent's hands are tied.

Plots should thicken, not thin. The only way to get where you're going is by moving forward and taking greater risks.

For example, if the primary action is "to confess," tactics could include (in order of safe to scary):

1. *To face the music* (The actor sees the heartbreaking challenge ahead, staring into the abyss.)
2. *To collect yourself* (Their focus rises, speaking directly to their scene partner.)
3. *To disassociate* (They go pale, just saying the words, for if they think too much they may retreat.)
4. *To fracture* (But they can't turn off, and they break.)
5. *To crumble* (They shatter before their scene partner, begging for mercy.)

Well-mapped tactics evoke truthful human interaction. Our brains process action at a certain pace, which is why we flag story events that seem to happen too quickly or slowly as we consume drama. A person asking politely, then firmly, and then blackmailing in ten seconds feels chaotic and unbelievable ("Well, this escalated quickly . . ."), but if each tactic lasted twenty to thirty seconds, they might feel more natural.

An easy way to think of this is by assigning tactics to sections of the song: a tactic for a verse, a tactic for a chorus, a tactic for the bridge, and a final tactic for the ending chorus. (This is often how writers approach their songwriting.) As audition cuts tend toward only a few sections, smart actors break down their primary action into two to four tactics, but a full song would require many more.

Sky's tactics might include "visualizing, praying, begging, demanding"; Little Red's, "recalling, reliving, forgiving herself, compartmentalizing"; and Diana's, "reminiscing, regretting, distinguishing, diagnosing, defying."

IN THE END, WHAT HAPPENS? (WIN/LOSE)

. . . *Until at last, you win. (Or you don't.)*

You work on your scene partner until you arrive at a conclusion: You either get what you want, or not. We should see in your expression and body language which one it is, and what that means to you.

Your conclusion creates **change in your life** ***that fulfills the stakes of your story.***

You now have a fiancé, you officially quit your six-figure job, or you tore up your yellow ticket-of-leave and are now a fugitive on the run. If something doesn't change by the song's end, nothing has happened. (In musical theatre writing parlance, such a song is said "not to function," and must either be rewritten or restaged to work harder—or risk getting cut.)

Which isn't to say that every song ends with a 180-degree turn for a character. At the end of "I Cain't Say No," Ado Annie . . . still cain't say no. The amateur decides that "nothing, like, *happens* in the classics," but it's the professional (like Tony winner Ali Stroker) who unearths the action and change beneath the repetition. Perhaps Ado Annie begins feeling pressure to restrain herself from the men she wants, but by the end she proudly proclaims she doesn't want to say no and she's going keep on keepin' on. In this way, a familiar refrain takes on new meaning as the song progresses.

We encourage you to choose winning in your first auditions, ushering positivity and optimism into the room. But if you must lose (perhaps in a comedic lament?), have a good reason.

Sky wins the bet, sends the gamblers to the prayer meeting, and gets Sarah back.

Little Red Ridinghood arrives at "Isn't it nice to know a lot? / . . . And a little bit not," achieving her objective by learning something powerful. Ironically, she also considers she might have been better off not acquiring the knowledge (Sondheim, you devil).

Diana dumps and flushes, her emotional life free once again.

EXAMPLE: "WHATEVER LOLA WANTS"

In the Faustian musical classic *Damn Yankees*, middle-aged Joe Boyd makes a deal with the devil (Mr. Applegate) to become young longball hitter Joe Hardy and help the Washington Senators beat their rivals, the New York Yankees—at the price of his soul. Torn between his exciting new life and his abandoned wife, Meg, Joe is running out of time before he forfeits his soul to Mr. Applegate. To ensure Joe doesn't renege on the deal over second thoughts, Applegate sends the hell-vixen Lola to get his mind off Meg *(context)*.

The song is sung by Lola *(character)* in the empty Washington Senators' locker room *(location)*. Lola has just asked Joe to spend the night with her, but he's resisted her increasing advances in favor of returning home to his wife *(moment before)*. This is new for the eminently talented Lola, who must get Joe *(scene partner)* to betray his wife *(objective)* or else risk losing her title as "Hell's Best Homewrecker" *(stakes)*.

Now the actress has her own individual choices to make. Music begins, and this Lola transforms into a dominatrix whose only mission is "to seduce a married man" *(primary action).* She likes adding "a married man," because it intensifies the brand of seduction she needs to do, which is to give Joe everything he won't be getting from his tired, vanilla-flavored wife. From here, she outlines her tactics across the sections of the lyric.

ACTION OUTLINE OF "WHATEVER LOLA WANTS"

Whatever Lola wants, Lola gets . . .	**Posturing** *She does not move much, presenting herself and watching him get nervous.*
Make up your mind to have no regrets . . .	**Teasing** *Slight motion, a smile, eyes moving up and down his body.*
I always get what I aim for . . .	**Demanding** *A step forward, an arm outstretched, pointing at what she will take.*
Whatever Lola wants . . . Give in!	**Taunting** *Having made him duly uncomfortable, she withdraws, knowing she has the upper hand. Satisfied she has the control, she makes it clear the ball is in his court . . . and he* will *pass it.*

By the end of the song, the actress has Joe right where she wants him *(win)*, cracking his impenetrable fidelity. (And even though Joe ultimately rejects her, both are shaken by the experience: Joe now has a taste for another woman and Lola faces her strongest adversary yet.)

ALL CHOICES ARE POSITIVE

Moment to moment, we do the things we want—whether that's asking out someone we like or eating a piece of delicious cake. Acting on annoying mandates like paying our bills is positive, too, because we want to keep the lights on. Self-destruction, it can be said, is no different. While the pub crawl might cause pain tomorrow, right now the alcohol feels good. So we order another round.

Every choice we make is inherently positive: In some way, it benefits us right now.

But what about the guy who punches his fist through a wall? He knows it's going to hurt and may even cause irreparable damage, so isn't this negative? No. In the moment, he's so filled with rage he *must* let it out or his body fears what else he might do, so he expels the excess in an act of violence. He *wants* to punch the wall, even *needs* to.

Actors keep this in mind as they analyze songs—especially dark, dreary, or depressing ones—by asking precisely what the character's *positive* want is, even when it seems positivity is impossible.

EXAMPLE: "I DREAMED A DREAM"

The tentpole song from *Les Misérables* might seem like an anthem of grief (it does end with "Now life has killed the dream I dreamed," after all), but a closer look at the story around the song reveals that it's much more.

In 1823 France, single mother Fantine *(character)* struggles to make ends meet while sending money to the innkeepers caring for her daughter, Cosette *(context)*. Fantine has just been fired because her foreman and the other workers learn of Cosette's financial burden and believe needy Fantine will drag them all down *(moment before)*. On the street *(location)*, Fantine sings to herself *(scene partner)*.

It's here, though, that things get murky. The gist of the lyric is:

In days past, the world was kind, but no longer. Young, hopeful, and naive, I dreamed of a happy life, and then catastrophe struck. I loved a man, and even though he abandoned me, I still believe he'll return. Yet now I see I am a fool. I had a dream once, but now life has destroyed it.

We guess this is why the show's titles translates to "the miserable ones." But what is Fantine actually *doing*? Reflecting on the past? Complaining to no one? Processing all she's lost? All of those are supported by the lyric, but none of these proposed actions truly accomplish anything particularly stage worthy; using our test, would you rush off to see anyone reflecting, complaining, or processing in the other room? Plus, through the song, each of those weak actions would be completed in only a section. But if we see these as tactics serving Fantine's larger primary action, we reveal the heart of the song's truth.

Looking to the end of the lyric, we could see the action as "to give up your dreams." That doesn't feel right because there is no objective positivity in it—unless we go further to figure out *why* Fantine giving up her dreams would benefit her. If we look before and after the song, identifying where she starts and where she ends, we learn something more. Before the song, Fantine lives a humble (if persecuted) life, employed enough to send cash for her daughter's care. Afterward, she sells her hair, her prized locket, and her body to make money. If Fantine's action were really to give up her dreams, she might as well call it a day and take her own life—but she doesn't. In fact, the song gives her the clarity and courage to make the hard choices that will keep her daughter alive, even if it ends up killing her (and ten show minutes later, it does). And so we see Fantine's action is really "to sacrifice herself for her daughter," which, while still sad, is imbued with hope and, yes, positivity.

Sacrificing yourself for the betterment of your child *(primary action)* is a big decision, and we now see that reflecting, grieving, absorbing, processing, accepting, and resolving are the ways *(tactics)* by which she arrives there *(win)*.

ACTION OUTLINE OF "I DREAMED A DREAM"

There was a time when men were kind, When their voices were soft And their words inviting . . .	**Reflecting** *Recovering from shock, for the first time seeing what must now be done.*
. . . I dreamed a dream in time gone by, When hope was high and life worth living . . .	**Grieving** *Holding each memory, letting it go. Some hurt more than others.*
. . . But the tigers come at night . . .	**Absorbing** *Facing what has happened to her with reluctance but bravery.*
. . . He slept a summer by my side. He filled my days with endless wonder . . .	**Processing** *Dividing emotional pain from hard truth.*
. . . But there are dreams that cannot be And there are storms we cannot weather . . .	**Accepting** *Gathering strength, confronting the coming storm.*
. . . Now life has killed the dream I dreamed.	**Resolving** *Deciding her happiness is over, but there's hope still for Cosette.*

EXAMPLE: "I'M NOT AFRAID OF ANYTHING"

In songs that are not from book musicals and have no larger context to pull from, you only have the lyrics to determine their story. In these exceptions, personalization is helpful to fill in the blanks.

In "I'm Not Afraid of Anything" (*Songs for a New World*), Woman 1 shares the fears of many people in her life but vows that she is (you guessed it) not afraid. Inspired to live an adventurous life, two-thirds of the way through the song she is suddenly distracted by thoughts of "David," who, she swears, *definitely does love her.* She concludes that he's afraid of her, but she is a fortress and won't let him or anyone break her down, because *she is not afraid!* (Or is she?) (Your authors think David is homosexual, but that's neither here nor there.)

This deceptively complex song can pose challenges for the actress and, if not thought through carefully, for her audience as well. We've seen many a performance where the actress begins the song warmly, even smug, telling us about how weak the people in her life are and how brave she is by comparison. Then in what appears to be a schizophrenic break, D-A-V-I-D crosses her mind. She fights a meltdown and decides not to let this get to her, "'cause after all, I'm not afraid." And it's this "after all" that further complicates matters, when we determine she is simultaneously aware of her fear but pathologically denying it, choosing delusion.

Jason Robert Brown is one of the most brilliant writers of our generation and we do not think this is the story he intended, nor do we think it's properly justified by his lyrics. The music, powerful and uplifting, has affection for its singer, so we don't think she's having a sudden, unexpected break about David; she must be thinking about him from the start. Otherwise, why does she begin singing? Just to list off the fragile failures in her life and build herself up? She must be surveying these people in an effort to understand something more about David.

She certainly seems self-aware and ambitious—likable even—and so we decide delusion is out. To give her the strongest, most positive journey, we also choose to believe she's telling herself the truth. She can't be talking to David because she mentions him in third person. Even if the actress decides that she's talking to her therapist, say, ultimately she's the one in her own way and the lyric supports a decision she makes on her own.

This leaves us with a story of a woman who is trying to figure out what to do about David—who *does* indeed love her but is hopelessly afraid of intimacy with her. She hears "the calling of excitement," will "never stop the calling of a challenge," is "sure to win with anyone at all," and is realizing that David "will always be" afraid of her. She must end things with him, and so makes the painful, terrifying decision because "after all, [she's] not afraid."

Now we have a story: Woman 1 plays David's partner (*character,* and her own *scene partner*) and must figure out what to do about David (*objective*), and so she is "coming to terms with ending things with her loving partner" (*primary action*) because the life they're living is doomed (*stakes*). To get herself there, she surveys her loved ones' fears, asserts her courage (building through ever more important examples, from small children to her mother), envisions a better future, faces the question of David, acknowledges his love, chooses to move on, assures her choice (*tactics*), and finally, steels herself for the forthcoming confrontation (*win*).*

All that's left for the actress to determine is her location, moment before, and the context for her relationship with David.

ACTION OUTLINE OF "I'M NOT AFRAID OF ANYTHING"

Jenny's afraid of water I mean, she swims so well, but still . . .	**Surveying her loved ones' fears** *beginning with the children in her life.*
I'm not afraid of anything, Be it mountains, water, dragons, dark or sky . . .	**Asserting her courage** *Reminding herself she's not a child, she can do hard things.*
Daddy's afraid of babies. I mean, he got through me, but now, He's afraid of babies . . .	**Surveying loved ones' fears (deeper)** *Facing her parents' emotional detachment, realizing perhaps she has found a partner who is much like her parents.*

* JRB has neither confirmed nor denied our analysis, but we think we're right.

. . . I'm not afraid of anything, Be it growing old or going out of style . . .	**Asserting her courage (deeper)** *With growing frustration brought on by facing her own childhood, she sees the full scope of her problem.*
. . . And I feel the calling of adventure And I hear the ringing in my ear . . .	**Envisioning a better future** *She sees that life could go on without David.*
. . . —And David loves me . . . He's afraid to hold me.	**Facing the question of David** *And facing the prospect of being alone.*
Listen to the calling of excitement . . .	**(Back to that better future)**
. . . Never stop the calling of the challenge, Blessing on the water and the stones David loves me—he's afraid to tell me . . .	**Acknowledging his love** *Knowing that his love is what has kept her from making the tough call, she accepts his love and also accepts it is no longer enough.*
. . . And he'll always be . . . He's afraid of me . . .	**Choosing to move on**
. . . And I'm not afraid of anyone! I am sure to win with anyone at all . . .	**Assuring her choice** *Like repeating a mantra, she can do this, and she will figure it out as she goes along. What other choice does she have?*
. . . 'Cause after all . . . I'm not afraid.	**Steeling herself for the forthcoming confrontation** *With a mix of fear and relief, she's come to a decision.*

Song interpretation and audition cuts

While we've used three full song examples, the process for interpreting an audition cut is essentially the same—just compressed.

For those who fear their cut might not have "enough story" in it, remember that a story can be told in just a sentence—or as Norma Desmond sings, "with one look." Your auditors likely know the song and show well. They're already with you.

You analyze the full song and excerpt your work just as you excerpted the cut, or save time and focus only on the bars you're doing—but make sure to create an arc, whatever you do. It can be small, but plan at least three tactics to build story momentum.

If your cut includes the end of the song, you'll naturally have a sense of win or lose. If it doesn't, either think of your cut's end as the conclusion of the song (if it's appropriate) or find an alternative conclusion (a different idea of win or lose) where you stop.

INTERPRETING RADIO MUSIC

While performing your radio song, should you act—or not? Actors hear conflicting answers.

Some casting directors and agents feel that radio music should always be acted in a theatrical audition, while others passionately feel they should *never* be acted because radio songs are not theatre. Making matters worse, when you walk into the room, how will you know which side of the argument your auditors are on without asking, "So, do you want me to act?"

We think there is a consensus for something in between, and we can safely say that *every* song you perform should tell a story, regardless of whether it comes from the theatre or radio. But in the case of the latter, it's on you to come up with your own circumstances.

When singing radio music,
you demonstrate how you sing in that genre,
while telling a simple story in a lower-stakes situation.

The primary reason for choosing low stakes* is that radio music is almost never character- or story-driven. The lyrics are universal, vague, metaphorical, or would sound a little silly if you sang them seriously. Have you listened to the words of Britney Spears's "Email My Heart" lately? We'll wait.

It's for this reason that some actors get the note that their radio song performance feels too "musical theatre-y," because their stakes are too high and they're confusing the material with contemporary musical theatre. It's not. It's radio, and if they wanted a complex, high-stakes narrative, they'd have asked for material written specifically for the theatre.

Avoiding weak scene partners in radio songs

One choice that comes up in radio or stand-alone songs (where no show context is provided) is that the actor opts to sing to a weak scene partner, like their best friend, loving parent, or therapist. The issue here is that these particular people aren't usually in the way. Rather, they're bound to support your desires and thereby dispel conflict. A best friend only works as a scene partner if, let's say, you're ending the friendship or telling them you're in love with the same person. A parent works if you're begging for their blessing to move away or fighting for a romantic relationship they disapprove of. Remember: Your story circumstances require tension to create drama (in both senses of the word).

Like it or not, most radio songs are about love (sad but true?)

Whether you're wistfully pining for someone or gunning for a hookup, the stakes must still be low. To do this, we suggest a safe, fun location like a bar or a club—a place you can let loose, "feel yourself," and move your body freely. Your scene partner is someone you want romantically, either a

---

* Sometimes called "baby stakes." Not to be confused with "baby steaks"—which would be gross.

stranger or a fuck buddy . . . but if it doesn't work out, you don't care *that* much—like in the Rolling Stones' "Let's Spend the Night Together," Marcy Playground's "Sex and Candy," or Taylor Swift's "I Can See You."

Story songs from the radio

Some radio songs (particularly folk and country) tell proper three-act stories, but to lower the stakes consider that you're telling the story to someone who needs to hear it, and though you enjoy telling it, it's not that deep for you (because you have a little distance from it): "Coal Miner's Daughter" by Loretta Lynn, "Fancy" covered by Reba McEntire, or "Goodbye, Earl" by the Chicks. (In other words, if you were to sing these songs as though they were *your* story, suddenly this would feel like contemporary musical theatre, not folk-country music. The original artists don't perform these songs as though they were their own true story, so you shouldn't crank the temp, either.)

Radio ballads: Ever so tricky

To that end, radio ballads are the most dangerous songs to interpret because singers often *really* want to suffer through them (who hasn't cried to a song on the radio after they've been broken up with?). Worse than feeling "musical theatre-y," these come off as purely self-indulgent. We recommend saving the painful performance for karaoke when your ex-girlfriend Amelia can finally hear how you feel (though, let's face it, she already knows . . . and doesn't care).

And even though the songwriter possibly wrote the song with personal circumstances in mind, the pain eventually subsides as they sing it a thousand times in concerts, on tours, on television, and so on, until the song becomes nothing more than a cash cow—er, gift for their audience. Best to treat radio ballads from the position of an experience you're on the other side of, looking back. (We're thinking of "Candle in the Wind," "Unbreak My Heart," "Driver's License," "When I Was Your Man" . . .)

Negative radio songs

Similarly, some radio songs appear negative—telling someone off or confronting someone who hurt you—but again, imagine that the moment is simply delicious and you don't honestly care that much if the person lives or dies, because you're over it.

While singing "Gives You Hell" (the All-American Rejects) or "Sorry Not Sorry" (Demi Lovato), maybe you accidentally run into him on the street . . . you're feeling yourself, and you've got some *excellent* news for this piece o' poo who broke your heart—and anyway, after the song you're getting margaritas with your friends.

These will yield matching lower-stakes actions: "to flirt," "to uplift," "to give closure," and so on, things we might not run into the other room to see but might keep an eye on if we spot them from across the club.

Avoid hyper-personal or professional circumstances

Personal stories (breaking up with your actual partner, your terminally ill relative fading away, etc.) may help you feel vulnerable, but if they bring you *actual* tears, pain, or anger, they're inappropriate for a job interview. Professional circumstances (what you'd like to say to your agent or telling off a cruel director) can be great backstage stories, but it's better to come into an audition with a positive mindset about the industry you're trying to break into.

DEPTH AND CONNECTION

Beyond the essential questions are more advanced practices to help you dive deeper into your interpretation. These techniques help you find more of yourself by placing a personal spin on the song. They're especially useful for Sondheim songs and other more complex pieces.

Paraphrase

Remember *No Fear Shakespeare*, those handy reference books featuring Shakespearean text on one side of the page and a rewrite in contemporary English on the other? These are excellent resources for the uninitiated student who wants to better understand the drama behind the beautiful yet challenging text. We can use a similar technique, called paraphrasing, to decipher the lyric.

In paraphrase, you reinterpret a lyric in your own words.

In "The Simple Joys of Maidenhood" (*Camelot*), future queen Guinevere questions her societal role as an eligible young woman. The original lyric is:

Where are the simple joys of maidenhood?
Where are all those adoring daring boys?
Where's the knight pining so for me
He leaps to death in woe for me?
Oh where are a maiden's simple joys?

One actress's paraphrase might be:

These are the precious years of my feminine youth,
And men should be pursuing me.
Strapping bachelors should desire me
So much that they lose their minds.
These years are slipping away too fast.

While another's could be:

I wanna feel sexy!
I want hot guys to want me,
So much they're practically
Killing themselves over me!
Ugh, I wanna feel sexy.

Here are two very different interpretations of the same moment, but both are rooted in truth and supported by the text. The first actress sees Guinevere as a thoughtful, sensitive darling longing for love, while the second sees a familiar fun girl jonesing to enjoy her youth while she still has it. Each is right for the actress who's playing her *because it came from her.*

Subtext

We rarely say exactly what we think and feel, especially when emotions and stakes are high—which is the case in almost any theatre song you sing. The lyric is only the tip of the emotional iceberg. Your character—and really, any real person in the same situation—is pursuing what they want while *risking as little as possible.* So they cloak what they really mean in other words.

> **Subtext is the unspoken, vulnerable sentiment "beneath" what is being expressed.**

Classic musical theatre is especially rife with subtext, but performers can miss it if they write the material off as too simplistic. For characters living in the historic past, resources are limited and opportunities few. Prospects are really life-and-death circumstances—which means greater caution in what they can express.

When a nineteenth-century young woman is interested in a man, her words must be chosen carefully, or she risks a damaged reputation (and possibly familial humiliation). If she fails to secure her prospect's love, the extraordinarily limited fish in her sea have diminished by a precious amount. For her, in this era, becoming a spinster might be a fate worse than death, whereas a girl today need only swipe right on the next profile. Unlocking the terrifying truth underneath the language plumbs the song's true depth and excavates greater connection to your material.

Or take another example: In the beautiful and unsettling television film *Evening Primrose,* nineteen-year-old Ella has been trapped in a department store with a mysterious group that comes alive after closing. When the poet

Charles—hoping to escape society—infiltrates their group, he and Ella are immediately drawn to each other. One day, Ella tries to recall to Charles her memory of the world before she arrived at the store . . . but realizes that they are being replaced by memories of the store. Ella knows that once you've joined the group, you cannot leave or else you'll be turned into a store mannequin. Though it isn't explicitly stated, the actor may discover that this realization sets into motion Ella's desperate need to escape at any cost *through subtext.*

Unlike paraphrase, which is interpreting the text in other words, writing out your subtext is writing out the character's secret, vulnerable thoughts—the words they *are net yet able* to say. Here is an example of how one actress might paraphrase their cut.

EXCERPT OF "I REMEMBER" (*EVENING PRIMROSE*)

. . . I remember leaves:
Green as spearmint,
Crisp as paper.
I remember trees:
Bare as coat racks,
Spread like broken umbrellas.

And parks and bridges,
Ponds and zoos,
Ruddy faces, muddy shoes,
Light and noise
And bees and boys
And days.

I remember days–
Or at least I try,
But as years go by
They're sort of haze
And the bluest ink
Isn't really sky
And at times I think
I would gladly die
For a day of sky.

I think I remember leaves,
But my memory is foggy . . .
Is my recollection real?
Well, I'm sure I remember trees–
They were just like . . .
No, they aren't like that at all.

Quickly! Remember it all,
Something must be clear to me–
Figures come into my mind–
A clear memory emerges,
I remember–a young man,
And how beautiful the world once was.

I do remember, don't I?
Oh, who am I kidding?
I will lose all my memories
Soon if I don't leave . . .
Nothing here is real,
And it never will be.
And I realize now I would risk my life
To see the world once again.
Charles, could you help me escape?

Never right or wrong, this paraphrasing interprets Sondheim's lyric specifically for *this* actress alone, informing her performance and sparking conversation for both her scene partner and her director.

Note that subtext exists even when we sing to ourselves. Though we're alone, we still might avoid saying certain truths aloud, especially if we aren't ready to accept our reality.

Elaboration

Paraphrase and subtext enrich a character's action, but this doesn't account for the nuance of history and memory, and their impact on the choices we make. Because you only have the given text to inform your character's past (let alone the unobserved scenes between the scenes we experience), this leaves a wealth of blank spaces for you to fill.

> ***Elaboration*** **fleshes out a character's history by using your rich imagination and creative voice.**

Line by line, you can dream up memories and specifics between the lines of the text. Like freeze-frame, stream-of-consciousness journaling, new details flow into the story. When a character sings a lyric like "You've always been kind to me," they're referencing many examples of their scene partner's kindness—examples that probably aren't seen onstage.

In elaboration, you can also clarify the rich details of a character's experience. As they say, no two people see the same color the exact same way. If you were to belt out, "I feel wild and free," this is rooted in sensations specific to you (and your version of the character). "Wild and free" for one person could be treating themselves to a McFlurry, while for another it's a booze and benzo-filled bender. If we're to believe you're authentically feeling wild and free, you must know what these thoughts are for you, just as the character would. When you don't have these details in your mind, you're just playing pretend, *acting* like the character instead of *being* them.

Taking only the first stanza of "Moments in the Woods" (*Into the Woods*), the long-suffering Baker's Wife processes her affair with the Prince:

Was that me?
Was that him?
Did a prince really kiss me?
And kiss me?
And kiss me?
And did I kiss him back?

Taking this line by line, you could elaborate:

Was that me? I've never kissed anyone but my husband the Baker, and even that was by accident the first time. How could I go through with that . . . then again, I always was impulsive as a girl, which got me into trouble until I met the Baker.

Was that him? Did a prince really kiss me? Maybe that wasn't him; my eyes have been playing tricks on me lately. Maybe I'm dreaming . . . certainly that experience felt like a dream. I haven't dreamed much lately . . . not for years, maybe.

And kiss me? And kiss me? The way he touched me, I've never been touched that way. His hands were so strong, like the butcher's, but uncalloused like the tailor's. And he smelled—oh, the way he smelled!—so good, not like flour and yeast and—oh, god . . .

And did I kiss him back? I couldn't have, wouldn't have, would never! I've always been a rule-follower, always done what was right. This isn't who I am.

Though the process can be painstaking, the effort pays off when you've colored in a world all your own. When you walk into your next audition or rehearsal, it's your pleasure to share the incredibly thought-out, personal tale that only you can tell.

TRUST THE PROCESS

Write down your answers to these essential questions and assignments. You can revise your answers later, but the physical expression of this critical thinking is something you should revisit to prepare for every audition. Later, your discoveries will also serve as a guide while discussing your performance with a director, music director, or writer.

We mentioned earlier that despite actors having learned these fundamentals (several times, probably, in every acting class they've ever taken), we're often disappointed to see extraordinary vocalists bring in stories totally underprepared. But why, given that they know better?

We wonder if some actors believe that once they've learned the process, written out some homework, and demonstrated it a few times for a teacher, the work is forever done and inside them. Now they can simply intuit their way through a performance, because "they get it."

Alas.

Just because a songwriter has composed hundreds of great songs doesn't mean that new tunes now appear out of nowhere. The process of creating a song will always be the same, no matter how many times they've done it: creating a vision, doing research, brainstorming ideas, sketching a draft, getting feedback, and refining it into something worthy of being heard.

So, too, is it for an actor. Every performance must be constructed from the ground up, no matter how many Tony Awards you have. What *does* get easier is the enjoyment of and confidence in the process.

When the work slows down, know that more nuanced songs pose an extra challenge and require extra work. In other cases (especially in new, underdeveloped musical theatre), the writer hasn't done you any favors—and you have to do the work they failed to do. When you struggle to identify exciting primary action or establish a clear conclusion, it's either because it's hidden under the surface (and you've got to keep digging) or it's not there—and if that's the case, it's up to you to tie the lyrics together with action and change, creating your own story.

But the *best* news is that, because effective storytelling eludes so many talented actors, by committing to a meticulously detailed, brilliantly crafted, and powerfully prepared story, you'll automatically start ahead of most everyone else.

Advanced Audition Techniques

The sheer volume of auditions a casting director sees requires a reliable system to expediently select the actors they're interested in, and excuse the ones they aren't.

One casting director put it even more simply: There is a "yes" pile and a "no" pile. The yesses comprise the most experienced, well-trained, mature, and prepared. The nos tend toward the green, the uncertain, and the confused. The first pile is considered for a callback and the second goes on to audition another day.

Considering how challenging a creative team's job is, we won't parse the ethics of this seemingly savage process. Instead, we encourage you to remember how quickly you're able to determine whether you're interested in collaborating with someone, being friends with them, asking them out, or the like. You, too, have developed this skill based on your experience—it allows you to navigate your world more carefully, and instinctively sense where and with whom you belong.

On one side, strong audition technique ensures you set yourself up for the "yes" pile. As each casting office gets to know you, you'll skip the first round of auditions altogether when they call you in for appointments.

On the other side, we learn to spot "red flags" (to coin a bit of dating parlance). As we see in the real world (and are often occasionally guilty of ourselves), people who know better commit off-putting faux pas all the time. So, too, do actors fall victim to contradictory or conditional advice culled from college courses, agent meetings, or master classes with high-level pros (who may not have had a first audition in a decade or more and underestimate the intensity with which early-career actors are judged). With this grab bag of mixed-up guidance, they unwittingly sabotage themselves.

This is a total bummer, because the better you understand what a casting director expects from you, the more resourcefully you show them who you are and what you're right for.

While there isn't an official Emily Post list of dos and don'ts, we've identified a core set of audition techniques to help you get to the "yes" pile. These come from the most common bits of constructive feedback given by casting directors' red flags. Keep in mind this is specific to a first audition for a project, not a callback or appointment where you've been given the sides for a role.

(ALMOST) NEVER LEAD WITH A BALLAD

For the many reasons we've already stated, it's nearly fatal to start your audition with a ballad in most requested genres.

When casting requests classic musical theatre, radio music, and *especially* contemporary musical theatre, *always, always, always* start with your up-tempo option.

Read that again. Then read it again. Tell a friend. Scream it alone in your room. Get a tattoo.

Yes, there are a few exceptions. Most notably, your contemporary legit song will often be a ballad, and casting is prepared for that.

Meanwhile, the genres of Sondheim, '50s–'60s, and folk/country *could* be a ballad if that song suited you best. In that case, if they request those genres, sing what you have. Avoid choosing ballads for all three of those spots, though, and if you find yourself singing from one of those genres a lot, you probably need an up-tempo as well—and then, of course, you should start with that instead.

So, unless you can't help it:

Don't lead with a ballad.
Do not lead with a ballad.
Don't lead with a ballad.

WALKING INTO THE ROOM

If you haven't already given your headshot and résumé to the monitor or casting assistant, you'll give it to them as you walk into the room. If you have, walk toward your accompanist while politely greeting the table. Keep it casual (but respectful) and confident (but warm). If you know someone in the room (because maybe you've worked together before), acknowledge them with a wave or a few words. It isn't the time to shake hands or get too personal.

COMMUNICATING WITH YOUR ACCOMPANIST

Greet your accompanist and place your music on the piano. Meet your accompanist on the side of the piano where your front (and not your rear end) is facing the table, which gives them a longer opportunity to see your face. Indicate where you're starting and ending, and point out any surprising trims you've made internally. Alert them to all tempo, time signature, or key changes (which, naturally, you've highlighted already).

Finally, you'll set your tempo by *gently* tapping your body or the piano and quietly singing a few bars of a major part of the song (probably the chorus). Never snap your fingers at them. You could conduct the tempo, but that could risk being unclear. Some actors nervously give tempos too fast or cautiously too slow, so if you discover you're in either camp, adjust accordingly.

If your cue is something *different* than slating and taking a moment to yourself (which is standard), let your accompanist know when you want them to start. If you have a strong reason why your cue will be different ("I'll be starting at the piano," "I'll begin standing against the back wall") let them know so they aren't caught off guard. We find nontraditional cues work best with comedy songs as part of a "bit."

SLATING AND INTRODUCING YOUR MATERIAL

After you've prepped your accompanist, walk to the center of the audition space. Place yourself in the middle of the auditors' table, and just behind the imaginary line separating the space between the table and the back wall. (Or, if they've placed a marking on the floor where they'd like you to stand, stand there.)

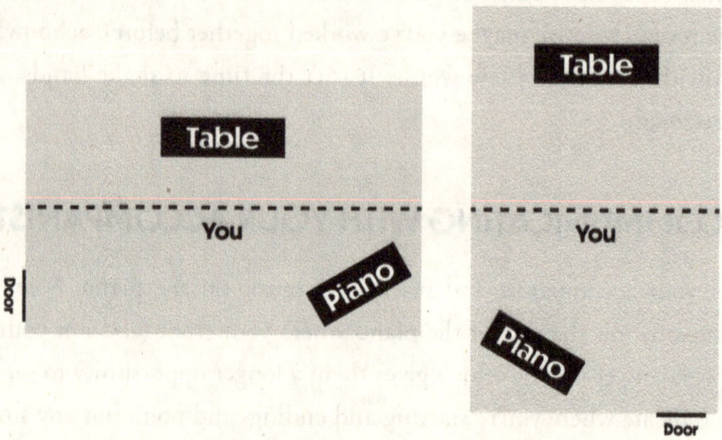

If you haven't already, you'll now slate and introduce your material.

You slate by stating your professional name clearly, and introducing the name of your song.

Example of a slate

"What name did they say?" "Is it Sammie or Samuel?"

It's best to give the name on your résumé and not jump to any nicknames (and if the casting team knows you by your nickname and is not your close friend, we wonder why your nickname isn't your professional name?). Speak slowly, clearly, and with confidence. A smile is always welcome!

TRANSITIONING INTO YOUR STORY

After you've slated, you now do two important things.

In the seconds before the music begins,
you seamlessly transition from **the human slating**
to the actor telling a story,
all while recalling your story's **moment before.**

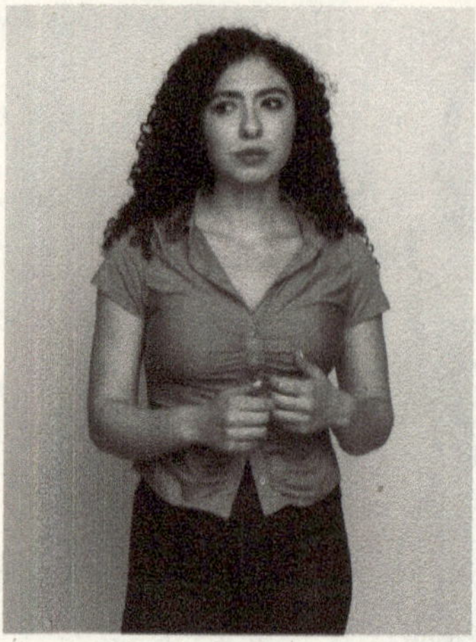

Actors recalling their moment before

If it sounds like patting your head and rubbing your belly, it is. Some coaches will tell you to lower your head, close your eyes, and fully enter your moment before. When you're starting out, this is a great and clear way to begin. When you're further along, however, blend this moment by focusing on the event that's just happened in your story more specifically—*seeing* it. After slating, you might look left where your lover has just walked out on you, or glance upward, thanking the heavens that she just told you she loves you, too. You pass a glance to the accompanist. You've just recalled your moment before, but the table only saw a beautiful transition.

When you raise your head or glance to your accompanist, the music begins. Because we've encouraged you to have a few bars of music rather than a bell tone or an a cappella start, you have time to see your location and your scene partner and remember what you want. As you open your mouth to sing, you take action with your first tactic.

"They really rushed into the song; they seemed anxious to begin."

We rarely hear about actors taking *too* much time before cueing their pianist, but we very often see them shortchange their preparation by taking too little. Take a few seconds more than you think you need. This is *your* time, and if a longer moment sets up a brilliant audition, everyone will forget the two extra seconds you took to get into it.

Use this time to *breathe.* Taking your full moment will also slow your nerves and create a more confident head space to work in.

PREPARATION TO PRESENTATION

To ensure a rich, detailed performance, you've arrived at your audition with extensive story work on the song you've selected. Now you're an expert on *your* version of *this* song. But unlike a lecturer reading off a paper or a politician reciting from a teleprompter, this work should never yield a fixed, unchanging performance.

A savvy actor memorizes the material, not the performance.

Excellent performances require that special spark of spontaneity and a feeling that every choice is happening for the first time, in real time. Though the table hopes you've got a method to your madness, they want to be riveted by an in-the-moment performance that isn't staged or choreographed.

Focus purely on the essential answers to your story's questions. Try not to predetermine your physical work: when you step forward, when you look left, the moment to giggle on a transition bar, clasp your hands, and so on. By keeping your physical presentation unplanned, you guarantee your work remains loose enough to look natural but prepared enough to feel intentional.

This will also help you should the team want to throw you a different take to see how well you take direction. Too often we catch a completely premeditated performance, and when we offer feedback for how to alter it, the actor does it again, identically, like a doll with a pull string. More notes, another identical performance. This is a quick tell that an actor isn't comfortable outside of their own over-rehearsed decisions, and getting their work to grow will be a challenge. The creative team will be anxious to see if the next actor in line is more up to the task.

Craft an expertly detailed story for every cut in your book. As you review your work ahead of your audition, be comfortable with a handful of choices (all in accordance with the action and tactics of your story), and remain open to what comes to you in the moment.

> *You create a toolbox of ideas to tell your story, making sure that—like live theatre—no two performances are ever exactly the same.*

NOTES ON VOCAL APPROACH BY GENRE

Every musical genre has certain conventions that define its sound. Through the songs in their book, actors demonstrate their understanding of each and their technical approach. We understand that an elderly church soprano warbling Ariana Grande's "Dangerous Woman" or a crooner singing "Empty Chairs at Empty Tables" like Frank Sinatra would be strange. Below you'll find a useful list of dos and don'ts by genre.

Classic songs/Sondheim

Placement: Always "legit," but head voice or belt depending on character type

Sound: On the darker side

Vibrato: Yes

Riffing: Absolutely never

Back phrasing: No

Ornamentation/Optioning up: Almost never. If there is a precedent from an established performance, you might integrate it into yours—but be cautious. The wrong option can appear like showing up topless to church—really.

Additional notes: Some characters falling in a "comedic" trope may have little to no vibrato in favor of a more spoken sound—characters like Aunt Eller (*Oklahoma!*) and Sarah Jane Moore (*Assassins*). It's important in this genre to sing what's on the page. Changing the full key of the song might be acceptable, but it's not advised if the new key forces the character into a different voice type.

Pop

Placement: Tending to mirror the original artist

Sound: Bright or dark, can be selectively breathy when appropriate

Vibrato: Hardly ever—only used purposefully

Riffing: Yes

Back phrasing: Yes

Ornamentation/Optioning up: Yes

Additional notes: Throw away ends of phrases. Key changes always acceptable, though questionable if the song is notable for its high range ("Chandelier" by Sia, for example).

Rock

Placement: Tending to mirror the original artist; rock tenors often use a bright, pingy falsetto

Sound: Gritty, full, bright

Vibrato: Sometimes, in certain styles

Riffing: Limited

Back phrasing: Sometimes

Ornamentation/Optioning up: Sometimes

Additional notes: Throw away ends of phrases. Key changes always acceptable, though questionable if the song is notable for its high range ("Barracuda" by Heart, "Beautiful Things" by Benson Boone).

Contemporary Legit

Placement: Head voice, belt, "legit" depending on character type

Sound: Dark, more open sound

Vibrato: Often, especially on longer notes

Riffing: Sometimes, especially if there's a precedent

Back phrasing: Often

Ornamentation/Optioning up: Sometimes

Additional notes: This sound is meant to combine contemporary pop sound and classic singing. Changing the key of the song isn't usually advised, except occasionally up or down up to step. Most characters in this genre, like classic musical theatre, are written for an established voice type.

Contemporary Musical Theatre

Placement: Forward, sometimes pingy, "in the mask"

Sound: Often very spoken, should mimic speech in verse sections and more of a "pop" sound in choruses

Vibrato: Sometimes

Riffing: Sometimes

Back phrasing: Sometimes

Ornamentation/Optioning up: Sometimes

Additional notes: This should sound simple and spoken, more so than any of the other genres. Changing the keys of these songs is usually not advised except occasionally up or down up to step (because these shows tend to be recent and their keys standardized); most characters in this genre, like classic musical theatre, are written for a specific voice type.

Folk

Placement: Mirroring the original artist, chest voice with "flips" into head voice, falsetto

Sound: Dark, mellow

Vibrato: Sometimes, for effect or to end a long note

Riffing: Sometimes, on long, open phrases

Back phrasing: Sometimes

Ornamentation/Optioning up: Sometimes—high notes tend to be gracefully approached rather than belted

Additional notes: Key changes are always acceptable, especially if they help the performer sing into the genre more.

Country

Placement: Full voice, hearty

Sound: Bright

Vibrato: Yes, especially on the ends of phrases

Riffing: Sometimes

Back phrasing: Sometimes in more recent country

Ornamentation/Optioning up: Sometimes in more recent country

Additional notes: Add some "twang" if it's appropriate to the song, and modify according to the show you're auditioning for (more for *Shucked*, less for *Bright Star*). Key changes are always acceptable, especially if they help the performer sing into the genre more.

'50s–'60s

Placement: Chest voice, belt, some falsetto for gentlemen

Sound: Very bright

Vibrato: Yes, especially on the ends of phrases

Riffing: Not really—more about ornamentation

Back phrasing: Not really; the melody lies "in the pocket" of the rhythm

Ornamentation/Optioning up: Often, especially as the song goes on

Additional notes: Though many songs from this genre get reinterpreted to a contemporary context later (like "Tainted Love"), and many more recent artists have been throwing back to this style (Amy Winehouse and Meghan Trainor among them), when you're singing a song from these decades, remember to perform them *vocally* in the style of these decades—not just rely on the vibe of the accompaniment.

FOCUS

Your eye focus should be centered over the table, just above the heads of your auditors. This is because you are standing, singing to one or more people who are also standing, and the folks at the table, being seated, are below your natural sightline.

> **Eye focus indicates to whom you're delivering your story, *whether it's one person, multiple people, or yourself.***

In a job interview, an interviewee always wants clear, comfortable focus—without their eyes shifting side to side or staring into space. Unlike in a job interview, however, you should almost never sing directly to the members of your casting team.

If the creative team is positioned evenly, your focus should be directly between the heads of the center pair, and if they're positioned in odd numbers (where one person seems to be dead center), it's slightly wider, a foot or so left and right of the central person's head.

This is your "center." When you're singing to one person, they're standing here.

When you are singing to a group of people, members of the group exist at center as well as left and right, but not further left or right of the table itself. (Consider that offstage.)

It's true that our eyes naturally wander regardless of whether we're alone or with other people. We think of what to say, recall a memory, get distracted by a thought, or briefly notice someone or something else in our location. It's normal and necessary to break your focus from center as you would in real life, but always with a sense of center in mind.

This is especially important when you're singing to yourself. When we're in mid-conversation alone, our eyes wander. Yes, we may focus on something while concentrating on one thought, but your song should have many thoughts—which means never singing to one central point, the way you would if you were talking to one person.

"Their focus was too high, off-center, unclear."

When our focus is too high, it looks like we're singing to a very tall basketball player, a giantess, or the sun (ow). We doubt these are the physical characters who can make substantive change in your story, and looking into the sun will blind you. Even if your song is technically a prayer ("Bring Him Home" from *Les Misérables*), still make sure your focus isn't too high.

Sometimes actors want to put their scene partner fixed to the far left or right, but this is confusing. Why is your scene partner standing over there? Is your moment before asking them to wait over yonder while you have a private moment? For many auditors, watching an actor talk to someone standing near the door or in the corner is unsettling. And please, don't let your scene partner flit around the room via changing eye focus left and right—unless your scene partner is a bat.

If an actor begins singing center and then spends the second half focused stage right—did their scene partner cross? Watching you watch someone cross stage will look like someone invisible is *actually* in the room (a ghost, perhaps), and is creepy.

The eyes being the windows to the soul and all, avoid closing your eyes for more than a second to make the most of your time in the room. If you must close your eyes, it should feel deliberate for the story (a painful thought you're pushing away, or experiencing sheer ecstasy)—and not for the joy of screlting, riffing, or listening to the sound of your own voice.

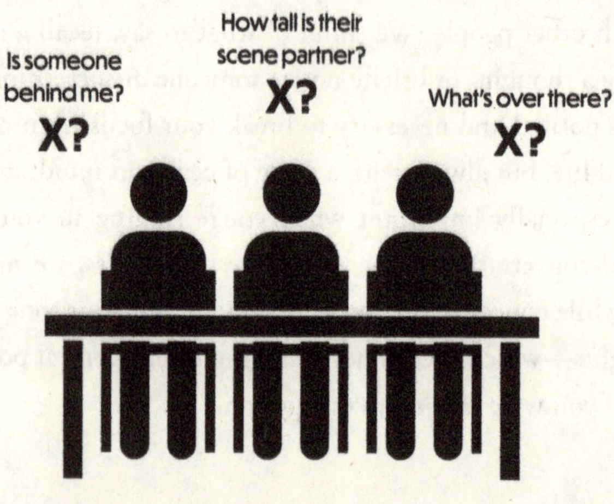

"Their focus was stuck most of the song."

If an actor stares into one space for too long, this icy, dead stare risks appearing like that of an up-and-coming serial killer. Break your gaze naturally with thoughts as they come, and make the world a safer place.

"I swear she was looking into my eyes during that love song. It felt weird."

Again, almost never sing directly to the casting team. In diegetic numbers where you are singing to actual audience members (like "Mein Herr" from *Cabaret* or "And You Don't Even Know It" from *Everybody's Talking About Jamie*), passing eye contact with your auditors can be acceptable (as they are part of your "audience"), but don't linger or overdo it.

When in doubt: Keep track of center.

GROUNDING

From where you've arrived, imagine a three-foot circle around you, roughly one step in any direction. Generally speaking, this is where you'll remain for the duration of your audition.

> ***Grounding is your physical foundation in the audition space, demonstrating clarity of story location.***

If you step out of this circle, it must be controlled and intentional—not a consequence of nerves or unfocused storytelling. If, in a job interview, the interviewee were to spin around in their chair, stand up unannounced, or shift their feet uncomfortably, they would appear uneasy . . . which makes everyone feel uneasy.

"He looked a little stiff."

Within this circle, your body is loose and committed to the story you're telling. It's wise to place one foot slightly in front of the other to maximize your hip mobility and range of motion, rather than keeping both feet in the same line, locking your knees with hips square to the front.

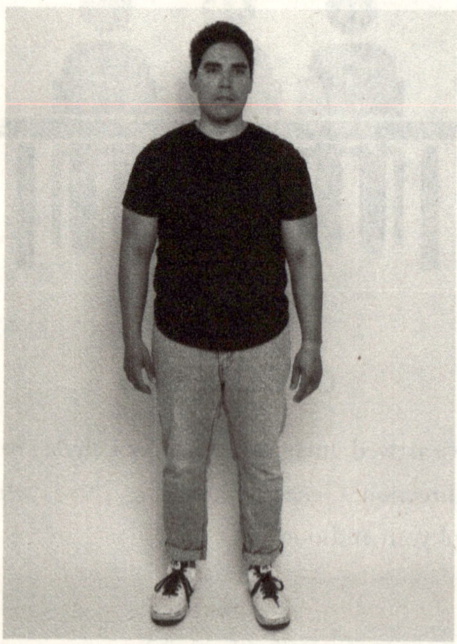

Stiff, square hips

When both hips face front, an actor looks (and feels) stiff. This causes discomfort and they inevitably step out of it. When you keep one foot slightly in front, you have the option of putting most of your weight on your front foot or your back foot—a choice that offers information about the stakes of your story.

A front-footed performance *indicates need, desperation, or aggression, perfect for your high-stakes story.*

A back-footed performance *suggests chill demeanor, indifference, or caution, useful for lower-stakes situations and especially radio music.*

Your weight may shift forward, back, or balance evenly with your tactics, but as long as both feet remain planted slightly askew, your body is fully supported.

"They were moving all over the place, totally ungrounded."

It's all right to take a step forward if your story calls for it, as in a moment of asserting power.

Some auditors find a dramatic step forward cliché, but others find it empowering. There's no rule against a step forward so long as it's motivated by story and used sparingly. (We once had an actor who continually stepped forward in their audition, crossing more than ten feet during their song. We feared they might soon climb the table.)

Avoid stepping backward. It's a quick indication of weakness—especially if you've just stepped forward. Unconscious rocking back and forth undermines your performance.

On some occasions, an actor chooses to feign "exiting" in their story, only to return with more to say ("My Stupid Mouth" by John Mayer), or consciously recoils from their scene partner ("Please Don't Touch Me" from *Young Frankenstein*). Both are exceptions supported by the lyric.

Stepping to the side also feels strange—unless you're dodging a flying object. Habitually stepping left and right can make your audience seasick.

Using the entire space

Some acting coaches appreciate more movement in the room than we're advising. We respect everyone's different tastes and find this absolutely works for more seasoned actors who have learned how to remain grounded wherever they move. If that's not you quite yet, better safe than sorry: stick to center.

Determine the borders of your playing space before you begin. Be conscious of where and how you're moving without letting it look staged. Have a good reason for why you're using all the space and ground yourself as you go.

Starting at the piano

Other coaches suggest starting at the piano as an effective and unexpected way to begin. If it's justified—you're crooning a jazz standard or lazing about in your story—it can work, but eventually find an easy cross to center to finish your story. If you sing your entire song from the piano, the instrument may appear more like a crutch rather than a prop.

Starting at other locations in the room

Some (particularly zany) actor friends of ours advocate for starting anywhere in the back half of the room . . . at the mirror, the curtain, the wall, and so on. While a seasoned professional may have the chutzpah (and support) to pull this off, the early-career actor might look unhinged. Best to leave the casting team impressed rather than unsettled.

Using a chair

In initial auditions, never use a chair. No matter how intimate a performance, deliver it standing with your focus right above the auditors' heads. Using a chair might be appropriate during a callback where the stage directions indicate the character is sitting and the creative team offers you a chair—but at an initial audition, never.*

RADIO SONGS: FEELING THE MUSIC IN YOUR BODY

You've learned that radio songs are best performed with lower stakes than musical theatre songs. Your body, too, should relax with simpler storytelling.

> ***When singing a radio song, feel* the music in your body, *gently moving to the song's rhythm and groove.***

We're not looking for a show choir step touch, nor are we leaving it at a tiny foot tap. Imagine listening to music you love while cooking, driving, or folding laundry. Your body moves with the song, enjoying the beat but not dancing so much that you spill the pasta sauce everywhere. We find this usually complements our radio songs' locations, actions, and scene partners, as though you're playfully luring someone to dance with you or sharing all your good vibes with that loser who ghosted you.

At the start, it's normal to feel uncomfortable or "uncool" while grooving to your radio song. Try not to overthink it. Remember, like your song, you're just having fun.

---

* One casting director used to simply write "CHAIR" in large caps where their feedback would have otherwise been. Not a particularly nice anecdote, but it gives you a sense of Chair's reputation.

GESTURES

"What do I do with my arms?" is a question so popular that it's the title of a contemporary musical theatre song.* And for good reason: Unnatural gestures are a scourge among early-career actors and a red flag for casting directors. Uncertainty around what is right and wrong gets so many actors in their head that their song is over by the time they let their limbs relax.

When you're completely immersed in your story, you move naturally, supported by your story.

Distracting and unmotivated gesturing is an epidemic among under-prepared, unfocused actors. It occurs when the actor themself is distracted by something other than their story and not motivating their body in a natural way. Usually, they're thinking about their voice.

If you're thinking about how your voice sounds, you can't be thinking about your story.

If you're regretting mixing and not belting that note, preparing for the forthcoming high note, or worried you sound raspy, you are *not* focusing on whether Jimmy the Paperclip Salesman could be the one for you ("Jimmy," *Thoroughly Modern Millie*). Remember, characters are not aware they are singing (unless they're singing in a performance within the performance). They think they're speaking.

In this way, voice-affected gestures are just another symptom of vocal tension. When you're fixated on your singing, your hands will betray you and all your prep will go out the window.

Unnatural gestures come in a few flavors.

---

* "What Do You Do with Your Arms?," lyrics by Sam Carner and music by Derek Gregor.

Distracting gestures

The hands move without relation to the story. Like a scene out of *Evil Dead 2* (where a demon-possessed hand terrorizes the protagonist), we're distracted by a wandering, mindless appendage and lose track of what the actor is doing. Not coincidentally, the hand is wandering because *the actor* has lost track of what they're doing.

Habitually symmetrical gestures

People only move their hands symmetrically on occasion, and rarely in consecutive sequence (unless they are a flight attendant).

Stuck gestures

The hands pick a gesture and freeze, leaving the actor looking like a doll stuck in a pose.

Over the years we've spotted certain stuck gestures so frequently that we've given them names, with equal parts affection (like a newly discovered star) and disdain (like a newly discovered disease). Again, these aren't a problem when performed naturally—only when the gesture becomes stuck.

Translating unnatural gestures into natural ones

As always, the solution is to return to your story—specifically, your tactics. Consider for a moment what "tease," "coerce," "plead," or "condemn" might look like in a production photograph, and notice how action correlates with posture and movement.

If you're struggling with unnatural gestures, the first thing to do is to learn what your habits are by watching video of yourself. Be ruthless and take notes!

Next, completely relax your hands. *You do not need them to sing.* Gently rest your fingertips on your thighs or clasp them behind your back and practice this way until you disassociate singing with gesticulating. At that point, you've arrived at "gesture neutral" and relaxed your habit.

From here, focus on your story and slowly invite your arms back into the song when they're ready to come back from their time-out.

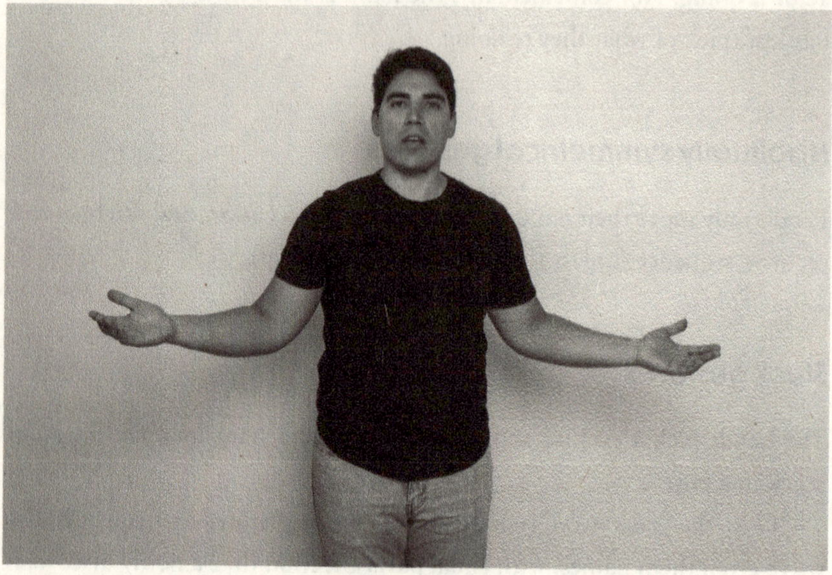

Muffins for sale

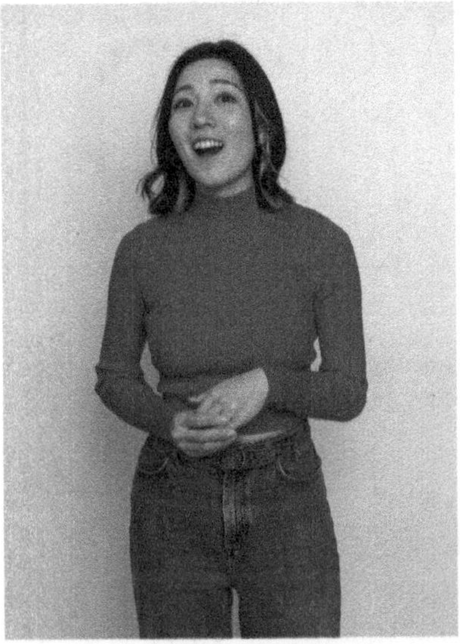

Hand glove

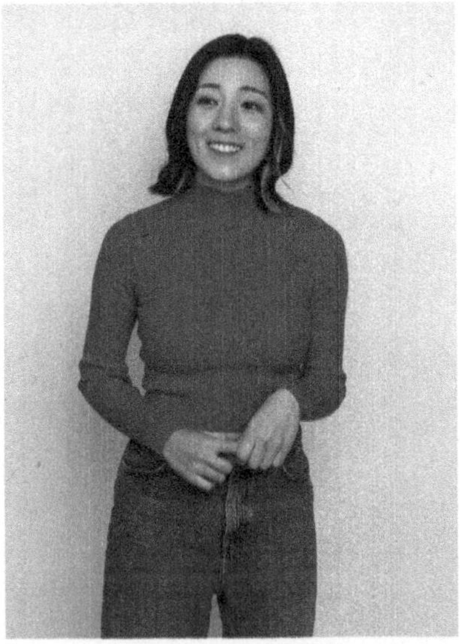

Warm finger

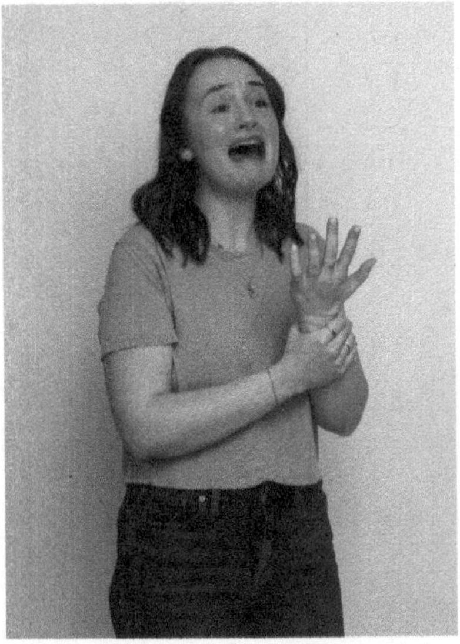

Hand tree

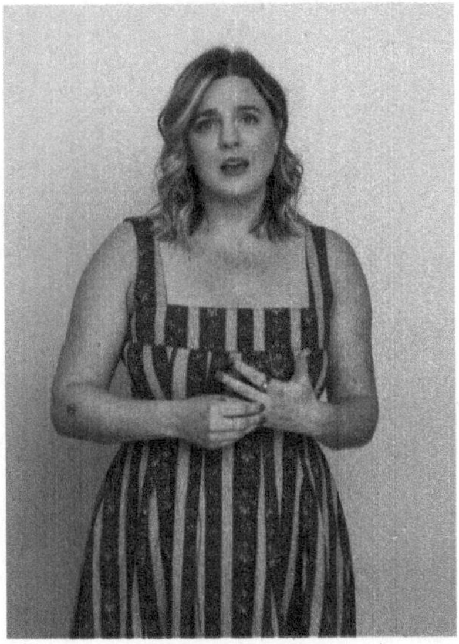

Wedding ring

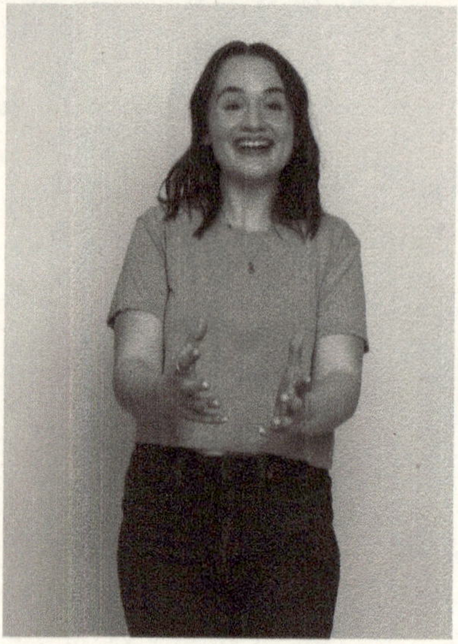

Bundt cake

Sheet cake

Taking your finger for a walk

Barbie hands

Steeple

Awkward pockets

Lady parts

(Invisible) locket

Don't be afraid of big gestures

Unnatural gestures stem from an actor's lack of intention, but when properly motivated, even the largest gesture can heighten a performance. Power poses, extreme stances, fingers pointed skyward, or ecstatic releases of physical achievement (or, as we like to call them, "whammies") can be extremely effective.

"Gimme, Gimme"

"Watch What Happens"

"I Can Cook, Too"

"Moving Too Fast"

Finally, fully commit to your movement, especially if it's large. An anemic finger point appears doubtful. A sad power pose looks forced. A half-hearted bit of choreography suggests you're being held at gunpoint by some mafioso growling, "Dance for me good." These, we hope, are never the story you're telling.

EXPRESSION AND ENERGY

Whether you're Pagliacci the Clown or Patina Miller, you're in the business of communicating clear emotions with your face. Sometimes, though, an actor isn't fully in control of how much or how little they're expressing—or are expressing something they aren't intending.

Facial expressions communicate emotion, and actors should ensure they are in complete control of the emotions they project with their face.

Remember the poster tacked to the kindergarten corkboard featuring animated characters in various emotional states, labeled HAPPY, SAD, CONFUSED, DISGUSTED, etc.? This introduced kiddos to understanding the meaning of facial expressions and how humans communicate without words.

Yet every face is different. Some naturally express more than others, wearing their hearts on their sleeves and empathically absorbing every feeling they encounter. Others appear always sober, thoughtful, and restrained, and may even admit to having a "resting bitch face." These people tend to be harder to read, and for an actor, this may be to their detriment. The former group may come off disingenuous or "fake," while the latter could appear cold and disinterested. To avoid these outcomes, more communicative actors work to adjust their expressions to each story on an individual basis, while more stoic actors may choose to express more generously. In either case, the result is a clearer performance.

By harnessing the power of our expression, we can also make stronger story choices. In a song like "Agony" from *Into the Woods*, a wildly emotive choice would highlight the Prince's foolishness, whereas a stoic performance ironically underscores that these gut-wrenching conquests are only business ("Look at my unmoving face: I'm in agony"). Each take offers a different perspective on the story and where the actor fits in the world of comedy.

Our body requires similar thought. Some people have so much energy it feels like caffeine drips from a special gland in their neck (maybe people tell them they're a little "extra"). Others appear perpetually at peace, like they just left a whole-body massage.

We must understand our own
inherent physical energy
and adapt for the song we're singing.

When our face or body causes confusion, we're often told we're over- or underacting—even though it's just a lack of body awareness. Early in your career, film your at-home rehearsals and private work sessions to get a sense of what your body is doing until you feel you're an expert on how you move. This expertise allows us to know our own strength.

END WITH A FIRE IN YOUR EYES AND LET THE MUSIC PLAY OUT

In production, your big 11 o'clock number likely ends with a strong musical button accompanied by a lighting cue or stage effect for emphasis. Though you can't throw a smoke bomb and disappear into the floor (well, you could try), you can allude to this experience by making sure the final moment of your performance surges with a bit of electricity behind your eyes. Something that says, "I see it" or "I won."

And finally, let the music of your cut completely end before you release your story and "return" to the audition room as you, the actor. That is, don't break your focus on your scene partner and location until the piano is completely quiet.

Once your song is done, the table will ask you for another song, give you a callback then and there, or thank you for coming in. Wherever it ends, return the thanks, grab your book from the accompanist, and exit. Simple, right?

Almost.

(EXTREMELY) COMMON STORYTELLING PROBLEMS

While everything you've just read may feel like Acting 101, know that the folks behind the table see the same problems day in and day out among actors with plenty of advanced training. Realizing we are all susceptible to them (especially when we're nervous), it's an actor's job to learn their bad habits and address them.

Here are the ones we see the most.

"Stop Thinking About Your Voice, Debra! (Reprise)"

Actors who identify as "singer-firsts" frequently perform while listening to their voice. They're judging their sound quality, worrying how sick they sound, or preparing for the high note—rather than, say, thinking about any of what we discussed in the last fifty-plus pages. When it's over, they hope they sang all right and no one noticed that their storytelling was distracted. In this very typical scenario, the good news is that *phewf*, no one noticed their storytelling. The bad news is that's because there wasn't any to notice.

> *An actor's career will remain stalled while they believe that the most important thing about their audition is their vocal performance.*

Their career takes off, however, when they enter the artistic period we call "post-voice." That is, their voice no longer interests them more than any other aspect of their skillset. Their singing is simply a tool—like their speech, movement, clothing style, or audition technique. All of it equally serves what they must graduate to: becoming a storyteller first.

Characters aren't acting

There is a terrific scene in the seminal classic *Mommy Dearest* where Hollywood actress Joan Crawford (infamously played by Faye Dunaway) dramatically pleads with her headstrong daughter Christina to behave in front of company, to which "Tina" replies, "*Don't . . . you . . .* act *for me.*" She's calling Joan out for manufacturing disconnected emotion for Joan's benefit, really, and not for Tina, the person for whom her words claim to be intended.

Remember that 99 percent of the time, your character isn't acting—not at their scene partner, and certainly not to themselves. They're telling a story, pursuing a goal, or traversing an emotional journey. Unless they're Sally Bowles at the Kit Kat Club or a master manipulator, they aren't consciously performing.

Characters don't know they're singing;
they think they're speaking.
We hear the music. They don't.

The problem begins with good intentions. Actors learn to perform from other actors. Imagine a fifteen-year-old belting out a mean "With You" from *Ghost*, and wow, what a performance it is. Of course, they've never had a substantive romantic relationship (let alone experienced the murder of their lover), but boy, they've picked up how to *look* like they have.

They're "putting on" what they think the performance *looks like*: the contorted face, the false tears, the anguished gestures—not crafting an emotional experience through action. Sometimes, this phenomenon continues into the same actor's twenties, even thirties, and some never get past this stage at all.

When we pursue acting seriously, we learn to strip away pretense and start from neutral. We allow an emotional experience to build organically inside out, where need creates action, action creates tactics, tactics create success or failure, and these create feeling.

Manipulators (and other bad actors) *use* emotion to cause other people to do things: I am angry, so you should cower. I am sad, so you should sympathize. I am certain, so you must be wrong. Honest people express thoughts and emotion follows. Feeling comes after the thought, not before it.

To avoid an inauthentic performance, practice starting in stillness—and make sure those hands don't rise reflexively when the music begins. Think the thoughts your character needs to sing their words and sink further into their emotional world. Repeat this until emotion surfaces organically—so naturally, in fact, that you can't hold back your joy, misery, or panic. Instead of wearing the costume of feeling, let it flow from within.

Focus on the other (invisible) person

As we speak to other people, they react to what we say as we say it. Whether it's a frown, a glance away, or a smile, these and hundreds of other microresponses give away how they're feeling and affect what we do next.

Considering how much you already have to do in the room, it's a challenge also tracking the reactions of an invisible person. But it's overcoming this challenge that separates excellent actors from merely competent ones. When we watch you sing to a scene partner who isn't there, we're searching for your eyes' response to something we can't see, and then to see how you, in turn, react to their behavior.

When you're singing to another person (or people), constantly ask yourself, "What are they doing? How are they responding to what I just said?" As you would with a living person, react.

Don't over-choreograph dance and comic "routine" songs

Songs like "I Can Do That," "Always True to You in My Fashion," and "Show Off" (*A Chorus Line*; *Kiss Me, Kate*; and *The Drowsy Chaperone*, respectively) are examples of songs heavily choreographed in production. Likewise, some comedy songs are so staged within an inch of their lives that they might as well be dance numbers; think "Worst Pies in London" (*Sweeney Todd*) or "Can't Stop Talkin' About Him" (*Let's Dance*). Brought in for an audition, however, you don't want to suggest you've copied a bootleg or hired a personal choreographer. Instead, develop a collection of gestures or steps as "movement vocabulary" for each moment in the song. You then organically pull from this toolbox of options in a way that feels spontaneous yet deliberate. The creative team gets the effect of dancing or staging while enjoying your creativity in the moment.

An exception to this advice would be if you want the team to see a necessary moment of choreography (doing the splits, a tap dance, or a triple pirouette). In this rare case, use your best judgment and fire away.

Change your story, not your song

One of the most useful audition techniques is adjusting your song's story to "point" at the character in the show you're interested in. This protects your well-constructed book of twelve or so songs, rather than searching for a brand-new song to accommodate each audition that comes your way. Maintain your shape, framework, and primary action, but consider a moment in the show where this song might be sung by the character you fit in the show, and modify location and tactics with them in mind.

Let's say your '50s–'60s song is "You Don't Own Me," and Rizzo (*Grease*) is your major dream role in this period. Accordingly, the story you've built is decidedly "Rizzo-esque"—guarded, sarcastic, and tough. Today's call, however, is for *All Shook Up*, and you don't think your Rizzo take will help you for the role you feel closest to, Miss Sandra. So instead of finding a "Miss Sandra song," you adapt "You Don't Own Me" to the moment when Miss Sandra rejects Chad in Act I (where she usually sings "Teddy Bear/Hound Dog"). For this take, you're less standoffish and proud (your "Rizzo" take) and lean flirtier and physically dominating. The action ("to reject him") is the same, but the tactics, posture, and location are altered.

AND THAT'S IT

By now you can see just how challenging it is to brand your strengths, pick the right song, make a good cut, craft a strong story, master effective audition technique, *and* deliver it all with ease under the powerful stress of a big-city audition. It's a ton of work building up your artistry to this standard—especially for what is most often a thirty-second audition.

Now you may more fully understand what we meant when we said:

Most early-career musical theatre actors confuse competence with **excellence.**

Try not to let this overwhelm you or brush past this essential work. Before you read on, take time to review this first part and make a list of work you still have to do—on yourself, on your book, on your storytelling, and on your performance. It's all right if the list is long; you still have plenty of time. The artist you are now wasn't built in a day, and the artist you're becoming won't be either.

Know that, regardless of how much work lies ahead, you have something to offer right now. Tomorrow, you'll improve it and get a little better . . . and the day after, and the day after, and the day after. Every day can bring a little breakthrough.

As our edgy friend Sweeney once said after having an epiphany of his own, "The work waits, I'm alive at last, and I'm full of joy!"

PART 2

DOING THE DAMN THING

The Actor's Ultimate Goal

Do great work. Get hired for well-paying jobs. Be recognized for your achievements. Climb the proverbial "ladder of success" as far as your time and energy allow—until you can fund a comfortable lifestyle and want for nothing. Isn't that what it's all about?

The ultimate goal is to make a life doing what you love.

That's big-picture, long-term thinking. Yet too many actors live day by day. They focus solely on booking the next job, convinced that once they do, things will get much easier. But most of the time, they find themselves back to the audition grind. Book the next gig, experience the same result, and on and on . . . until they wake one morning from uneasy dreams to find that they have become an audition machine.

THE SAD, SAD TALE OF THE AUDITION MACHINE

The audition machine has only one function: to find auditions, book jobs, and repeat. Every morning, it boots up early, scans for the nearest casting call of highest value, and initiates its mission: It must book this show. If it fails, it powers down until the next day, when it will reactivate and try again.

But when the audition machine succeeds, something strange occurs: It enters a temporary "human simulation mode"—participating in rehearsals, engaging in performances, and even experiencing what carbon-based life-forms refer to as "joy."

But inevitably, the production ends. The machine updates its résumé firmware and the cycle resets: audition, book, repeat.

Over time, the machine comes to realize there's a glitch. Despite all the production operations it's experienced and the great fun it's had pretending to be sentient, something feels . . . off. Its core processor starts to wonder: Is there more to existence than just running the same program day in and day out?

Eventually, the audition machine calculates that its ultimate purpose remains light-years away—and finding its function futile, it breaks down forever.

Woof! Thank god *we're* human, right?

You are not an audition machine . . . you're an artist.

Whether you're in the ensemble of a national tour or starring on Broadway, living life audition to audition, opening to closing, becomes a self-consuming ouroboros—until you see your career as part of a challenging, rewarding journey.

The audition machine is programmed to believe that after the first big job, everything will click into place: join Actor's Equity, land a fancy agent, get into bigger rooms, finally be seen for who they are, and then play their dream roles in Midtown. Except . . . joining Equity doesn't guarantee you jobs. Your agent can't plan your retirement. And no matter how great the role or show, every contract ends. Every show closes.*

---

* Yes, even *Wicked* will close one day. We're sorry.

***Being an artist means also being a* small business.**

Strong small businesses aren't just aiming to make this month's bottom line. Instead, they're focused on growing year over year—and growth requires a plan. Even if a major windfall comes their way, they invest it in their grand design so it can pay off long-term.

Like knowing what to sing at an open call or strategizing where you best fit in a show, getting control of your business is a puzzle. Putting this puzzle together can be tricky, but it's the greatest one you'll ever solve. It's designed to be challenging, and will take longer to complete than you think—but with patience, solving the puzzle helps you to reach the ultimate goal.

The key to solving this puzzle? We're glad you asked. Why, it's . . .

DOING THE DAMN THING

Doing the damn thing means accepting that you're in control of your future. It means acknowledging that what you think is stalling your momentum isn't actually insurmountable. Being non-Equity, agentless, or inexperienced are just obstacles to work around, as so many have done before you. Realize that once you do, new obstacles will emerge, and you must then work around those.

***Doing the damn thing means spending less time waiting for others to choose you, and more time* choosing yourself.**

Choosing yourself means realizing your own power. By investing significant time in your business *outside* the audition room, you see that those you admire and want to become are mostly focused on the elements of their career they can control. Like watching paint dry or water boil, somehow when you stop waiting to be chosen, you get chosen much faster.

Being a professional means
investing **substantial time in your chosen line of work.**

Many early-career actors believe that the only way they can be a full-time artist is to be in a show—rehearsing six days a week, performing nightly, and occasionally attending put-ins or understudy rehearsals. Beyond that, they think the only ways they can propel their career are through auditions and submissions to book the next show. But this is far from true.

In part two, we'll learn to nurture our careers by building our business. We'll gain a sense of purpose to stave off the aimlessness and despair that artists are so prone to suffer. We'll find reliable solutions for getting through the dark times by keeping our minds, bodies, and bank accounts healthy.

Because while we are on this incredible artistic journey, as each day ends we must be able to say: "Today I worked as long as I could to pursue what I love. I made sure that even if I worked for someone else today, I gave my best hours to myself and my passions. I have a plan that's in my control. I'm taking care of myself and actively choosing growth. My finances are stable. I'm maintaining a presence online. I'm regularly connecting with people who can help me, and whom I can help. I'm making my own opportunities when things are slow. I'm keeping disciplined with my time while nurturing both my professional and personal lives by staying organized."

Every day that you can say these things are true—all of which are completely in your control and accessible to you right now—is a day that, regardless of whether you were seen at this afternoon's audition, if you got a callback, or if you booked a job, you can safely say: *I'm doing the damn thing.*

GETTING THE DAMN THING DONE

There are seven equally important and interconnected parts to doing the damn thing:

1. **Prepare an artistic business plan.**
2. **Grow through training and self-care.**
3. **Stabilize your finances and get a job that works for you.**
4. **Build a digital presence through a website and social media.**
5. **Foster inspiring and mutually beneficial relationships.**
6. **Create your own opportunities.**
7. **Manage your time effectively.**

These steps can be approached in any order, because as you work on one, you help the others.

Don't overlook any of these areas, and see each as integral to your larger objectives. You've already seen what happens when one of them is ignored: "I'm lost and my career needs some direction" (get a business plan), "My materials stink and I'm exhausted" (continue training and amp up your self-care), "I'm broke" (stabilize money), "I feel invisible" (increase digital presence), "I need to make better connections" (foster relationships), "I just want to do what I love" (create your opportunities). Disregard one and it creates a gap in your business that drags down the others. If you're exhausted, it's harder to have brain space to make your own opportunities. If you're broke, it's tough to afford meeting people where they want to meet. If you don't have a plan, you'll struggle to find the materials you need.

The next six chapters will inspire a hefty list of to-dos. Luckily, the seventh chapter breaks down time management to organize it so that these life-changing projects are more manageable. If you get overwhelmed with all there is to do, begin in whichever area you have a healthy head start so you can hit the ground running.

You the Actor, Inc.

Lindsay started training at age three. She attended the Orange County High School for the Arts in Southern California and pursued every opportunity to sing, act, and dance that she could find. Her plan: Attend a BFA musical theatre program, come out the other side with an agent and a clear path ahead, and move to New York City.

But when she applied to colleges, she was accepted by exactly zero.

She believed she had the talent. She'd won numerous citywide awards and had worked professionally starting at seventeen. But whatever the reasons were, what was done was done. Hope shattered, her options seemed to be waiting a year and applying again or trying to make a career in SoCal.

Lindsay didn't like those options. You could say a voice from right down in the bottom of her soul told her she was destined to become a Broadway actress. If these colleges didn't want her, then screw 'em. It was New York or bust.

She came to the Big Apple with only a couple of credits and even fewer contacts. She enrolled in a two-year musical theatre certificate program—but she left after a year to focus full time on auditioning. Her perseverance paid off. Before long, she'd booked an international tour.

What guided her savvy decisions was a business plan.

A business plan outlines your vision for the future, mission in the present, and the values that guide your actions forward.

No one but you should make your life's toughest calls. No one will profit more from your accomplishments or suffer harder for your missteps. Only you travel in your skin every day and only you know what you've been through. Your heart alone has borne, nurtured, and carried your dreams to this point. Many colleagues and collaborators will enter and leave your orbit. You will outgrow some, and others will outgrow you. But you will never outgrow yourself. You opened this shop, and you'll be the one to close it.

It's time to figure out just how your business works.

THE BUSINESS PLAN

In entertainment, there is one truth above all.

Show business has more to do with business than with show.

A business plan identifies who you'll become, how you work, and what you care about, in the same way your branding statement helps you define what you have to offer. When you find yourself lost, directionless, and unmotivated, the plan reminds you what's next. When deciding between two competing offers, the plan advises your choice. If you're feeling overworked while simultaneously like you're not working hard enough, the plan holds you accountable or gives you peace of mind. You set the bar to reach.

To do this, we determine where we want to go (our vision), figure out how we'll get there (our mission), and prioritize the things we'll take with us (our values).

VISION STATEMENT

RSO had one retail job during college, working at a popular bookstore*—his first experience in the corporate workforce. During onboarding, he learned the store's vision: "to become America's best-loved bookstore." As part of training, the manager took the new hires on a field trip to the other major bookstore down the street. That store's vision? "To become America's most successful bookstore," the manager said, pointing out the cultural differences between the two.

Bookstore B was sleek and minimal, laid out in three bold colors. Staff wore crisp button-downs and aprons, giving the impression that every book was a curated object to be handled with care. In contrast, RSO's bookstore A was full of color. Employees wore whatever expressed their personalities. Books were loosely organized, inviting you to sit, sip tea, and lose yourself in a new story. The staff was also more diverse in queerness and color, which made bookstore A's hometown vibe even more appealing to him. In the end, the biggest lesson was clear: A business's vision shapes everything—its look, feel, layout, practices, and people. Both stores sold books, but what they were really selling was an idea of how books should be sold.†

> ***A vision statement outlines the personal and professional achievements you intend to accomplish in a set amount of time.***

When you imagine your future, you're blending aspiration with realistic expectation. Your vision should feel reachable, inspired by your own

---

* Lindsay had a survival job, too, working as a bouncer at the *American Girl Doll* store, but she doesn't want to talk about it.

† For what it's worth, the "best-loved" bookstore A filed for Chapter 11 bankruptcy a few years later, while the "most successful" bookstore B has managed to stay afloat all these years later. On the bright side, RSO figures everyone got what they wanted in the end—"best-loved" suggests nothing about "longest-lasting."

momentum and the successes of your peers—because if they can do it, so can you.

Looking ahead *specifically* means your business plan must include measurable goals—clear achievements you either complete or don't.

We recommend planning five years out, though college-aged actors may prefer three or four.

Brainstorming your vision statement

It's time to dream in draft.

Looking to the next few years, sketch out as many goals as you can think of until nothing is left unconsidered. We're thinking about professional and personal goals, because our work feeds our homelife and vice versa. Start with what's top of mind and then dig deeper for everything underneath. As if goading a psychic, ask questions about where you'd like to be on today's date five years from now.

What city will you be working in? New York City, or elsewhere?

How and where will you be living? Comfy in a two-bedroom uptown? A studio in the village? Cozy with a roommate in Boystown, Chicago, or with a signif-o in Silverlake, California? Do you have an office space or a puppy in your pad?

What will your résumé look like? Broadway, Off-Broadway, Off-off? Consider tours and regional credits, ensemble tracks and principals.

What kind of work will you be known for? Are you a queen of reading new works, a master of classic revivals, a great interpreter of rock opera? How will you have nurtured your strengths and interests?

With whom will you have worked? Are you besties with new composers or established directors? Do you have a dream choreographer in your phone's favorites, or a group of actor friends you regularly devise new work with?

What else? Do you have other personal or professional goals to consider, such as landing representation or joining Actor's Equity? Will you have mastered a hobby or thrived in a secondary profession?

Think about what you're working toward now and imagine it paying off in the future. If you're working toward something (like moving to a certain city or building pounds of muscle), have you succeeded in your vision? If something already feels complete (a great relationship, peak fitness), include maintaining it in your vision. You can also reverse-engineer your goals—if you're tired of touring, reframe "I won't be touring" as "I'll have put down roots."

Make a long list with examples (e.g., "working at the MUNY," "collaborating with writer Adam Gwon"). Use names and places, but not so specifically that it limits your possibilities. Give yourself ample time—let ideas flow naturally or brainstorm under pressure. Don't overthink it. Aim for twenty-five to forty items.

Here's an example of what it might look like for Charlie, a twenty-three-year-old actor who just got to New York with a BA in acting from a well-known school. He's living deep in Brooklyn and his résumé has a few credits from back home in Seattle.

CHARLIE'S VISION LIST

In five years, I will . . .

Be Equity
Have 1+ B'way credit
Have had three principal roles in major regional theatres
Have done 2+ B'way national tours
Be regularly asked to sing at a major NYC cabaret venue like 54 Below
Have performed my own solo show at a major NYC cabaret venue
Have traveled to Europe 2x
Have performed in London
Have done 5+ readings of new musicals
Have worked with 2+ B'way directors
Have worked with a B'way star
Be living with my partner
Be living in Manhattan
Be living in a one-bedroom
Have a cat
Be able to take at least one nonholiday week off a year
Be financially stable without help from parents
Be known for my folky voice (offered a role because of it)
Make at least $80,000 a year from all sources
Have an agent who gets me 1+ appts./mo.
Have been called in by 5+ major casting offices
Be working actively with a composer I respect (1x+/yr.)

Notice that each item on Charlie's list is specific and measurable. For example, he could have an agent he loves, but without defining "loves" he could convince himself that an agent half-assing would suffice. Here he specifies he wants nothing less than monthly appointments.

Once your list is as comprehensive as possible, the next step is to collect the goals of highest priority and pare away those of less importance. Life is short, and we only have so many hours in our day. Below are two ways to go about this process.

List and pen

In this method you grab a pen or pencil and form a list of goals in no particular order.

Step 1: Pick five goals. Circle the ones that stand out as paramount among the others.

Step 2: Cut twelve or so. Go through the remaining uncircled items and cross out about half. As you pass over your circled highest priorities, ask yourself, "Is this as important as that?" Be ruthless!

Step 3: Win some and lose some. Circle a few more keepers and cut out half of what remains.

Step 4: A final look. Without adding more, pit what's left on the chopping block against what's been circled. The undecided have survived thus far, so they must carry some importance. Consider crossing out something you've circled and trading it for one of the leftovers.

End with a final list of eight to ten items.

Corkboard method

This process is ideal for those who like to get hands-on. Write each goal on an index card or scrap of paper and shuffle them up. Sit at a table with plenty of space, and place each item in front of you one by one. Those placed in the dead center are most important and those furthest out matter least. Only so many things can occupy the center of your attention (just like in life), so rearrange your cards until the centermost items (about eight to ten) make up your goals of highest value.

Charlie opted for the list and pen method, and here's where he ended up.

CHARLIE'S VISION LIST—FINAL

In five years, I will . . .

Be Equity *
~~Have 1+ B'way credit~~
~~Have had three principal roles in major regional theatres~~
Have done 2+ B'way national tours*
~~Be regularly asked to sing at a major NYC cabaret venue like 54 Below~~
Have performed my own solo show at a major NYC cabaret venue*
Have traveled to Europe 2x*
~~Have performed in London~~
Have done 5+ readings of new musicals*
~~Have worked with 2+ B'way directors~~
~~Have worked with a B'way star~~
~~Be living with my partner~~
Be living in Manhattan*

Be living in a one-bedroom*
~~Have a cat~~
~~Be able to take at least one nonholiday week off a year~~
~~Be financially stable without help from parents~~
~~Be known for my folky voice (offered a role because of it)~~
~~Make at least $80,000 a year from all sources~~
Have an agent who gets me 1+ appts./mo.*
~~Have been called in by 5+ major casting offices~~
~~Be working actively with a composer I respect (1x+/yr.)~~

Charlie's focused on booking Broadway but doesn't want to obsess over the finish line and lose sight of the path. So he drops the pressure to book it in five years—still hoping, just not forcing it. Goals like working in London or with major stars feel out of his control, so he cuts those, too. Touring stays—it's practical and he loves to travel, especially in Europe.

He keeps joining Equity and finding a strong agent, both essential to him. As a great sight reader with close writer friends, he'll lean into new musical readings. A solo show excites him—it blends his love of music and performance. And while he values lifestyle and relationships, he knows meeting the right person can't be scheduled—just like Broadway, it happens when it happens.

Working with your results

What do you notice about what you kept and what you let go? Did you choose business over pleasure? Family over fame? Comfort over conflict? The only "right" answers are the ones your heart and mind agree on. If you choose something because you think you *should*, you'll likely pay the price for that choice later—so be honest with yourself now.

Rank your results by number or categorize them into groups of "high," "higher," and "highest" priority. Here's how our man Charlie ranked them:

1. **Be Equity**
2. **Have traveled to Europe 2x**
3. **Have done 5+ readings of new musicals**
4. **Be living in Manhattan**
5. **Have an agent who gets me 1+ appts./mo.**
6. **Have done 2+ B'way national tours**
7. **Have performed my own solo show at a major NYC cabaret venue**
8. **Be living in a one-bedroom**

Writing your vision statement: I WILL . . .

Like your branding statement, your vision statement should be a short masterpiece. It's written in *future tense*: I will be . . . , I will live . . . , I will have . . . Begin with the highest-ranked items and continue to the lowest, and on your first pass don't self-edit. Revise until every word excites you.

CHARLIE'S VISION STATEMENT

In five years, I will be an Equity actor with a communicative agent who gets me at least one appointment per month. I'll have done at least two Broadway national tours, my own solo show at a major NYC cabaret venue, and will participate in at least one new musical reading a year. I'll be living in Manhattan in a one-bedroom apartment and have traveled to Europe at least twice.

The power of a vision statement

A business without a vision is like a road trip without a destination. Cruising with the top down is fun for a while, but eventually you need to decide where the heck you're going. Life won't go exactly as planned, but having a plan ensures you'll always have direction.

Some goals will come quickly, others more slowly, and some may fade as new priorities emerge. You'll revisit and update your vision over time.

MISSION STATEMENT

While your vision statement imagines where you'll be in a few years, your mission statement outlines who you must be today to get there.

A mission statement details the practices and standards to make your future vision a reality.

When RSO began his professional career, he made a few promises he still keeps. Every year, he writes at least one new musical—whether it's a commission from a producer or studio, or a passion project he does for himself. Each month, he pays his bills on time, checks in with his five-year plan, and fills his calendar with friends and collaborators. Weekly, he writes at least twenty-five hours, clears his inbox, and stocks up on groceries. Daily, he wakes up at 7:45 AM, goes through an extensive morning routine, works ten to twelve hours blending creativity and business, exercises, and cooks most of his meals. Between 8 and 9 PM, he sits down with his husband and dogs to reflect on the day and enjoy something on TV.

It's easy to see how these habits support success. New shows expand his portfolio and income. Meetings grow his network. His routines nurture his body, his work hours feed his creativity, and time with loved ones fills his heart. Best of all, these promises reinforce the control he has over both his career and his life.

Our mission statement points to our future vision by taking actions in the present to fulfill us today.

Some days you'll fear you're not working hard enough. Other days you'll burn out from overwork. A mission statement tells you exactly what you should expect of yourself: no more, no less.

Brainstorming your mission statement

You'll create your mission statement using the same process you chose to create your vision statement. Start by asking, "What habits would the accomplished person in my vision statement perform regularly? What standards would they set for themselves?" We answer in the present tense—whether we do them presently or not.

How many voice lessons and dance classes do you take per month? Do you regularly explore new acting, improv, or on-camera classes? How many auditions do you attend each month? How often do you rent a practice room to sing for fun, update your website, post on social media, or work out? On a personal level, who are the people in your life you keep in touch with?

As before, start with a comprehensive list, then narrow it down to the dozen or so practices most aligned with your vision.

Writing your mission statement: I DO...

Form a new paragraph from this list, but this time in the present tense. I do... I take... I go... I work out... Here's Charlie's final mission statement.

CHARLIE'S MISSION STATEMENT

I submit to different agencies at least once a month and audition at least three times a week, especially focused on tours. I go to the gym five times a week, take three dance classes a week, see at least one show every two weeks, and attend at least one concert or

> cabaret a month. I update the reel I've pinned on my social media and update my website every other month. I foster relationships with new writers and up-and-coming directors and MDs, aiming to meet up at least twice a month. I read one book related to the business per month, plus one for fun. I listen to new music weekly for at least two hours and make at least $800 a week.

Just like your vision, your mission statement will change. As you progress, attending dance classes may become a rarity since you're dancing all day in rehearsals. When you're comfortably booking television work, you put your coach on pause. Suddenly your mission becomes about the number of mornings spent with your toddler at the playground, the number of scripts you read per month, and the hours spent prepping for the triathlon you've registered for.

The power of a mission statement

Sometimes the little things are really the big things that make a life well lived. To leave your house each morning, you already practice many necessary habits to feel like a put-together person. Trivial as they may seem, having our morning coffee, showering, and brushing our teeth are prerequisites for going to work, meeting friends, or being with our partners. Or they're the very activities that keep us in touch with our humanity, like listening to a favorite album or calling a supportive sibling. Imagining our lives without them proves how great their absence would be.

Your mission statement outlines the upgraded routine you need to activate the pro that's locked inside you. It serves as a constant reminder that you are, right now, the artist you want to be—regardless of what your résumé currently says.

VALUES STATEMENT

The actor and singer Josh Groban was a senior at the Los Angeles County High School for the Arts (LACHSA) while RSO was a sophomore.

During a rehearsal break for their all-school production of *Fiddler on the Roof,* RSO asked Josh why he had come to LACHSA as an acting major, given his already incredible singing voice.* This was perplexing to RSO, a voice major, who figured a person should focus on their greatest talent. As Josh saw it, he knew he was an excellent singer, but didn't know as much about acting. Josh valued working on his weaknesses more than exploiting his strengths.

Lindsay, too, has relied on her personal values to make big career decisions. In 2010, she faced a tough one. As a darling of the new musical theatre scene, she'd originated a role in a new musical practically written for her—an underestimated young woman longing for recognition. She loved the show and hoped to stay with it as it moved forward.

But between development steps, Lindsay joined Sherie Rene Scott's *Everyday Rapture* Off-Broadway. Even as a backup singer, she loved the experience—being part of Sherie's story, and thrilled it was heading to Broadway.

Then came a conflict: the new musical got a major regional production—scheduled for the exact same time as *Rapture*'s Broadway transfer. She had to choose: lead a regional production or sing backup on Broadway? Despite the different scale, the pay was nearly identical.

Lindsay returned to her values. Ultimately, she felt that joining another Broadway production—even in a supporting role—better aligned with her long-term goals. It was a hard call, and she worried it might hurt people or burn bridges. Worse, the new musical's director called to scold her, insisting she was making a mistake—and claiming they'd seen *Rapture* Off-Broadway and "forgot she was even in it." (LOL . . . The fuck?)

---

* Their entire high school production of *Fiddler on the Roof* is on YouTube if you're clever enough to find it. Josh was Tevye and RSO was Perchik, which is funny because Josh is ten times the singer you need for Tevye and RSO is ten times *not* the dancer you want for Perchik.

Even backed into a corner, Lindsay stood by what mattered to her. As Sondheim wrote in *Follies*: "Chances that you miss: ignore. Ignorance is bliss—what's more, you won't remember . . . at all."

Who's to say if it was the "right" choice? But we know it was the right choice for Lindsay.

A values statement lists the ideas and beliefs we hold most important.

Our values already influence the decisions we make every day. The person who ignores the free cookie and goes to the gym values their health, while the person doing the reverse values personal pleasure. The person who does both believes most in balance.

When it comes to larger decisions—which contract to take or which city to live in—a values statement is the blueprint for making the most informed choice.

Our values help us make decisions in the present that lead us toward our vision of the future.

Writing a values statement is, at its simplest, taking stock of your priorities. Who fills the cast of characters in your life? What opportunities do you go after? How do you make your living? On a night free, what shows do you buy tickets for?

You live in Astoria because you value space above convenience. You are aggressively single because you value your independence over a relationship. You go after Broadway shows and tours over regional work because you value NYC and money over traveling and easier-to-get credits. You're a gig worker because you value freedom over stability. These values have guided your decisions up until now, and as you identify others, you prepare for the trickier ones to come.

A values thought experiment: The Secret Garden *versus* Dirtbag

At its most complicated, a values statement is a mind-bending game of "Would You Rather?"

> **Would you rather** be a chorus member in Pittsburgh Civic Light Opera's production of *The Secret Garden* with a busy, working director . . .
>
> **Or would you rather** be the lead of a new rock musical Off-Off-Broadway called *Dirtbag*, written by a promising twenty-five-year-old, for virtually no money—but that is sure to be reviewed by New York critics?

You probably knew your answer as soon as you finished the question—because of your values. Maybe *Secret Garden* is your favorite, building active contacts is a priority, or making decent money is your thing. You choose the first. Or . . . working in New York, getting your name in print, screlting rock, and working with new writers is top of your checklist, so you choose the second.

But let's get interesting. For a moment, consider the option you didn't pick. What details would have to change for you to reconsider? For those choosing *Dirtbag*, what if PCLO were doing a show you liked more, the track were bigger, or you were understudying Lily Craven with a weekend of guaranteed performances? For our *Garden* gnomes, what if this rock musical blew your mind, or your agent got you a particularly fabulous deal? Conversely, what if you heard *The Secret Garden* director was a hack, or you found *Dirtbag*'s script a bit, er, questionable? Or, or, or what if two of your best friends were also in *Secret Garden*, or the producers guaranteed an original cast recording of *Dirtbag* . . . ?

Head spinning? Knowing exactly what is most important helps you make your life's tough calls.

Writing your values statement

For the final time, whittle down a long list of values to that magical dozen. Form them into a paragraph like the other two statements, or leave them alone as a list. Here are some questions to get you started.

- What city do you value most?
- What aspects of a job (money, notoriety, creative team, etc.)?
- What performers?
- What titles?
- What writers from the past?
- What writers from the present?
- What genres of musical theatre?
- What genres of stories?
- What genres of music on the radio?
- Revivals or original musicals?
- What forms of mental or physical health?
- What qualities in collaborators?
- What career milestones matter to you?
- How does family factor into your professional pursuits?

A final word from ever-so-helpful Charlie:

CHARLIE'S VALUES STATEMENT

Charlie values New York City. He chooses his jobs based on being paid a fair wage and the collaborators involved. He values musicals like *City of Angels*, *Guys and Dolls*, and *Honeymoon in Vegas*, writers like Frank Loesser, Cy Coleman, Marvin Hamlisch, Jeanine Tesori, David Yazbeck, and Jason Robert Brown. He values revivals, comedies with heart, and jazz music. In his personal life he values his personal fitness, focusing on weightlifting and running. In others, he appreciates loyalty and a commitment to hard work above all.

Based on this statement, we think hypothetical Charlie would hypothetically choose the hypothetical *Dirtbag*. He values New York City, and the genre of the show is much closer to his personal tastes. Though he knows he won't be paid as well as going to Pittsburgh, he senses that the "scrappy" nature of the Off-Off-Broadway show will bring together the kind of tough-as-nails workhorses his city is known for.

While out on a run, Charlie briefly fantasizes about going on for Dickon and singing "Winter's on the Wing," but with a push, he trades that daydream for another more exciting—one that quickens his pace and makes him suddenly aware of how brightly the sun is shining.

USING YOUR BUSINESS PLAN IN PRACTICE

Your final draft combines all three statements and should fit on one page.

This business plan is for *you*—keep it in a notebook or saved on your computer. No one else needs to see it. Your dreams, habits, and priorities don't require approval. (But if feedback helps you dream bigger, feel free to share it with someone you trust.)

Yet the details of your plan will come up more than you think. You might bring up your goals with a prospective agent ("I want to go Equity in the next two years—do you agree?"), share your weekly habits with a friend ("I'm hitting two open calls a week—join me?"), or passionately defend your values during a drunken debate about *Anyone Can Whistle* ("We need to mek ssspace fr orginal musscals, an bussides, *Whistle* iss not, **hiccup**, hiz besssssssst . . .").

Revisit your plan every few years—or sooner if your goals shift. Who you are at twenty-two won't be who you are at thirty-two, and by twenty-seven, you might already feel the difference. Make it a habit to reread and reflect on how it's serving you now.

Your business plan is a guide, not a blood oath. Sometimes you'll set it aside. That's okay. But too many compromises blur your vision, weaken your mission, and chip away at your values.

With a plan in hand, you're officially open for business.

Training and Self-Care

When Alisa's friends notice that she's been in a particularly great mood lately, they assume she's booked something big and hasn't told them yet. They try to get it out of her, but she insists that nothing much has changed in her professional life. She *is* busy—busy taking care of herself, inside and out, and it's made all the difference.

Alisa isn't letting her career lull get her down. She's also not waiting until circumstances improve to get her act together. Doing the damn thing is hard enough when you're at your best, but it's nearly impossible when you're not. Alisa knows there's no hack to maintaining her talent, mental health, and physical strength. It requires discipline, planning, and ongoing effort to find the instruction, habits, and routines that make a real impact. Because while taking care of herself is nonnegotiable for a long-lasting career, *how* she does it is entirely up to her.

Smart, healthy businesses are run by smart, healthy humans. When their owners grow, their business does, too.

For artists, nurturing yourself is its own art form. In this chapter we'll break this down into three areas:

- **Continued training:** Confirming, maintaining, and expanding our skillset
- **The process-oriented perspective:** Remaining open to growth and releasing beliefs that no longer serve us
- **Physical and mental self-care:** Staying present, processing the ups and downs of our lives, and holistically protecting our health

Alisa used to wonder if she had trained long enough to be competitive. Some of her peers didn't go to college for musical theatre and booked Broadway before they could drink wine. For a moment she even contemplated going to grad school, but after a good nap she instead scoped out the right classes and teachers (outside the academic system) who could help improve her progress confidently in her work.

She also released the notion of a "finish line"—because it was driving her crazy. Instead of focusing on where she was "supposed to be" according to the arbitrary timeline she made at nineteen, she instituted monthly check-ins to reflect on recent accomplishments and identify the right questions that would continue her growth.

Like many of us, she also struggled to care for her mind and body with consistency—despite knowing what was good for her. Tempting as it was to take shortcuts, she decided instead to lean in, making a clear plan to build healthier habits.

Take it from us, who've also wrestled with our volatile industry and leaned on our personal well-being to get through it—in the same way that, as a small business, you learn to become both your own boss and the board of directors, as an artist you're your own gym coach, guru, and sounding board . . . sometimes, even your own parent!

TRAINING: THE BEGINNING

Whether you're considering college, currently in college, or have already finished college and are wondering what the heck happened, this deep dive into the value of higher education is for you—and will set the scene for what training you may still want to pursue.

To BFA or not to BFA, isn't that the question?

Most actors are introduced to the basics of performing musical theatre in high school:

- How to sing—understanding music and the voice
- How to act—breaking down and interpreting text to tell a story
- How to move—picking up choreography and communicating with their body

If, after this period, they decide they want to make musical theatre their profession, their next step is traditionally to pursue higher education: earn a BA in music, dance, or acting, or combine them by getting a BFA* in musical theatre at a prestigious institution. Through four years of acting, dance, voice, music theory, history, and audition techniques, they carve out their niche, try to get cast in mainstage principal roles, and finally get an agent at showcase.

Cue Fiyero.

The trouble with schools is . . .

If four years of theatre school sound like a challenge to get through unscathed, it's because they are. And that's before factoring in the cost of admission, the struggle to find the right teachers who will inspire you, and dealing with a tricky community of competitive peers, while still nurturing your competitive self.

Musical theatre programs have many brilliant educators—but also some who aren't. Unlike other majors, many adjuncts aren't required to have terminal degrees, just strong credits. And while some say, "Those who can't do, teach," it's also true that "Those who can do . . . aren't always great teachers." Some educators repeat the harsh, unsympathetic methods

* The difference between a BA (Bachelor of Arts) and a BFA (Bachelor of Fine Arts) is that in the former you'll take more general education classes during your four years, and in the latter you'll concentrate on your major with more arts classes.

they were taught, mistaking performative toughness for care. Often, students have no choice but to endure these teachers due to how their program is structured.

Students may also be pushed down a path that isn't right for them. While some schools have moved past "type," there's still pressure to stay in a lane—one often shaped by the subjective views of faculty and peers. In this book, we've emphasized the control you have over your career and the importance of knowing yourself. But in many programs, the final word belongs to the faculty. Disagree, and you risk being seen as difficult. If there are too many belters, and one who can both belt and sing soprano, she may be nudged in the latter direction simply to balance the program.

Bias is another real issue. Students of color or size may be cast only in shows written for them, limiting their college résumés. Queer students may be overlooked in favor of more conventionally "leading" actors. In large programs especially, students can be led to believe that their most marketable traits are their stats or identity—and that their careers should be shaped around those alone.

Spoiler alert! College is not the real world

A BFA musical theatre program can breed unrealistic competition—not because the professional world isn't competitive (it very much is), but because there are different factors influencing casting decisions. When only three sopranos can play Clara in *Light in the Piazza*, casting may hinge on seniority, who hasn't had a lead, or whether the director feels your classwork has improved. The best person for the role isn't always cast, and the real reasons are rarely stated, leaving everyone guessing.

In the real world, you're only competing with yourself. The hundreds auditioning beside you don't matter—you're judged only on how you fit the production's vision. You'll never know what someone else did, or get a chance to outdo them.

"Cut programs" (where students may be asked to leave the major if they don't live up to the faculty's expectations) are fading—but so is arts funding, leading some schools to keep weak students and relegate them to the back, simply to keep their tuition revenue. Exceptionally talented students may be urged to stay in school and forgo a major professional opportunity—not because they need more training, but because the program benefits from their eventual graduation. A hyper-self-aware sophomore may still be pushed in classwork to go against her strengths just to expand her wheelhouse, even if she's ready to work now. Growth is valuable, but why ask a job-ready student to pay $1,200 per credit when she could be earning $1,200 a week in a show?

And then there's showcase

Somehow the whole fraught experience leads to an even more fraught senior showcase—that fateful day when agents decide whether to sign you. If they don't, it can feel like you "failed" college; if they do, you "won." Showcase becomes the final exam—but no amount of studying guarantees you'll "pass."

Anyone who has left college without an agent knows the emptiness that follows. You were sold the lie that if you did the work, took the feedback, and trusted the process, representation would be your reward—but agents are looking to fill a roster, not award "A" students: They're looking for more dancers, more film actors, more men of color, more spooky girls, more bubbly gays. Their needs aren't your business until you become theirs.

The BFA obstacle course almost ensures that each student will, at some point, seriously doubt themselves. Some will leave so discouraged they quit altogether.

People say rejection builds resilience. But if you could get the same rejection for free in the real world—why pay $200,000 for it?

Your degree doesn't matter (that much)

Unlike in other fields, a degree in musical theatre is not a prerequisite for getting hired.

We asked 322 casting directors, casting associates, directors, writers, music directors, and choreographers—anyone involved in casting—how much an actor's alma mater impacts their audition.

- *50 percent said: "Little to no bearing. Rarely affects whether they'll be called in and isn't weighed when considering two evenly matched performers."*
- *46 percent said: "Some bearing. It may be used to thin the pool or to select between two evenly matched performers."*
- *4 percent said: "Heavy bearing. A prime consideration for calling them in, and it's weighed seriously in final casting."*

Actors are hired based on how they align with the creative team's vision. Training helps—but it can be gained elsewhere. An alma mater sets expectations. A top school signals strong training; one lesser known means the actor must prove themselves. But a UMich grad can still flop a callback, and a gutsy newcomer from community college can land the role. Auditions decide, not schools.*

College may occasionally help narrow the casting pool, but building real relationships can open just as many doors. And as for getting an agent at showcase? More often than not, showcase doesn't actually matter.

A poll of 220 working actors in New York City found this:

- *62 percent said they did not get an agent at showcase.*

* One exception is if you are more focused on acting in straight plays. In that case, getting your MFA in acting from an established university can greatly affect your trajectory. In the non–musical theatre acting sphere, a high-level degree can even be a prerequisite for getting seen—or cast. (Film/TV also seems not to care about school.)

- *21 percent said they did, but within seven years they had moved to another agent.*
- *17 percent said they got an agent from showcase and are still with them.*

Why you should go to school

Many program heads might say, "Yes, that was true—but we're part of the change." And we believe them. We admire these schools and see real progress. Their reputations are growing, and we're hopeful they'll soon be known more for building students up than breaking them down.

If you're pursuing a BFA in musical theatre, seek a program that nurtures autonomy, rewards savvy, and hires compassionate, curious faculty who challenge and support you. Before seriously investigating a degree in musical theatre, consider the following.

- DON'T GO to theatre school if booking roles in college shows is essential to your path. Would being rarely cast ruin your experience?
- DON'T GO to theatre school if one of your top reasons for attending is to get an agent from showcase. If you don't get one, will you be all right?
- DON'T GO if constantly competing with your close friends would crush your spirit.
- DO GO if you believe that, regardless of college shows and showcases, you are confident in your ability to find performance opportunities outside of school, and that when you're ready for an agent, you'll get one.
- DO GO because you want to learn the craft of musical theatre: to study voice, acting theory, history, dance styles, and more, and to plan your path post-college.
- DO GO because you want to meet other brilliant artists—both friends and faculty—and learn from both. You can distinguish

competition from collaboration, and you won't let the opinions and decisions of others bring you down.

- DO GO because the structure and schedule of a college program are important to you. If you don't feel confident creating your own schedule, you may need guidance.
- DO GO because you might want to teach someday—and *definitely* go if you want to teach at the college level. After your undergraduate degree, consider getting an MFA.

TRAINING II: THE REVENGE

Lindsay didn't go to theatre school and she won a Tony Award by thirty-five. The list of successful Broadway actors who didn't get a degree is long and convincing.

That doesn't mean, however, that we're advising you to come to a major market and simply shoot your shot. Regardless of your talent, continuing your training is nonnegotiable. Talent is a muscle—and if you don't exercise it regularly, it will weaken over time. No one is "fully cooked" at eighteen, no matter how talented they are or what credits they've acquired. Growing is a lifelong project.

New York or bust: Skipping school

Without college, you must create your own education—which takes an incredible amount of time and, yes, money. Your schedule will resemble a BFA program, but at a fraction of the cost, the flexibility to customize your faculty, and the agency to choose the environments that are right for you.

- First, find someone who will help to keep you accountable—preferably someone you can't avoid, like a parent. Especially if you're just entering adulthood, the transition from a teen's life (which is organized for you) to an adult's (when you must remain disciplined and on task with little supervision) takes time. Think of this person as your "advisor."

- Attend dance class at least three times a week. Move to harder classes and teachers regularly and explore different styles.
- Take weekly voice lessons. If you're still strengthening your vocal technique, go twice a week until major issues are resolved.
- Take straight acting classes outside of musical theatre, focusing on Shakespeare, comedy, improv, contemporary acting, clowning, and so on.
- Take a dedicated audition techniques class weekly.
- Attend master classes with industry pros whenever you have the opportunity.
- Get a mentor or two (or three)—people who can offer guidance throughout your journey.
- When you're ready, attend showcases for casting directors and agents at least once a year. Early on, go for the experience, not the outcome.
- Film footage and share with trusted pros for feedback.
- Review part two of this book at least once a year. As you grow, certain elements will gain new relevance.
- See shows big and small, and attend concerts put on by others in your industry. Meet people. Build a community of artists around you.
- Audition when you have go-to songs polished by coaches you respect (especially your classic, contemporary, and radio uptempos). Early on, audition for the experience, not the outcome.

Create a detailed, weekly schedule and establish an education budget that you use up regularly. This isn't the time to cut corners on training. It's the time to go all-in.

TRAINING III: RESURRECTION

You got into this business by watching others on stage. Even today, when the going gets tough, a brilliant performance can replenish your spirit. Just as a body needs food to function and a car needs gas or an electric charge to drive, you need inspiration to feed your creative expression. Sure, you can operate on fumes (some days, you have no other choice), but to put good work out you need to put good work in.

Here are some approaches you can take to keep your creative cup topped off:

- **See shows, read plays, learn new musicals, and fill your cup.** Sometimes when we're burnt out, we avoid experiencing other work (because, perhaps, it depresses us), but this is actually counterintuitive to reviving our artistic selves.
- **Check in on expert skills.** Even masters refine their skills. Before auditions, refresh with a voice teacher or acting coach to stay sharp and improve in new areas.
- **Maintain your managed skills.** Skills that took years to build need practice to maintain. Dance, vocal work, scene study, or the gym keep actor instincts fine-tuned.
- **Address weaknesses.** No one excels at everything, but weaknesses can become liabilities. In top markets, they can come to define you if they're left unchecked. People avoid work that makes them feel bad (especially as they get older), but improvement takes less effort than expected. Prioritize training where growth is needed, because progress (however small) makes you more competitive.
- **Most importantly, learn something new.** During the pandemic, Lindsay expanded her skills through vocal pedagogy. Strengthen your craft—dancers learn new styles, actors explore improv, musicians refine their sight-singing. Or as RSO did, pursue an unrelated passion (he started learning Italian)—juggling, poker, parkour—to provide balance and mental recovery. Growth fuels creativity. *Capisce?*

PROCESS-ORIENTED PERSPECTIVE

When Lindsay was cast in *Godspell* in the role of, well, "Lindsay," it was unfamiliar territory. The show was built from improvisation—no real script, no clear character arcs—just the room, the props, and her fellow actors.

Never one to back down from a challenge, she dove into rehearsals, trusting director Danny Goldstein and her cast. Though she hadn't attended college, *Godspell* became her "undergrad," pushing her out of her comfort zone and unlocking a freedom to play that would shape her future work.

If *Godspell* was her undergrad, *Dogfight* was her master's. Working with Joe Mantello, she had to set aside many of her instincts—bold vocals, big comedy—and trust her quieter, deeper self. Living in the character's pain, even wearing nearly nothing in one scene, forced Lindsay to open up to new, uncomfortable experiences. But she trusted the team—and herself. That year, she earned nominations from the Drama Desk, Outer Critics Circle, and Drama League.

In both cases, Lindsay embraced a process-oriented mindset. Unconcerned with past achievements, she knew growth required facing the unfamiliar. Without discomfort and the growing pains that can accompany taking risks, she wouldn't be the artist she is today.

Our work is always evolving. Performances shift from table read to final rehearsal, through tech, previews, and weekly shows. Some roles we understand deeply; others remain a mystery long after closing night. So why does the industry expect early-career actors to present as finished products? How do we balance the pressure to be "ready" with the reality that we're always a work in progress?

Theatre kid versus the process: Fight!

The cognitive dissonance between being Officially Talented and a Perpetual Student can sabotage an actor's path forward. From theatre camps to college programs, we give time and money to achieve guaranteed readiness—yet leave our expensive programs hearing that we still have "a lot to learn."

A process-oriented perspective means acknowledging that we know a lot—it's what got us here—but we don't know everything. Some things we "know" today *were* true once, but aren't anymore. Other ideas were never true to begin with.

The truth is that we carry things we've learned that we don't need anymore. When we do this, we leave no space to take home anything new. It's better to travel with only the essentials and leave room to pick things up on the adventure.

Have we mentioned that RSO is a type-A Virgo?

RSO knows these dangers all too well.

He grew up a bit of a wunderkind—skipping eighth grade, graduating second in his class at sixteen, getting a full ride to UCLA, and finishing NYU grad school with multiple writing awards. His rapid rise came from fierce confidence and motivation—bordering at times on delusion. Nothing could challenge what he believed about himself. He embodied a product-oriented mindset, making it hard to see beyond his own ideas. But the baby of the group who was "wise beyond his years" eventually became a man, and by his late twenties, his talent had outpaced him. New opportunities began to dry up. Something had locked him out of rooms he'd once been in, but he couldn't figure out what that something was.

At thirty, he switched agencies and his wonderfully direct agent told him the truth: He'd gained a reputation as someone who "couldn't take a note." His grip on an outdated self-image had become his identity, and he hadn't allowed himself to grow up . . . because when someone tells you you're brilliant at twenty, why would you want to change who you are at the risk of losing what you've got?

From that moment on, everything shifted. He began saying "yes" where he once said "no," took genuine interest in collaborators' ideas, and became a true teammate. He still knew a lot—but now he understood how much more there was to learn. New opportunities came quickly, shut doors reopened, and best of all, doors he'd never noticed before suddenly appeared.

The process-oriented perspective in action

Say yes to "yes!"

Enter unfamiliar processes openly, putting thoughts that compete with what you may now learn into "storage." Try new ideas, see how your craft works without old practices, and discover what you miss from what you've put aside.

It's powerful to say, "I don't know." By saying "Sure, let's try that!" we build trust with the room. When someone gives you a note or a suggestion, remember that you're both on the same side. If the idea doesn't *feel* helpful, ask someone, "Say that a different way?" to see if you can better understand it. The best idea always wins—if everyone is willing to accept that the best idea may not be their own.

SELF-CARE FOR THE ACTOR

"Being an actor is a really hard life," said your strangely competitive uncle. And your uncle is right—but not for the reasons he thinks. Above all, the emotional wear and tear of being an artist easily drains our will and can make our profession feel like a never-ending slog.

When it comes to your motivation, no one else but you is in the driver's seat. Each morning you have to say, "Today, I have something important to do." Self-belief like this can be a bear in the face of frequent rejection. When we're pressured by dubious parents, tempted by quitting peers, or crushed by inarticulate coaches, the cave of hopelessness beckons (to say nothing of the total deflation that comes from watching classmates' dreams come true on social media). And that's just the day-to-day. In extraordinary times, you may get fired, lose a loved one, or experience the crippling despair that comes to sit on your heart like a rehearsal cube.

Every artist battles with their mental health at some point. But there are many ways to protect it, and though they may be familiar to you, it's vital to revisit them year after year.

- **Meditation** reduces stress and enhances self-awareness. It can be a morning ritual, midday focus, or nighttime unwind. Free YouTube guides, affordable apps, and expert-led sessions offer options. Beginners should start small—practice improves focus, making meditation a daily essential.
- **Journaling** brings clarity, turning fears into manageable thoughts. It helps explore worries, assess control, and find solutions. Whether it's a quick "rose and thorn" or pages of reflection, writing offers self-therapy and a rational dialogue with your inner voice.
- **Therapy** fosters growth, processes trauma, and builds resilience. It's available in person, in groups, or online. Find a therapist who understands your needs as an artist specifically. Many services offer sliding-scale fees or affordable e-therapy options to ensure cost isn't a barrier.
- **Self-help and philosophy** have gone more mainstream in recent years. Either may encourage personal development and emotional clarity, and usually at very little cost.
- **Exercise** boosts mood, confidence, and sleep while fighting depression. Whether gym workouts, classes, or just walking, find a routine that fits. Start small, stay consistent, and lean on friends for accountability. Soon you'll crave the feeling that only a finished workout can bring.
- **Protecting our minds from negative influences** is key. Motivational speaker Jim Rohn said we're the "average" of the five closest people in our lives. Do yours inspire or drain you? Set boundaries with negative personalities who discourage your forward momentum. The same goes for social media. Be mindful of its impact and find a balance that won't leave you taxed (or worse, tormented).

Checking back in with our thriving friend Alisa, keeping up with her skills and practicing self-care offer her a daily achievement fix. On an ordinary Wednesday, Alisa has a breakthrough in therapy, does a killer workout in dance class, and takes an audition techniques seminar with her favorite coach to ease the dull little ache of finding out she didn't book yesterday. The daily "wins" of practicing mindfulness, bolstering her confidence, and encouraging all those good brain chemicals have become essential for her well-being. Most importantly, living a healthy, stimulated life doesn't require anyone's permission but her own.

And in a profession brimming with rejection, that's quite a relief.

Money and the Hustle

Jonah's older brother is worried about him. Jonah's been saving money over the last few years and finally feels ready to move to NYC, but his big bro aims to persuade him to stay home in Tampa, Florida, for a few more years. What Jonah knows, however, is that his overprotective bro—a lawyer—doesn't think Jonah will survive in the big city.

"Dude, there's no money in theatre. Everyone knows that."

But Jonah's brother is wrong. There's a ton of money to be made in the arts—if you know where to find it, and what to do with it when you do.

"Think of Brett," his brother goes on. "He didn't last three years before he came home." He's referring to the star of their high school who left for New York, wiped out his savings, fell into debt, and struggled to find time to audition with his day job's demanding schedule.

Jonah does think of Brett. A lot. But two things can be true at the same time:

> **True:** Many artists wrestle with their financial welfare because they never learned healthy financial habits, nor were they shown how to support themselves between high-paying gigs without resorting to straining nine-to-five "survival" jobs.

> **Also true:** Thousands of artists are thriving financially today. They achieved this *primarily* through a steadfast drive to generate ongoing creative income (stability) and *secondarily* through sporadic professional success (bonuses).

In his brother's defense, right now Jonah is mystified by the whole "money thing" (though he's not going to tell his brother that). He had a class in his junior year of high school where his gym teacher (substituting for the social studies teacher who quit after her messy divorce) covered the "finance unit." He learned about making a budget, a little about taxes, and some about the stock market. But Jonah was checking out the girl seated in front of him and wondering when the cast list for *Thoroughly Modern Millie* was going up, so he didn't absorb it as much as he now wishes he had. After all, Jonah thinks nervously, this is the country that once decided cafeteria ketchup counted as a vegetable, so why should he have trusted the folks in charge to make sure he understood the difference between a 1099 and a W-2?

But if Jonah is going to make the big move, he's got to take serious control of managing his bank account—or else he'll end up like Brett. It's time to answer the money question before it becomes the money problem.

A healthy financial life means earning the money you need to live the life you want, staying out of debt, and saving for the future.

Ignorance is not bliss

The first reason so many suffer from the money problem is that they effectively ignore the money question altogether. It's stressful to think about, so they just don't.

"Oh, I'm definitely *thinking* about it. I am, in fact, *worrying actively* about it," Jonah says on a phone call with Brett.

Since leaving New York, Brett's had time to reflect. Back in the city, even as his checking account dwindled and his credit card balance soared, he often felt paralyzed to do anything about it. Looking back, he realizes he was clinging to a misguided belief: "Once I land a big Broadway job, all my money problems will disappear. Once I'm famous, I'll never have to worry about money again."

But after watching several friends achieve the success he dreamed of, Brett learned the hard truth: that belief was just wishful thinking. If only someone had told him sooner . . . but at least now he can help Jonah avoid the same mistake.

Being a green witch isn't as green as you might think

When Lindsay played Elphaba on Broadway, she was making the best money of her career to date, earning in six weeks what the average American made in a year—and she stayed in the role for nine months. You'd think she'd be set for a while—but you'd be wrong. After taxes, agent fees, tipping dressers, paying off debt, upkeep, periodic medical bills, and simply living the Broadway witch life, she finished her run not much better off than when she started.

She discovered two fundamental truths. First, the more an artist makes, the more an artist tends to spend. Second, the older you get, the more you want and the less you'll tolerate. As your personal baseline rises, any extra money gets allocated to support a more exciting lifestyle. Put simply:

***If you're struggling with money now,
you'll likely struggle with it later—
regardless of how much more you make.***

"The problem isn't your income," Brett said. "It's how you manage it. If you aren't responsible with $1,000 in the bank, you probably won't be responsible with $100,000 in the bank."

"Woof."

"No one is coming to save you, man. When it comes to money, you've gotta save yourself."

"But for how long?" Jonah asks.

"For the rest of your life!"

NO ONE TEACHES YOU THIS STUFF

When RSO had to cash his first check at the bank, he realized he didn't know how. He asked his mommy for help. He was seventeen.

RSO didn't come from money. As a kid, his dad worked endless overtime as a cross-country car hauler, while his mom worked for the school district. There were few dinners out, no vacations—certainly no private training or expensive summer camps. So he chased every free performance opportunity available, wrote constantly to build his portfolio, and applied for every scholarship he could find. He left his undergrad at UCLA debt-free and arrived in New York with just $1,000—but finished grad school at NYU $45,000 in debt. Not exactly a strong financial start.

RSO was determined not to let the money question send him home. To maintain a healthy financial life, over the first few years in the city he developed six rules for himself, rules he still follows today:

1. **Establish a budget for the lifestyle you want.**
2. **Find your artistic Hustle and make it grow.**
3. **Track your finances regularly.**
4. **Save at least 10 percent of your income.**
5. **Stay out of debt (and if you get into debt, pay it off quickly).**
6. **Never live off your savings (and if you borrow, pay it back quickly).**

Over the past two decades, he's paid off student loans, avoided credit card debt, saved consistently, filed his taxes on time, bought a home, and invested. That may not sound extraordinary—until you consider that many of his theatre friends have gone broke, accumulated major debt, or struggled to save, even with more impressive bios. The peace of mind in not stressing over a paycheck or affording a new computer is something he continues to rely on.

In this chapter, we're going to break down these money rules, while teaching you—and Jonah—about the essential key to a financially healthy artist's career: building the Hustle.

Though Jonah wasn't great at math in school, Brett says that if he can put away his laundry, follow traffic laws, and light a match without burning himself, he can learn how to successfully manage his money. Jonah doesn't totally know how those examples relate to money yet, but for now all he needs to do is open his calculator app and get ready to write some things down.

NOTE: We're not financial advisors—just artists who've learned a few things about money. If something here resonates, talk to a money-savvy loved one and discover more about the best financial practices.

ESTABLISH A BUDGET FOR YOUR LIFESTYLE

The first step to answering the money question is to determine your cost of living.

Your cost of living is how much sustainable income you need to live the happy yet practical lifestyle *you want.*

Picture the life that would make you happy today, one that feels past where you are now yet still reasonably within reach. Where do you live? How often do you eat out or fly home? How much do you spend on clothes, entertainment, and training? The goal isn't luxury, it's contentment—for now.

Since most people will spend how they want anyway, it's smarter to meet your practical needs than to start off defeated by strict budgets and cutbacks. Because we don't believe in an approach of spending less, we believe in making more—which means working hard enough to support the life you want with as little compromise as possible.

How to identify your cost of living

Let's assume you make and spend the same amount every month, give or take. Add up the total expenses that make up your month, including:

- Rent
- Loan payments
- Phone, internet, etc.
- Public transportation, gas, etc.
- Gym, fitness
- Utilities (power, water, etc.)
- Subscriptions (Netflix, *New York Times*, etc.)
- Insurance (health, dental, etc.)
- Classes
- Anything else

Next, estimate your **daily expenses.** On an average day, how much do you spend on casual things like coffee, lunch, movie tickets, drinks out, groceries, and the like? You're probably looking for a number between $20 and $75.

Now estimate your **monthly miscellaneous expenses,** which occur haphazardly and tend to be large—anything from a plane ticket home, to a new pair of LaDucas, to paying for a dental procedure out-of-pocket. On average, you're looking at something between $500 and $1,500 per month.

Add all of these together for a number between $3,500 and $7,500. A number higher or lower is okay as long as it accurately reflects the life you're living on the resources you have available.

As a final step, add **10 percent on top for savings** (more on that in a bit). If your final number were $3,500, you would add $350 ($3,500 × 0.1), for a total of $3,850.

This is your monthly cost of living.

Brett points Jonah to his financially clever friend Tavia for an example, who's happy to help.

TAVIA'S EXPENSES

Rent	$1,250/month
Loan payments	$380
Phone, internet, etc.	$140
Public transport, gas, etc.	$140
Gym, fitness	$90
Utilities	$175
Subscriptions	$60
Insurance	$0
Lessons and classes	$450
Daily expenses	$35/day × 30.5 days in the month = $1,067.50
Miscellaneous large expenses	$500
	Subtotal = $4,252.50
Add 10 percent for savings	$425.25
Tavia's Cost of Living = $4,677.75 per month	

A few notes on Tavia's lifestyle: She shares a small two-bedroom in Inwood (northern Manhattan) with a roommate, her phone bill also covers half the apartment's internet and a few streaming services, she has a cheap gym membership, and she takes a couple of spin classes each month. She's still on her parents' insurance because she's under twenty-six. She takes voice lessons almost weekly and sees a therapist on a sliding scale. She hates shopping, and with family nearby in New Jersey, her other expenses stay low.

Identify your monthly income

What do you make in a month, after taxes? If you have multiple jobs, add them together.

Tavia works at a cute little café around the corner. She also babysits in Midtown an average of eight hours a week, where the parents pay her under the table (we make no judgments on either party).

TAVIA'S INCOME

Barista....... $17.60/hr (after taxes) x 40 hrs × 4 wks = $2,816
Average babysitting hrs/mo .... (32 hrs/mo × $35) = $1,120
Tavia's Total Monthly Income = $3,936

In order for Tavia to live the lifestyle she wants, she has to make up the difference between her cost of living and her income.

Cost of living $4,677.75
- Income $3,936.00
Difference = $741.75

Making up the difference

If you were honest about your cost of living, your monthly expenses will probably exceed your monthly income. This also would explain why your bank account might always look stressed—because the life we choose to live naturally tends to exceed our means. But hey, we're human!

Now we have to close the gap between the money we're making and the life we want. The solution to this—and the answer to ultimate financial stability as an artist—is the Hustle.

THE ARTIST'S HUSTLE 101

At the beginning of their career, when consistent acting work is difficult to come by, most actors take on a "survival job" to, well, survive. This work usually eats up to thirty or forty hours of their week and pays minimum wage (or just above it), somewhere between $15 and $30 per hour. It's inflexible, unstimulating, or so exhausting they have no energy to pursue their craft—maybe even all three.

An actor cannot survive—
let alone thrive financially and artistically—
on most survival jobs.

To solve this dilemma, some get a better-paying full-time job, which creates a new problem. They love their new office gig, with all its benefits, high salary, and room for promotion . . . but wait, are they a receptionist, or an actor? Are they a bar manager, or are they an artist?

A forty-hour-a-week job working for someone else
won't support your artistic career.

Juggling both worlds, they miss auditions, skip rehearsals, and struggle to stay focused like their peers. It's just till they get on their feet, they swear . . . but what starts as a momentary detour silently becomes a lengthy sojourn, while their acting career goes on indefinite pause. Sadly, most never return to it; over time, the steady paycheck makes it harder to go back, and they settle into a career they only kinda sorta like.

This is where the Hustle comes in.

The Hustle is a job you create
to close the gap in your cost of living,
live the life you want,
and pursue your artistic career.

The Hustle is there when you're waiting at auditions, between contracts, or even rehearsing on Broadway. It grows over time, boosts your income, supports your lifestyle, and—most importantly—is fully in your control.

Don't confuse the Hustle with a "side hustle." That's your survival job—something you do just to get by and drop as soon as you can, because it takes time away from what you really love: acting.

The Hustle doesn't compete with your artistic work,
it supports it.

Virtually every successful actor you can name has a Hustle—you just don't necessarily know about it. (And we posit that their Hustle is *part* of what has made and kept them successful.) That awesome soprano who just closed a year starring in her Broadway show? She's got her own private voice studio. That baritone's doing regional symphony gigs, and his dance captain husband is offering master classes. The ferocious beltress you were surprised to see in an Off-Broadway show this season also runs a lucrative videography business.

***The Hustle* is not a backup plan.**
***It's a forever plan, and it's* for everyone.**

It's not just for Broadway actors. If a movie star makes ten million, they'll want twelve next time to match their new lifestyle. When that big role doesn't come, they need to fill the gap—so they Hustle too. They hock merch, establish Patreons and Cameos, launch a tequila brand, or take a slew of bizarre TV roles—because, like you, they have bills to pay.

No matter how high you climb, your Hustle gives you the stability a selective industry can't.

The qualities of a good job

To understand what we're looking for, we judge work on three qualities.

***The first quality of a job* is income.**

Does the job pay well, relative to where you live, your situation, and what your peers make? For a ballpark estimate, we're looking at substantially more than minimum wage—$40 or more an hour. Insurance, benefits, and perks can also be factored in, too.

***The second quality of a job* is flexibility.**

A flexible job lets you leave for a callback, take six weeks off for a contract, or work from the road. You can take time for a cabaret, make up hours later, or have someone cover for you. It never gets in the way of your art.

***The third quality* is stimulation.**

Do you enjoy the work you're doing? Do you like your boss, coworkers, clients, and customers? While you're there, do you like *yourself*? Does it, in some way, contribute to your work as an artist?

***A great job fulfills all three qualities.* Never let go!**
***A good job fulfills two of them.* Cool, keep it!**
***A bad job fulfills one or none.* Quit ASAP!**

If your job fulfills one or zero of these qualities, quit as soon as you can. You will find a better one.* If you like your job fine, it probably fulfills two. This is a good survival job on which you can build a Hustle.

The Hustle has all three qualities

Any job that checks all three boxes—pays well, offers flexibility, and stimulates you—is a dream job worth keeping. That's the Hustle.

The Hustle is usually a job you create and run yourself. It's flexible because *you're* the boss, stimulating because it's something you enjoy and excel at, and it pays well because you're using real expertise to charge what you're worth.

It's why your roommate makes $16 per hour in retail, while your voice teacher earns $225 for fifty minutes. The difference? Your voice teacher has

* Yes, you heard us! For over a decade we've told actors to quit these low-paying, inflexible, unstimulating jobs and promised them they could find a better one—and we've yet to be proven wrong.

built a small business selling a high-value skill—just like you can. You don't need to rely solely on acting gigs to earn a living.

In fact, Actor Therapy is the Hustle your authors built for themselves years ago. When Lindsay's between contracts, she teaches. When RSO has a free spring, he adds classes. When we're booked, other teachers step in. Over time, we've built a company with a team of ambitious artists who've made A.T. their Hustle, too. We're living proof of its power.

GETTING AN ARTIST HUSTLE

The size of the Hustle you need right now is the same as the gap between your cost of living and your income.

Previously, Tavia's difference was $741.75 per month. If we divide this number by four weeks, we see Tavia is looking to make an additional $185 per week via her new Hustle.

Where to find your Hustle

What do you enjoy doing? How do you spend your free time? What skills have you been trained in—even ones that didn't seem important at the time? Your answers reveal potential options for your Hustle.

When RSO moved to New York, he didn't want to take a retail job like he had in undergrad, so he had to rely on his artistic skills to pay rent. He sang as a tenor section leader at a church* ($600/month), did freelance graphic design ($100/month), and music directed for a local opera company ($200/month). Most profitably, he returned home a few times a year to direct children's theatre—eventually taking over the Pasadena Musical Theatre Program ($8,000/year). For years, these flexible, well-paying, and creative gigs fully supported him.

---

* This is despite being a lifelong atheist. In fact, he quite enjoyed the people, the routine, sight-reading great music, and doing the crossword on his phone during the sermon, tucked away unseen in the choir loft.

As his writing career grew, he sold sheet music ($300/month) and taught as an adjunct professor ($1,600/month). Over time, he dropped graphic design, then the church job, and eventually stopped directing and adjuncting as other opportunities took over. His income—and lifestyle—rose accordingly.

This kind of gradual shift is common for artists who harness the Hustle: starting with smaller creative jobs and growing into bigger ones.

Here are a few more Hustles we've seen (and the list doesn't stop here):

Personal assistant
Freelance personal trainer
Private yoga teacher
Voice teacher
Dance teacher
Acting or monologue coach
Musical theatre college audition coach
Private tutor for high schoolers
Essay or interview coach
Home organization
Gigging musician
Small-time interior design (offices, dressing rooms)
Photographer/Videographer
Social media manager
Graphic designer
Craft artist selling their work
Influencer (yep)

Each Hustle commands a high price, can be scheduled around your availability, and has room for growth as you improve. It's maximized if you're working for yourself and not losing a cut to someone who is managing you (as with a personal trainer working for a gym, or a tutor working for a parent company). The administration and advertising they're handling for you is work you could handle yourself.

Just like in an audition, people are looking to purchase something from you that is in line with your strengths and aligns with their needs. Decide exactly what you're offering—and to whom—to find clients who are right for you.

Your demographic

Who is your product for?

What is their age? If you're looking to teach, begin with students about ten years younger than yourself. If you're twenty-four, another twenty-four-year-old might not be interested in you as a monologue coach—but a fourteen-year-old might be.

Where do they live? Early on, your Hustle may not be as competitive in big cities, but smaller areas need to fill the void left by those who abscond to larger markets.

Your rate

Factors like your age, education, and experience affect your rate. Starting out, charging less is an advantage against others offering your service, especially those who are further along and more expensive. If your brave first customers think that working with you is a "steal," you're not selling yourself short—you're rewarding clients with a good eye for early talent.

If the personal trainers in your area are charging $80 per session, you might start at $60 to attract more budget-conscious beginners. As you gain experience, you'll charge more.

Decide how to accept payments

You can take cash in the beginning as you're working out your Hustle's kinks, but eventually that won't be practical—or legal.

Services like PayPal make accepting payments easy but will assess a fee for the convenience and security of their platform. Others like CashApp,

Square, and ApplePay charge a smaller fee for business transactions and credit card purchases. Venmo and similar peer-to-peer cash exchanges aren't intended for business transactions and will charge a fee for those that are.

• • • • • •

After some experimenting with different skills, you'll gradually discover a strong candidate for your main Hustle. When you're raising prices because you can, gaining clients, working more efficiently, and dedicating more time to it? That's a sign that it's time to make your main Hustle official.

GROWING YOUR ARTIST HUSTLE

Tell the world about your Hustle (or at least, your community). Start with sharing information about it as subtly as an Instagram post from a personal account, or shout it far and wide by creating a dedicated social media account or building an entire website. It needn't be impressive looking (yet) . . . it just has to *be.*

Reach out to at least ten people. Let them know the new work you're doing and ask if they know anyone who'd be interested. Your first clients are likely to be friends of friends, friends of your parents, and the kiddos who orbit them. The good news is that people want to help a motivated young person make a living on their passion—especially when they have a personal connection. As you get on your feet, don't be shy about offering freebies and discounts.

People will tell others, and those others will tell *other* others. Some clients will naturally disappear, but if your total number is growing, then your Hustle is, too.

Announcing your business

Our favorite way of telling the world about your Hustle is to post about it online as though your business is already *in motion.*

Hey friends, I have an opening in my voice studio at 3:00 PM and 4:00 PM this Thursday. Direct message me if you're interested!

Some close friends may be confused to see this story pop up on their socials—because they didn't know you had a voice studio. And until that story, you didn't either!

"Uhh, Sasha is a voice teacher now? Weird," you imagine your "friend" Amy texting your mutual pal, Caren. "Who does she think she is? Imagine taking a voice lesson from *her*." With all due respect to Amy: F off, Amy. We're trying to survive without retreating behind the Lululemon sales counter, and it doesn't matter if Amy thinks you'd be a good voice teacher as long as your students do. If you don't think you've got something to offer the world, why should anyone else?

Everything your authors have accomplished they did by taking a leap. Our peers were occasionally surprised by our bold moves, but in no time at all, our good work caught on. Your outer circle might get jealous, but that's not your business. Your Hustle is.

Feed your Hustle, watch it flourish

The Hustle starts small, but the more time and energy you invest, the more it grows into a stable and reliable support system.

When your Hustle gets going, you might make $200 a week with three clients. This means one or two fewer shifts at the bar. As months pass and positive word of mouth spreads (because you're awesome at what you do and continuously improving what you offer), you grow to six clients and $400 a week, and it's another shift you can forgo. Then after a year, it's nine clients for $750 weekly, and you go part-time. Then one day a week. A few days a month. Finally, you quit your survival gig altogether.

The final step of the Hustle is to overtake your survival job as your primary source of stable income.

Your flexible Hustle will adapt its schedule around whatever life throws at you, but you must feed it to keep it alive. If you build a client base and then go on tour for nine months, forgetting all about it, your clients will move on and your hard work will have been wasted.

With flexibility comes control. When your bank account is as packed as your busy schedule, you can pull back a little if you need to focus on rehearsals. When you're cash poor and have extra time, you circle back to past clients to pick up some extra income. Because you genuinely love the work, you expand it over time, possibly bringing on others to expand your team and turn your one-person show into a small cast.

Soon you might find your business promoting your artistic life as your artistic life directly promotes it. For your authors, teaching Actor Therapy has made us a better actress and writer. Just as our artistic careers feed our student base, by constantly exploring the crafts of acting and storytelling we stay curious students ourselves.

ARTIST HUSTLE FAQ

"This seems like a lot of work. Wouldn't staying a temp be easier?"

Yes—in the short term. But with that mindset, you'll likely return to temping again and again throughout your career. At twenty-five, that might seem manageable. At forty, facing three months between gigs and an empty cupboard, the café is a lot less cute.

Make no mistake: The few years it takes to build a sustainable, supportive Hustle are worth it. This investment will save you decades of frustration, not to mention the regret of wishing you'd started sooner.

"I'm afraid I'm not ready—or my Hustle isn't."

Like so many daunting life changes, we're rarely ready to take the leap. But somehow we do, and realize we couldn't be "ready" because we couldn't know what exactly we had to be ready for, until we did it.

Likewise, your Hustle doesn't have to be perfectly ready to go to get started. Remember, when the iPhone first came out, it wasn't "ready" either, released with an inferior network speed, lack of features, and even software bugs. Put yourself out there as soon as it feels reasonable.

"My Hustle isn't growing. What should I do?"

All businesses ebb and flow. It's normal to troubleshoot slower times. But if you feel you've done everything you can for your Hustle (including offering free sample classes, sales, lowering your prices, getting feedback from clients, and asking for advice from savvy mentors) and it's not helping, it may be time to look elsewhere.

Not every idea will be right for your long-term investment. For RSO, doing graphic design, leading a theatre company, directing, and teaching at a university were fun while they lasted, but he didn't see a future in those fields. While he had talent in these areas, he couldn't make the necessary loop happen:

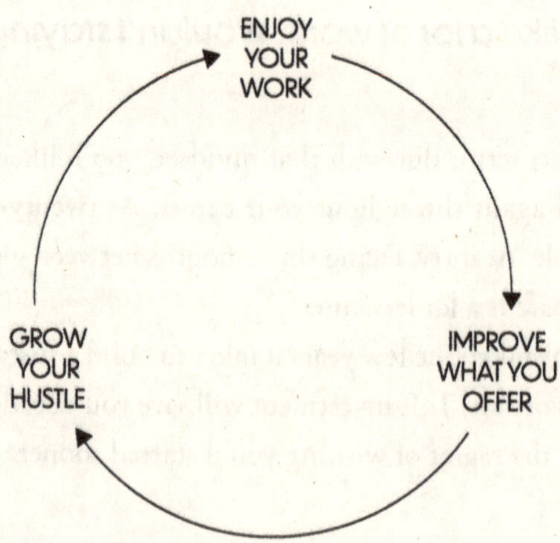

There's a perfect Hustle out there for you. Keep experimenting until you find it.

"Do I have to pay taxes on my Hustle?"

YES, you criminal!

You are legally obligated to pay the government taxes on any and all income you receive. Starting out, you'll claim this total cash on your taxes as "miscellaneous income," and a tax professional can advise you on what you owe.*

"Do I need to open a bank account or form an LLC for my Hustle?"

While you're still figuring out your Hustle, no. Income can go directly into your personal checking account.

When your Hustle's income grows so great that it's too mixed up with your checking account's acting and additional survival job income, consider forming an LLC (a limited liability company) and opening an official business bank account to keep your Hustle separate.

Note that LLCs do cost something to form, ranging from $200 to $2,000 or more, depending on whether you set it up yourself or work with a lawyer. However, the personal tax benefits (which are too variable and complex to get into here) can easily offset the cost, especially over time.

TRACK YOUR FINANCES

You need a method to track your income and expenses, and compare them to your projections. Are you spending according to your cost of living, and making what you expected you would make?

* If you decide to take cash "under the table" (not claim it to the government or pay taxes on it) because what you're making from your Hustle is still quite small, then you may not need to report this to the government. Amounts under a certain threshold don't need to be claimed.

Tracking your finances regularly ensures you don't get into a hole.

We suggest tracking at the end of every week: checking your credit card statements, bank accounts, and reviewing any receipts you got for things you paid for in cash. Later, when money is freer and you're more comfortable, you could check by the month.

Tracking your income also allows you to estimate cash flow, keep track of any outstanding payments owed to you, and compare with your expenses to ensure your net (income minus expenses) is going up. If things aren't looking so good, it's more advisable to add hours into your work schedule and make the money back. We've found that most artists struggle to cut back, no matter how much they promise themselves they will.

Some days you'll overspend, others you'll be under, but always know your personal balance. Use a budgeting app, like the one offered by your bank, or a service like Mint, YNAB (You Need a Budget), or Simplifi (or construct a psychotically designed Excel spreadsheet you love, like RSO does).

Whatever method works for you, stick with it.

SAVE YOUR MONEY AND SAVE YOURSELF

The key to avoiding paycheck-to-paycheck living is simple: Always save a portion of your income.

The artists who don't save believe they can't afford to—but that's rarely true. If you get $100, you'll likely spend it all. If $10 is set aside, you'll adjust and live on $90. People adapt. Whether you make $5,000 a month or $50,000, you'll find a way to live within it, shifting your lifestyle as you need.

Saving a portion of your income is essential to providing any life security beyond paying your bills, and must begin today.

A savings account isn't just there for the future. It's also there for the present as "liquid" assets in case you have an unexpected major expense, if you run into an emergency, or if your checking account can't pay the rent. And of course if you do borrow from your savings, pay it back as soon as you can.

Save at least 10 percent of everything you make

Saving 10 percent is a good place to start. If you're an aggressive spender or have debt you're trying to pay off, you might put aside 20 percent or more until you become more responsible with your money.

You can manually transfer every payday or at the end of every month. Even better, set your banking app to automatically transfer 10 percent of every deposit from your checking to your savings whenever new money hits your account.

STAY OUT OF (BAD) DEBT

Some debt can be good for you. Some debt is not.

College debt and long-term financing like the kind you take on from a car purchase help to build the credit you need to lease an apartment or buy a home—as long as you pay the minimum on it every month. If you don't, this hurts your credit.

Meanwhile, credit card debt is among the worst kind of debt. It savages your credit, drags down any income you make, and stresses you out.

Always pay off your statement balance each month IN FULL.

At the end of each one-month period, the credit card company notifies you what you owe them (your "statement balance"*) and gives you another

* Your statement balance is different than your account balance. The former is only what you spent this month, while the latter also includes whatever you didn't pay off last month (which we hope is nothing!).

month to pay it off. If you don't, you lose the game called Credit Card (by paying extra interest on top of what is left). If you keep losing at Credit Card, you may soon lose the game of Money altogether.

If you do pay off your statement balance each month, though, you win. You get cash back, points toward free flights or upgrades, gift cards, vacation discounts, and so on. When you pay your statement balance off in full every month, you essentially get free prizes for beating the credit card company. But they're hoping you *won't* do that, so that they can assess their fees and make money off you.

DON'T LIVE OFF YOUR SAVINGS

Brett did get a great contract during his time in NYC, enjoying a nine-month stint on Norwegian Cruise Lines. It came just as his career was hitting a slump—he was keen to travel, and the pay was killer. With the boat covering his room and board, Brett came back with $11,000 in his savings.

But then Brett made the fatal mistake of thinking that this $11k meant he didn't have to go back to his survival job (or better, get a Hustle). He thought he could live off his surplus until Broadway rang. When Broadway didn't call in time, he squandered what he'd earned over just four months. He was back to square one.

Brett learned too late that when you have a windfall, you take it as a major contribution to filling up your savings, not as permission to stop working. Your savings account is there to cover an emergency or otherwise protect you from hardship. It's meant to go up, not down.

Ain't too proud (to get help)

If someone in your life is willing to support you financially, it's okay to accept.

Artists work in an exponential growth field—there's no real cap on what we can earn. One week it's $100 for a reading, the next year it's $3,000 a week in a Broadway ensemble. One year brings a $6,000-a-week principal contract, and another, a $10,000 yogurt commercial. That's not how it works for our parents and siblings in steadier professions.

Financial support, when offered, should be seen as an investment in your career—not a sign that you can't take care of yourself. When you're able, pay it back creatively: a meaningful gift, a dream vacation, or a shout-out in your Tony speech.

If a potential supporter is hesitant, show them a clear, actionable plan. Map out how you'll use their help—what classes you'll take, which auditions you'll attend, and how it impacts your finances. Set milestones they can track, like performing in a cabaret or hitting fifty auditions by a set date. Defining a clear endpoint makes their support feel purposeful—and makes them more likely to say yes.

Order of events as your income increases

As our bank accounts grow, it can be tricky to understand what to do with our money and when. Here's a handy guide.

1. Make sure you have opened both a personal checking and a personal savings account. If you have an account meant for a college student and you're finished with school, consider moving to a regular account.
2. Build your checking account to just about twice your cost of living, and don't let that number sink below it. So if your cost of living is $3,500, always keep about $7,000–$9,000 in that account.
3. If you have an outstanding credit card balance (or any other high-interest debt), once your checking account is full, use additional income to chip away at what you owe until it's zero.
4. Move 10 percent of all income into your personal savings account, until it reaches four to six times your cost of living. If your cost of living is $3,500, you're working toward a savings account of $14,000–$21,000.

5. Once your savings is maxed in this way and large debt is demolished, seek out the right investment strategy—or better yet, strategies—to put your money to work. Talk with your parents, your bank, or a smart friend about your options.
6. When you're ready and your accounts have accrued enough, decide if purchasing a home is the right next step for you.

Jonah's big brother is impressed. Now Jonah is a wizard at Excel, regularly tracking his finances; he's made moves for his Hustle (starting a private personal training business); and he views his savings as something to continue to build, not drain in his first few months. Jonah's big bro is so pleased that he offers to pay for Jonah to take a quick trip to the city a month before he planned to leave, just so he can scope out a survival job.

It takes a village to teach us how to manage our money, warn us about mistakes, and show how many paths there are to getting good at it. It's clear to Jonah that this will be a lifelong project—but so is pursuing a life in musical theatre. Now Jonah is prepped for both challenges.

Websites and Social Media

Sammie's been on tour for three months, with six more to go. They were nervous to lose the relationships they'd built in Seattle while they were away, but they realized that they had two incredibly valuable assets at their fingertips.

Though auditioning in person is thrilling, Sammie knows that in the digital era the fastest way to be seen—faster than getting seen at an Equity open call—is through their social media and website. While they're gone, they're regularly updating both.

Digital visibility makes them feel even more connected than they were when they were home. Sammie knows that people get interested in others' work while going about their day. By the time a casting director has finished their bagel sandwich, they've shared two videos and texted a friend: "This person is so good. Do you know them?"

Websites and social media won't replace a callback, but both can be invaluable for grabbing that initial appointment. Seeing impressive work through a mutual friend's mutual friend's shared video can make a casting director feel like they've discovered someone. After catching Sammie a few times while the algorithm works its magic, they just might just ask Sammie to submit—which sounds much better to Sammie than waiting around all morning, hoping the monitor will call their name.

In this chapter we'll take a page from Sammie's playbook and explore how to create and maintain an impactful website. You'll learn about the relationship between social media and musical theatre, both in the short term—surveying the landscape today—and the long term, as platforms inevitably change in relevance.

YOUR WEBSITE: COME TO MY GARDEN

Launching your website is like holding a cotillion, except instead of joining adult society you're entering the professional world.

Like an audition, a website tells people what you can do—but unlike an audition, you have total control of what they see.

Having a website tells the world you're ready to work.

If you don't have a website and someone looks for one, it signals you're still figuring things out. Some actors wait to be told they're "ready" . . . but remember that *children* book Broadway. Like so many things in life, you'll never be ready in the sense you're waiting for. If you're reading this book and you don't already have a website, it's time to seriously think about making one.

How people find your website

People often visit your website before ever meeting you. Maybe your name was on a list, they saw something on your socials, or heard about you and googled your name. However they got there, they're curious to learn more.

They're usually looking for certain information—and fast. Their visit might last thirty seconds (checking your headshot and résumé), a few minutes (sampling your work), or longer (exploring all your pages). From there, they either find what they need and make contact with you—or move on, just like in an audition.

WEBSITE BASICS AREN'T BASIC

Your website should communicate what you want people to know with efficiency. It shouldn't be complicated, but each choice should add flavor to your brand. There are several elements to zero in on.

Get a domain that is clear

"YourName.com" is the ideal actor domain name, but that presumes it's available—and it's probably not. Most actors have no choice but to get creative.

Following your name with "actor," "music," or "MT" works ("YourNameActor.com") works, but we wouldn't use "theatre" because of the age-old uncertainty of its -RE or -ER spelling. Some people use ".net" at the end of their domain name, and, of late, others get cute with "TheRealYourName.com."

Don't revise your professional name with a middle name, initial, or nickname unless you already use it when you work. If you go by Brooklyn Jones, but "BrooklynJones.com" is taken, don't get "BrookJones.com" or "BrooklynKJones.com"—but instead consider "BrooklynJonesMT.com" or "BrooklynJones.net."

Whatever you decide, let it be simple to say and easy to remember.

Pay for website hosting . . .

You can secure your domain name and web hosting (where your website's files "live") from companies like Squarespace, Wix, GoDaddy, or another similar service. When deciding whether to opt for your web host's free or paid version, invest in your career by paying for the lowest-tier paid version at minimum to avoid ads. Like quality headshots, paying for your website is a necessary start-up expense. One day, you'll hopefully be so well known that you don't need a website anymore. (LindsayMendez.net was retired in 2019.)

. . . But you don't need to pay for someone to design it

There are many web designers out there who will handle your site for a few thousand dollars, from obtaining your domain hosting to designing it top to bottom. While we're sure they'd do an amazing job, we don't think it's necessary to shell out this expense when all-in-one sites like Squarespace and Weebly have sleek and easy-to-use templates that make the design paint-by-numbers. They're also easy to update.

A picture's worth a thousand callbacks

Greet visitors arriving at your homepage with an image (or images) of you. This is an opportunity for them to "meet you" in the same way they meet you as you walk into the audition room in person. Ideally, this isn't a headshot but a "lifestyle shot."

Lifestyle shots are professionally taken photographs that focus on your full body, personality, and interests. The attire is casual, in clothes you'd wear on a night out with friends or to attend an exciting event (incidentally, this is also audition attire). You could add bolder options in formal or niche attire depending on the brand you're selling. For example, if you're very focused on classic and legit work, you might have a shot in a suit or dress. If you're a musician, you might have one with your instrument. If you're a geeky gamer, there might be a stylized artistic set up of you with a controller in action. This isn't the time for cosplay of any kind (no Elphaba, Cinderella, or Spiderman), but otherwise let the shots tell us about who you are as a human being.

Shout your name out loud

On or above your homepage shot is your big, bright, beautiful name. Use a readable font that isn't so fancy we have to squint. Style and color should fit your personality. As always, make sure the name on your headshot, domain name, and the name they're looking at on your website are consistent.

[Your branding statement here]

In part one, you learned how to build a branding statement—those two or three brilliant sentences telling us how you sing, look, feel, and identify. Your landing page is a great place for it, alongside your initial photos and name.

You could simply opt for "actor, singer, dancer" as many performers do. But using your branding statement hooks in your hurried visitor—who is checking out dozens of recommendations—and tells them quickly whether or not you could be what they're looking for. Just like a first audition, your branding statement sets expectations. Now they explore to see if they're going to be met.

THE VERY IMPORTANT VIDEO PAGE

Next up is a page of performance videos. In navigation, you might call them "videos," "media," or "performance."

The ideal video page starts with a handful of single-song videos—not a reel. Each video should be a separate song because most people coming to your website are looking for something specific. They're casting a new rock musical, a regional *Carousel*, or a Joni Mitchell jukebox musical, and they're keen to see your rock cut, your classic cut, or your folk cut, respectively. The rock musical casting director doesn't care how well you sing folk or Golden Age right now. They have a job to do—and a reel of many genres will only delay them.

Each individual song is clearly labeled with its title and the show it's from or artist it's by. You might also label it with the genre: "Many a New Day" from *Oklahoma!*—classic up-tempo. It won't hurt and will only help your visitor's navigation.

Cuts or full songs are all right. If your visitor has the time (they probably don't), they'll watch the full video (we hope they do). If they're in a rush and looking through forty websites, they will—like asking for just eight bars—scrub the time bar two-thirds of the way through and see how things are going at the climax. If you're nailing it, they'll go back and check out more, but if not, they'll move on. (Presumably, you've put this video up because it's an excellent demonstration of your skill from start to finish, so don't worry too much about that.)

Once your book is at a comfortable place, a video of each cut (including one or two full songs) makes your website an interactive audition book.

Is it "reel"y me? (No)

Single-song videos contrast with a vocal reel, which combines short clips of several different tunes. A reel might be requested by a prospective agent, a casting team working on summer stock or a cruise ship, or someone else looking to get a "tiny taste" of the many things you do.

Like an appetizer platter, a vocal reel can be delicious—but a plate of apps, cheap as it is, doesn't replace the power of a spectacular entrée made to order. A vocal reel effectively shows you as a jack-of-many-trades. Worse, it can be frustrating for your time-crunched visitor. It's as if you're saying, "I know you've only come here looking for one or two things, but I'm going to make you sit through ten instead. Good luck finding what you're looking for!"

Your video page should be made of *mostly* single-song videos clearly labeled—*not* reels.

Because you may be asked at some point for a vocal reel, you can put one together and make it the last video of your singing work . . . if you desire.

Quality control

Your videos don't have to be cinematic masterpieces. They can be self-tapes, footage from a concert, or even videos of you singing in a class—so long as the video is a strong performance by only you and the audio is clear. Make sure there isn't audience noise, someone else in frame distracting us, or a band overpowering you.

You don't need to pay for an expensive recording of you singing, but consider booking a rehearsal studio for a few hours. Hire an accompanist and use your phone to film a few cuts. Don't overthink it—extensive editing isn't necessary.

Dance reels and acting videos

Monologues, scene work, film/TV samples (including student films), or a reel of acting clips pulled together can be terrific. Contrast styles, like a classic comedy with a contemporary dramatic monologue. Having a reader is fine as long as they're off-camera.

In a dance reel, all the same advice applies. Confirm that the video clearly features you (rather than hiding you among a group), start with your strongest styles, and then upload any other dance styles you're comfortable performing.

Beware of production videos (and photos)

Videos from a production you've been in can work if they're extraordinary, but it's easy for your viewer to get distracted by everything around you. There you are, playing Sarah Brown in *Guys and Dolls*, singing a glorious "I'll Know"—but your Sky Masterson is miscast, the sets are paper, the five-piece orchestra is out of tune, the spotlight is shaky . . . better to have a self-tape than footage in this case.

No matter what, your video page should be a brilliant representation of you. If you crack in the video, it doesn't matter how good the rest is, because anyone can do a hundred takes. When you put a video up, we assume that's the best you can do.

As you get older, if you rewatch a video and see an "old you"—whether less trained or physically unrecognizable—get rid of it.

OTHER PAGES

Headshot and résumé

We'll dive deeply into these materials in part three, but for now don't worry if your résumé isn't chock-full of credits. Your visitor could be looking for new talent. If you feel you're ready to work, whatever's on your résumé is good enough.

It's fine to have one headshot, but many actors show two or three contrasting (neutral, comedic, serious, etc.). We don't think anyone needs more than four options, because it suggests the actor is telling the visitor, "I dunno which one is me. You decide?"

Make both your résumé and headshot viewable in-site rather than only as an annoying link to download. However, being *able* to download the materials is useful, should they want to.

Mad about the About page

You don't need an About page. Really.

What they need to know "about you" is, first, your branding statement on the landing page, and then the contents of your headshot, résumé, and videos. Still, many an actor is tempted to share their life story.

Nobody:

Actor: When I was four and three-quarters, Gran-Nana took me to *Wicked* and something changed within me. Growing up in Cornwank, Indiana, I always had a

```
love for singing and dancing, and after Gran-Nana's
embolism, I swore to her that I would be famous one
day. If only she could see me now! I'm not famous
yet, but if she could see me it would mean she was
alive. I miss her.
   Anyhoo, over time, I realized that being Elphaba
wasn't going to be part of my special journey. I'm
really more of a Glinda! Then when I was six . . .
```

Nothing contained in an About page will get you cast, and like your blind date oversharing, it really asks more questions than it answers. Your online visitors will learn about your education from your résumé and your artistic taste by the songs you've chosen. Your "passion for collaboration and truthful storytelling" should be a given. If some personal fact matters to your work, include it in your branding statement.

Don't nobody bring me no bad News page

News pages, like About pages, are a dicey proposition. The problem starts when the actor posts about the production they're currently in, and nine months later—long after the show has closed—the News page isn't updated. Scanning the backlog, we see the News page has been updated every eighteen months or so. Again, it distracts us with information we didn't ask for.

If you can keep it updated every month or two with useful news, it can work—though embedding your Instagram feed could offer updates just as easily. Your visitor already has access to that, and your Instagram is probably updated with both the personal and the professional more frequently, which is an easy way to tell people what you're up to.

Making contact

The point of your website is to interest your visitor in working with you, so make sure it's clear how to get in touch.

Whatever you've put as contact information on your résumé could be repeated here. If you have an agent or manager, include their information first ("For professional inquiries, contact . . .") including phone and email, and then list your own ("For personal inquiries . . .").

If your design template offers you a contact form like the following, we recommend not using it:

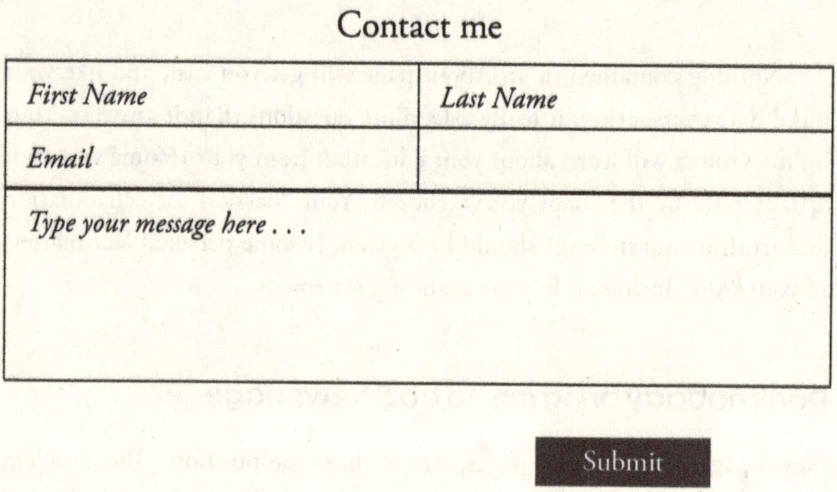

Contact forms look like an obstacle to reaching you. Some actors step away from the business or stop checking whatever account the form sends messages to. Emailing you directly is the way to go.

If a time comes when you're so booked and blessed that the number of personal inquiries in your inbox is getting out of hand, delete your personal info on the contact page and let your reps handle everything.

DON'T BLUR YOUR BRAND ON YOUR WEBSITE

Even when you find a Hustle, don't blur the fact that you are an actor by having a page dedicated to your work as a yoga instructor, personal trainer, or custom greeting card designer selling work on Etsy. If those areas are ready for webspace, give them their own site—just the way a restaurant might open a sister restaurant to sell a different cuisine.

An exception would be skills related closely to acting, like writing, directing, or choreographing. Many artists are successful multi-hyphenates, and that's terrific. If you're unsure if your secondary passion or skill should be included on your actor website, ask yourself what assumptions you might make if you were a visitor on a website with that combination.

SOCIAL MEDIA: ALWAYS TRUE TO YOU (IN ITS FASHION)

Social media moves quickly. From Friendster to MySpace to Facebook to Twitter to Snapchat to Instagram to TikTok to BeReal to whatever's next, the cool kids tire of the platform their parents join, and move on. This makes a guide on mastering a platform obsolete as soon as it's published, so instead we'll provide general tips to make social media work for you, with examples from today's media landscape.

Two approaches: Public versus private accounts

Those who keep their account private (requiring permission to access their page) don't want strangers seeing their posts. Perhaps they feel their accounts are personal or silly, or maybe they're protective of family-oriented content.

For those who make it public, their accounts—like their website—are viewable by anyone, and they consider this when creating content. They use their accounts to share their adventures and business with people they work with, new friends, old friends, and strangers alike.

Between these two opposite groups are those who attempt to make their pages both public and private. They block access to the masses but accept almost anyone who asks. They create content they understand could be shared far and wide, but don't want just anyone to see it. They're neither gaining the benefits of true privacy nor the usefulness of sharing their life and work.

> *Your social media account is either public or private, and trying for both makes either approach ineffective.*

Marketing is expensive, social media is free . . .

One of the largest expenses for a business is advertising. This is why productions of any size rely on every angle possible to get the word out and will pay exorbitant sums to do so. But with social media, you have the most useful marketing tool at your fingertips—for free.

The people who are most likely to come to your show, find your work, or call you in for an audition are already-captured followers and friends. They routinely drive past your digital street and catch the billboards you put up (posts, stories, tweets) at no cost to you.

Keeping your profiles as public as possible guarantees that the most people see you, and so we question why an actor shouldn't take complete advantage of that.

If you have pictures you want to keep private, go to Kohl's and get a scrapbook. If you don't want people to see your tweets, allow us to send you one of the dozens of empty journals we've received over the years, or make a group text chain with your closest friends.

> *Social media is a free, accessible, and effective way to promote your work, so we encourage you to make your accounts public.*

. . . Well, almost free

Using social media is totally free except for the wasted time, compromised mental health, damaged family relationships, and yes, lost privacy. It's no conspiracy to acknowledge that your phone is listening to you and tracking your interests to push ads upon you. Yes, social media is free . . . except for all of that.

Social media is far from perfect, and we know intimately the pain and stress it can cause. But we think the price of being unknown, unfindable, and inaccessible may be a larger price to pay.

Still, if social media has become a serious problem in your life, there are ways around it, which we'll touch on here.

Social media: Then and now

Lindsay's career ascended alongside social media and put her in a group of artists who didn't have to work very hard to build their following. Rather, her following was built *for* her *because* she worked.

RSO, on the other hand, had a more typical journey. Around 2007, as YouTube began its global rise, so did his music reach the masses of musical theatre undergrads. He'll never forget when a stranger approached him and said, "You're the guy who wrote 'Mrs. Sharp'!" They'd seen a video of Carnegie Mellon students singing the song—one he didn't even know had been posted. Back then (he says with a creaky voice), these moments felt brand new, and in so many ways, both he and Lindsay credit YouTube with helping to launch their careers.

Depending on your age, you're likely somewhere on this same trajectory. How excited are you for the next platform after TikTok? Probably not very. But just as you felt about the platforms of your time, when the next one emerges, those younger than you will take the bait. Probably.

At any given time, certain platforms are considered "professionally acceptable," while others are divided between the olds and the children. Your job is to stay aware of what's relevant and use it wisely. As of this writing, Instagram remains a go-to space to scope out creatives and actors alike. Alongside a website, it's a professional tool—but that will change. Staying current is part of the job.

You don't have to be an influencer to make the most of social media

For those currently sweating, you don't have to be active on social media as long as you're findable. It's all right to make an account, post a few basic things (the same way you'd post things on your website), and leave it alone. Maintain access to messages you receive and keep notifications turned on for when you do.

It's okay to have additional, private, exclusive accounts

Some have personal, just-for-now accounts (where they post truly private—and often silly—content for only their inner circle) in addition to their regular public profiles, and that's okay. You might have a secret Twitter/X and of course you can get weird on TikTok (or merely lurk). None of this is a problem, as long as the accounts you want the business to see are easily in reach—and the first ones they find when they search your name.

POST IN FOUR DIMENSIONS

Everything you share on social media can be separated into four different types, based on the four different experiences you create for your viewer.

All posts made on social media fit
into one of four categories:

Self-promotion

Humor

Activism

Recommendations

Self-promotion

The most common type of post, self-promotion, shows off the many parts of your individual life. This includes the obvious: videos of performances, show graphics, ticket links, and "First day of school!" script photos. These posts say, "I'm doing things!"—fans cheer, critics shrug.

But self-promotion goes beyond that. Photos of your LA life, trip to Aruba, or a fancy cocktail show your lifestyle. A video of your dog or a tribute to your grandma reveals something personal. These posts spark reactions like "Proud of you," "Yum," "Aww," or "I'm so sorry." Even without comments, they invite others to care about your life. Like it or not, it's all self-promotion.

That's why posting only self-promotion can be tiring. Seeing forty posts about your college roommate's *White Christmas* might be too much—but so would forty from his Scotland vacay.

When we mix self-promotion with other types of posts, we create more depth.

Humor

Make 'em laugh by sharing a hysterical meme, reposting an idiotic video, or spreading a clever tweet in the hopes that others with your sense of humor will find them funny, too. This isn't self-promotion because, like a good joke, it's a gift you give your audience they can now pass on to others. Even if *you* created the comedy, people are better off for it. Everybody likes to laugh.

Activism

Telling people what you believe in, encouraging your friends to vote, raging against a terrible injustice, and letting everyone know the location of the march are all examples of activism on social media. The world can be a scary place to live in, and social media is a place where we can help to change it for the better—at least as we see it.

Not everyone will share your beliefs. Just as you would in the real world, be mindful of what you're sharing and get clear on what the consequences could be.

Recommendations

Tell people about the movie you just saw, the book you're reading, the comedian you just found, or the album you can't stop streaming. Unlike self-promotion, where your viewer can't share your experience, recommendations encourage other people to see, read, or listen to things you think are fantastic—or stay away from what you think is terrible.

By mixing up what you share, you maintain an honest image of yourself as a fully formed human. There is a whole world offstage, so show people you're living in it.

OTHER UNSPOKEN RULES OF SOCIAL MEDIA

There are a few other things to consider in our engagement with social media.

We are pleased to announce (!!!) you don't have to brag about it

"After months of keeping it a secret . . ." "The cat's out of the bag!" "I'm so thrilled to announce this summer . . ." A peer shout-posting about their next gig in the most unbelievably smug, clichéd way makes everyone cringe. You've been on the other side of this, so don't do it to other people.

You *should* be proud of your achievements, and when you're leaving town for a contract people need to know where you're going and how long you might be gone. Acting is your job, so keep announcements on social media simple and direct, telling us the facts. "Next up . . ." "Hey friends, I'll be on tour until September . . ." "Broadway debut!" Keep the excitement, but don't rub it in the face of your out-of-work friends any more than you'd be willing to in person.

You could also be clever, silly, or even cute about it, in a way that expresses humility while telling your community what you're up to. We once had a student book a major contract and post a photo of himself onstage in costume with the recognizable set behind him, captioning it with an unrelated fact about Whoopi Goldberg winning an Academy Award for *Ghost* in 1991. His followers learned three things about this actor that day: a bit of film trivia, he was now in *Hamilton*, and their friend had a sense of humor about his big break.

Pack old stuff into the digital attic

The people we were ten years ago aren't the people we are today. Sometimes the people we were *six months ago* aren't the people we are today.

Yet with enough scrolling, those old selves remain for anyone to find. If you get an ick thinking about someone time-traveling to meet eleven-year-old you belting out "Empty Chairs at Empty Tables," you can archive the content while hiding it from the general public.

This is especially true of past YouTube performances, a platform of varying usefulness that is easy to neglect. Maybe your voice was still changing, you've lost weight since then, or you didn't quite hit that note. Make sure anything anyone can find represents what you offer today.

Google yourself—because others will

It's wise to Google your professional name every now and again to see what comes up. The dream is that your website or social media page comes up first, followed by major press or production information. If they click the images or videos search, they find your best first.

If you discover search items that you own and *don't* want people to see, remove them. If someone else owns them and it's appropriate, ask them to remove them. If you can't get rid of them or would prefer these items not show up so early, the best thing to do is to share and engage (click, update, comment) with the pages you want people to see first. Eventually, search engine optimization will work its magic for you and push the unwanted material down.

Your followers aren't your therapists

Sometimes you're just having a bad day. Maybe you're looking for a friend, can't get out of bed, or just got fired and you're pissed. People post about these things all the time—but should they?

Some see it as oversharing, while others view it as important mental health advocacy. More than anything, we hope you have someone closer—your partner, best friend, or parent—who's better equipped to support you than your followers. Sharing raw emotions with acquaintances, coworkers, or strangers (including future collaborators who only know you from Instagram) is risky. Now they also know that your ex is a toxic narcissist—or at least that *you* think she is—and they're texting mutual friends for more gossip.

It's worth asking how you'd feel receiving a similar post. Would you wonder if your friend was okay? Why they got fired? Would your first thought be "This person should definitely be in a high-pressure show right now"? What you gain in likes and sympathy might come at the cost of your professional image.

As Curtis says in *Dreamgirls*, "Effie, we all got pain." Everyone's going through something, and that's understood. But when it comes to bad days, it's usually better to turn to a trusted person—or an actual therapist—than to the cold, confused, and often cruel world of social media.

It's meant to be diverting, not destructive

The best way to handle social media is the way that works for your life and protects your heart. Try to remain present for those looking for you by posting with some frequency (however sporadic), and make sure all of your accounts have contact information for you.

But of course, if necessary, it's okay to step away or delete your account entirely.

• • • • • •

Back to our savvy Seattleite, Sammie. They've just gotten back from their nine-month tour, and it feels like no time has passed at all. Reuniting with actor friends, they're already up to date following Sammie's adventures on Instagram. At Sammie's first audition back, the casting associate credits one of Sammie's performance videos from the ship as the reason they've been called in. In the room, one of the casting associates mentions that she checked out Sammie's website this morning. She loved Sammie's version of "Heaven on Their Mind" and requests specifically that Sammie sing that for everyone else. The casting associate thinks the writers will be impressed, and she's right.

Netwerqing

When Maggie thinks about networking, she gets the ick.

Her best friend, a press rep for a big Manhattan agency, has invited Maggie to a big Broadway opening night party. Feeling the pressure to network, she suddenly sees all the humans walking around the room as playing cards. Here comes a king. There, a pair of queens—and look how a full house of sixes and sevens draws toward them. Far in the back in a discard pile, a tragic two has captured an eight in conversation because he had the misfortune of coming alone.

Maggie, as a self-assessed four, sort of pities the two—but realizes she actually knows a few of those sixes. She wonders if maybe they'll introduce her to one of the queens—when the familiar shiver of anxiety courses through her bones.

While her best friend is thriving in her element, Maggie feels terrible. She understands that every profession has a hierarchy of experience and seniority, but to her it seems that networking is really about kissing up to higher cards and looking down on lower ones. Upward mobility is all about who you know, which she gets, but—

"Not exactly," her best friend says. "The key to networking is to never 'network.'" Maggie's trying to understand exactly what that means. "Don't *you* want to work with your friends?" Of course, that makes sense. When millions of dollars and hundreds of jobs can be at stake, people are inclined to work with someone they trust over a total stranger.

Still, Maggie wants to treat people like people, not playing cards. Maggie doesn't want to feel small, but also doesn't want to make someone "bigger" feel like she's taking advantage of them. No one wants their time wasted by someone who sees them only as a job opportunity.

Her best friend tries to calm her down. "Building relationships isn't about trapping people who can do something for you. For sure, you *need* people—but remember they also need *you*. Without each side of the table, no one can do their job, girl!" Maggie's bestie is wise.

Whether it's at a party, over Zoom, through an email, or via a follow on social media, connecting with others in your industry is an essential part of how we get closer to our dreams. In this chapter we'll explore how to engage with people who can (and want to) help you—and learn how you can help them in return, which sometimes simply means helping them help you. Regardless of how big your circle is now, you'll learn how to harness your personable, interesting, and curious self to expand it.

Maggie has a sudden realization. Her best friend said that the key to networking is never to network. But nobody said she shouldn't "netwerq"—that is, connect with others in a way that feels reciprocal, sincere, unapologetic . . . and fun.

NETWERQING LIKE A PRO

Some people are born skilled netwerqers (like Lindsay). Others find it an ongoing challenge (like the other guy). It's as much a talent as any other skill in musical theatre, but it requires maintenance to be—and stay—good at it.

The following tips refer to initial conversations at a party, in passing, through a digital exchange, or at a first meeting. As you get to know someone better, your discussions will deepen and many of these "rules" will fall away, but here's where to start.

Be warm, curious, and generous

When meeting someone, focus on what you have in common—like a show you've both seen or a mutual friend's project. Foster a mindset that good things happen to good people, and show that you're good people, too. Optimism and gratitude are easy to join and hard to resist.

Ask more than you answer. Show real interest in the person, not just their job. Most people are happy to talk about anything *but* work—so ask what they're drinking or what they got up to today. If you know something about their public personal life (indeed, in entertainment there is such a thing), ask about their vacation or new puppy.

Be generous with words and actions. Compliment their outfit, offer to grab them a drink, or share a light story for a laugh. Like your favorite up-tempo, show up personable, warm, and full of that awesome, professional charm.

Poor child

This is especially key for younger actors who may feel awkward in conversation. Since they often know a lot about older professionals—because, perhaps, they're fans—they may avoid asking questions they already know the answers to. This can lead to the temptation to overshare about themselves. But if you want to be seen as a peer in the industry, focus on learning about *them* first—*then* they'll be more interested in learning about you.

Unworthy of their love: Conversation assassins

Some behaviors will end a conversation as quickly as they start. Avoid negativity, self-obsession, and ingratitude.

As tempting as gossip can be, a poorly timed comment can have consequences—including trash talking shows you've seen. Everyone working on a production is doing their best, so lead with kindness and give others the benefit of the doubt.

Everyone has tough experiences in the business, but venting at the wrong moment can put others in an awkward spot. If you walk into a conversation angry, you're forcing the other person to choose a side—when they'd rather be laughing over the questionable crudité.

Keep unsolicited talk about yourself to a minimum. If someone's interested, they'll ask. It's great to share exciting news—like a recent contract or engagement—but spark the topic once and see if they engage. (This rule does not apply to puppies. Everyone loves puppies.)

If the conversation winds down, end with warmth. A simple "It's so great to finally meet you!" or "Congrats on the new apartment" leaves things on a positive note.

THE LIFE OF THE PARTIES

Parties, events, and social gatherings in public spaces (like theatres and bars) are special situations where everyone in attendance has signed up to meet and chat with the other people there. It's a great opportunity to reconnect with people you know and enter new orbits you'd like to join.

Putting them together

The easiest people to meet after connecting with your host and your friends will be your friends' friends. To make their world a friendlier place, they'll want you to meet the other people they know. After all, your mutual friend saw something in each of you they liked, and you may find that same thing in one another. Sometimes you might even discover a connection that is even deeper than the one you have with the person who introduced you!

Never underestimate the importance of body language

Body language will guide you through a gathering, so be mindful of social cues.

If people are talking with their bodies facing in several directions or moving around, they're open for you to join. After all, everyone showed up to be in a large group, so this means that you can try squeezing in (if they wanted a one-on-one, they'd go for coffee).

If someone's body is squarely facing another person in close quarters, it's likely a moment for just the two of them. Don't hover nearby waiting for them to stop their conversation (which might not be over), as though demanding they give you their time now.

If your partner's feet turn in a direction away from you, or their eyes start to wander, it may be time to let the chat go. A simple "It was so good talking to you! Make sure to try the corn fritters!" can be a graceful exit for you both to move on with your night. Try not to take it personally and remember you deserve to talk to people who want to talk to you.

The more the merrier, usually. If you want others to join the conversation, open your own body up while still giving energy to your partner. This invites others in, without forcing your friend out.

Please, please, please, don't ask, "What are you working on?"

Most social gatherings happen after work. People have been on the clock, writing in their studio, rehearsing, or taking class . . . and this isn't the desired question you think it is. They're tired, or maybe just excited to have some fun. They don't want to go back to work.

Any career milestone or project someone would share with a stranger is probably already in the press or something you should be aware of if you're both at this party. If it's not, they'll gladly share. If you ask this question and don't know, you look uninformed.

The better question to ask is a version of "What are you excited about lately?" This opens the field to learn about what shows they've binged, their spouse's promotion, the vacation they returned from, the new puppy they just got, or yes, what they're working on.

That's personal (and that's okay)

Certainly, anything you've shared on social media is fair game to bring up at a party—people may have seen it and would be glad to talk about it with you.

It's also okay to share more personal details if it deepens the conversation. People going through similar life stages—getting a first apartment, moving to a new city, getting married, or having a second child—often feel seen when someone truly relates. If you can, bond over that.

More sensitive topics, like medical issues or breakups, may need caution—especially if they're too intimate or heavy. Use your best judgment, and if it feels right, a little humor always helps!

Other party etiquette

Here's a grab bag of other rules to follow:

- Most people are looking to deepen their relationships and leave this party with more friendship than they entered it with, so it's better to have a few conversations of depth rather than collecting as many trivial encounters as possible.
- If you're bringing up someone famous you "know" simply to imply your own importance, name-dropping is a turnoff. If the relationship has relevance to the conversation, go for it.
- Follow instructions. Whether it's dress code or party end time, respect the people throwing the event and what they've asked of you.
- Don't get overly intoxicated—even if others seem willing to. In a professional setting, the extra high is never worth the risk.
- For our introverts, it's okay to set a time limit for how long you'll stay. Whether you drop by for thirty minutes or gab for two hours, set a vibrating alarm and have a believable excuse ready, which can be as simple as you're exhausted and need to sleep.
- Or "Irish goodbye." If the gathering is large (there are more than a handful of conversations happening at once), you can just leave when you wish and bid adieu to whomever you run into. Your host

or guest of honor is likely busy and will enjoy receiving a "Thanks for a wonderful party!" text the following day.

- Always bring something to an event at someone's home. Ask if there's anything they'd like you to bring, and if you're unsure bring a bouquet or a bottle (if they don't drink, they may keep some for guests)—but don't bring food unless you've been asked to. You might conflict with dietary allergies, a theme, or what the host has prepared.

SURVEY YOUR TEAM

Why do so many artists think that the people they *really* need are people they haven't met yet?

The people most likely to influence your career are the people you already know.

So far, we've focused on you as the one-of-a-kind owner of an exciting small business, the one who cashes the checks and makes the tough calls—but you're not alone.

You have a network of people working for you. Take stock to respect and nurture these invaluable relationships every day.

This network works for you in various ways, and you compensate them in turn.

Heroes

Every artist was inspired by another artist who came before them. Learn from your heroes shamelessly. While they might not know you exist, by following their work as an example, they work for you. We "pay them back" by counting them among our inspirations.

Mentors

A mentor can be a teacher, artist, or anyone further along in their career. They support you by paving the way, sharing lessons they've learned, and investing in your personal and professional growth. You repay them with gratitude—buying a drink, treating them to dinner, thanking them in your bio, or acknowledging their impact on your journey.

Some mentors are paid, like voice teachers or acting coaches. That's perfectly valid, as long as both sides signed up for it. Just don't expect someone to offer a service for free that they charge others for, even under the label of mentorship.

An ideal mentor has experience in areas where you need support, and may be retired or working in a different capacity. They might welcome the chance to stay connected to their passion through you.

Representation

Your agents and managers make it their business to handle your business. They're always thinking of ways to advance you and thereby advance themselves. They literally work for you, so we pay them back with whatever percentage we've contractually agreed to.

Collaborators

Members of the creative team rely on your work to do theirs. After the show closes, a strong relationship means they'll be more likely to think of new ways to collaborate with you in the future. You repay them through your dedication and hard work.

Co-workers

These are your fellow actors and colleagues. You pay them back with respect and effort in kind.

Investors

Everyone else in your life—friends, family, and fans—invests in a multitude of ways. Whether it's playing therapist, supporting you financially, or buying tickets to your show, they back your career and life. You pay them back in quality time, gratitude, and by returning their investment in all the ways you can.

You are on many other teams for many other artists

Don't forget: You're an investor of time and resources for friends and family, relied on by peers, and a patron in your own right for others' businesses. Your reps count on you to book work and your mentors hope their investment will pay off. And one beautiful day, you'll continue the cycle your role models continued with you, becoming an inspiration for an artist just starting out.

Keep the love

In any workplace, it's normal to be frustrated with someone on your team. At home, vent away! In professional settings, however, talking poorly about your costar, agent, director, or patron weakens the relationship—even if they aren't in earshot of your criticisms.

A core rule of netwerqing is to speak of everyone on your team the way you want them to speak of you. This is especially true of past relationships. It may be tempting to dish about how awful your music director was on your last contract, but whether or not she hears about it, you're sparking fire on an important bridge. You'd be shocked how often people get jobs because they were recommended by someone they didn't like—or who they thought didn't like them. In fact, sometimes people try to heal negative past experiences by connecting folks with opportunities.

Make a list of your team members in each category. If you're lacking in an area, it's a cue to explore it. No mentor? There may be someone in your life who just needs to be asked. If your support system of parents and friends feels distant, reach out to reconnect with your loved ones.

MAKING THE CONNECTION: EMAILS AND MESSAGES

Before we become proper friends who broach the boundaries of humor, opinion, and bald honesty, there's etiquette to engaging others in the industry through email, text, DMs, and (gulp) the phone.

A very important note on time

When you're young, your entire day is school, extracurricular activities, homework, and free time. As an adult, there are work hours, dates with friends, errands, and fewer periods of free time. Eventually something shifts, time changes, and suddenly every hour is accounted for.

The busy professional rarely has time to sleep in. They wake, have a moment to center themselves, and get to work. After a long workday, they exercise, see friends or colleagues, then return home to chase as many minutes as possible with their spouse, children, and pets, while preparing for the next day of work. Finally, they spend an hour—maybe two—relaxing and decompressing, before crawling into bed and doing it all over again tomorrow.

> *Time is by far the most precious resource to any busy professional.*

Even if this isn't already your life, you understand this in your own way. Let's say you're in your mid-twenties. Consider if your mother's best friend's fifteen-year-old daughter wanted to hop on the phone for an hour to talk about the theatre camp they're auditioning for. If you knew them well, we expect you'd gladly impart your wisdom (and hey, it feels good to be looked up to). If you didn't, you might feel odd but otherwise amenable. If they hounded you, demanded to meet urgently, or insisted on more of your time, though, at some point you'd arrive at the same conclusion: There are better people in their young lives for these questions, closer to their age and experience.

The people you look up to are busier than you realize. With this in mind, respect their time by keeping the relationship rewarding and manageable on both sides.

Start by reconnecting

As you dive into expanding your network, first contact those closest to you who might feel a similar need to connect as you do.

See if a former castmate or colleague has any free time coming up. Every hour spent with them enriches your relationship, and when opportunities arise, you're each more likely to think of each other. If you discover complementary needs—like your music director friend is looking to play more in the city and you're wanting to do a cabaret—make the match.

These serendipitous moments fill memoirs of many artists, including your authors. We met because RSO was looking for performers for his debut show at Joe's Pub in New York and Lindsay was anxious to meet new writers. A mutual friend sent him a video of Lindsay singing "Meadowlark." From a single concert, a lifelong friendship was born.

Cold emails: Into the unknoooown

Before contacting someone cold (as in, you have never met or spoken) or lukewarm (you've met in passing but they haven't contacted you first), decide if this is the right person and right time to make an ask. If it is, follow professional email etiquette.

If you don't already have one, get a clear and intuitive email address, like Your.Name@gmail.com, YourNameActor@yahoo.com, even YourInitials@YourName.com. Avoid being "cute" for the local part that isn't your name, like SugarSparkles625 or EverybodySaysDont555—and if you can, move on from educational domains (nyu.edu, etc.).

Keep your email signature brief with your name and website link. You don't need to include your phone number, but you might include links to social accounts. No need for an inspirational quote, inset headshot, or other text that will multiply like bunnies over the reply chain.

As you draft your email, be clear and direct about what you're asking of them. Most people welcome a quick request for advice ("I thought you might help me find the booking agent at this cabaret space"), providing information ("I'll be around if you need a reader on Thursday"), or a straightforward question ("Any tips for someone moving to the city this summer?"). These are fast to read, flexible to address, and are likely to get a quicker response.

If you have more than a few questions, ask in your introductory email if you can send a separate follow-up ("Would you mind if I sent you a few questions to get your take?"). If the answer is yes, prepare a short list and impress upon the person you're sending why they *specifically* are the person you're asking. In exchange for their wisdom, you're giving them respect, acknowledgment of their position, and the chance to help out a young artist.

Because their time is precious, asking someone to take a phone call, hop on a Zoom, or meet in person is a bold (and often frustrating) ask. Carving out an hour (plus travel) to meet with someone they hardly know or providing services they're typically paid for puts older professionals off. Leave it to the recipient to suggest moving past email if they have time and interest.

Emails: Short and sweet

Keep your emails simple, brief, and direct, with personality and warmth. Consider this structure:

> Warm greeting here,
>
> If you haven't met the person, you might open with who connected you to them. Warm opening line about how great it was to see them recently or how much you enjoyed their work last week!
>
> Direct sentence about what you need from them. A sentence or two of context. If you're asking more than one question, bullet point them

briefly. If what you're asking for could be delivered several ways with varying time commitments, offer those options here. Keep everything under 150 words.

A warm sign-off about the near future!

Your name
E-signature including your website

If this feels like email writing 101, you'd be floored by how often young actors write emails so long you have to scroll five times to get to the bottom of it (a "five-scroll," as we call it)—and to a person they've never met! *The nerve!*

When someone receives a long email or text, it's an immediate signal that the sender doesn't respect their time. This email may never be replied to, or not for a while.

And of course, proofread times three. You're likely to reread the email after you send it, and nothing is worse than realizing it contained an embarrassing typo or incorrect information.

I'm young, and I love to be young

Many early-career artists are afraid to come off "too green," and so will write incredibly "PRO-FESH-UH-NAL" emails that are firm, ice-cold, and devoid of any personality at all. Unfortunately, this fools absolutely no one.

It's okay to be in an early stage of your career—everyone started there!—and put naturally youthful energy in your message. Despite our comments about time, most people want to help younger artists in the ways they're able to, paying forward the help they got when they started.

Are you there?

You've sent your email, several days have passed, and still no response. Did they get it? Did it go to spam? Do they hate you? Does everyone hate you? Should you never write an email again?

If you're cold contacting, don't follow up if they don't respond. You sent the message to a stranger, and now it's up to them to get back to you. We hope they do! It's possible your message went to junk, but don't write again to check because your second message might be seen as *actual* junk nonetheless.

If someone told you to contact them or they contacted you first, you're welcome to follow up after ten days if you don't get a response. Maybe they've been busy or had pressing matters to deal with first, but if they *still* don't respond, leave it there.

Sometimes people will tell you that they appreciate your message but are currently too swamped to give you what you're asking for, but "please contact them in a month or so." Follow instructions and follow up when they suggested! If they again put you off, it may sadly be that they are politely telling you that they are simply too busy.

We know that this kind of rejection can feel personal, as though this person doesn't think you matter. But see it instead as an opportunity. You might have overestimated their interest or could have been asking too much of someone unavailable. Now more informed, you can reach out to someone who is more eager to help you.

Reply quickly

Sometimes younger artists take their sweet time replying to professional emails. Maybe they're swamped with their tour guide job, are overwhelmed by how to respond, or even pretending to be busier than they actually are . . . but in any case, it can be very frustrating to the sender who is giving you their time—and possibly an opportunity.

When someone in the industry emails you, do your best to respond to them within twenty-four hours. If you get the email in the evening, it's fine to respond in the morning, and if you get it on the weekend, you could delay it until Monday—though their emailing you on the weekend may indicate urgency. Don't be afraid to reply immediately if you can—you won't look desperate; you'll look enthusiastic, which they hope you are.

If someone messages you and has cc'd members of their team, keep them cc'd. If someone has messaged you among a larger group and you're replying as an individual, don't reply all.

Play the long game

In networking, some relationships develop gradually over time. You may have admired someone from a distance for years, consistently engaging with their work and inviting them to your shows. One day, they realize you've been trying to connect for over three years. It dawns on them—they recognize your name, they know your work, and despite never attending your performances or always responding to your emails, they suddenly have a free Tuesday this month. Seeing your persistence and genuine investment, they decide it's time to finally give you a chance. (Little do they know, you've hardly noticed the time passing while living your own life, connecting with others, and doing the damn thing without them!)

LET'S GO OUT TONIGHT

If you contact someone and they agree to meet up, it's right that you should pay for the person you've approached. They're giving their time, energy, and know-how to you, so the least you can do for them is cover a couple of mojitos. If they've contacted you for a meeting, it's appropriate that they pay, but if they don't, splitting is fine. If they do pay, tell them you'd like to pay next time.

As to location, if you contacted them, you should always offer to come to their neighborhood and to a spot of their choosing. If they pass it back to you, suggest a few places and let them choose. If they've contacted you, suggest meeting in the middle unless they offer to go your way.

Keep the meeting to an hour (the basic unit of "meeting time") unless they're game to stick around longer—and as long as you want to be there, too. Zooms and phone calls are usually around thirty minutes.

This week's no good

If scheduling comes up, most people aren't free this week because busy pros tend to fill up their week by Monday. Start with dates next week, but whatever time they suggest, go if you're available—even if it's tomorrow!

Preparing to meet

Follow up the morning of your meeting with a "See you today! Does [the location] and [time we set] still work for you?" This way everyone remembers the details. Include your phone number if they don't already have it, in case they need to text you that they're running late.

If they last-minute cancel on you, as annoying as it is, don't sweat it. Follow up in a few days to reschedule.

If you don't know the person well, do your research and ask informed questions. No need to rattle off their own bio at them, but knowing to whom you're speaking greases the wheels of conversation.

Inviting people to shows

Most people welcome an invite to your performances, big and small. Most people will also decline—or not respond at all if the message doesn't feel personal. And that's okay!

We don't need to reexplain the value of someone's time—especially their evenings—but rest easy in the fact that it's often *more* beneficial for someone to simply be *aware* that you're working rather than to physically experience the work itself (which they may form an opinion on at your risk). If the concert is recorded, you can follow up with videos to share.

Always offer complimentary tickets when sending a personal invite. If you haven't been granted comps to give out, you'll have to pay for their seats yourself. Expensive as it can be, if they do agree to attend, they have serious interest in you. The dollars you've spent are very likely to come back to you later on.

If there's a food and drink minimum at your performance venue, you aren't expected to pay it for your comped guests. (You can also ask to get the minimum waived for your comps.)

If someone offers *you* comps to their show, they're telling you they would like to share their work with you. Maybe they want to collaborate, or they value your opinion. If you're available and it's not a total inconvenience, accepting is an excellent way to cement a relationship.

NETWERQING MISCELLANY

Here are some additional quick tips to improve your netwerqing.

Stay up on the (theatre) news

Get to know the names, faces, and major credits of those working on Broadway or in your area by keeping up with the Broadway Briefing, *Playbill*, *The New York Times* theatre section, or anywhere else delivering up-to-date, unbiased theatre news.

Support people you want to work with

Attend the productions and concerts of people you respect, whether or not you already know them. If they're a peer, post about their show generously and tell the world they deserve attention.

Seeing so many shows might be pricey, but the relationships you nurture are well worth the cost. And hey, plain seltzer with lime looks an awful lot like a vodka tonic.

Thank-yous

Nowadays, a handwritten thank-you note to someone you hardly know, but have recently met with, can be hit or miss. Some find it endearing. Others get confused.

You absolutely never need to send a casting director a thank-you note, whether it's after an audition or a class. If someone else got you the appointment, you can send a quick email or text after the audition process is over to thank them—but don't request feedback. They did you a solid by getting you into the room, so do them one by not making them regret it.

The rooms just outside the room where it happens

If you're interested in meeting more of the people who make the business run, go to the places where they do their business. Coffee shops, bars, and busy hot spots in your city's theatre district are a great place to hang out with friends or work during the day. Before long you'll see someone you know (or would like to know), and all the previous advice about making contact will be resolved for you.

• • • • • •

"Hey, girl—you okay?" Maggie's bestie says, tapping her on the forehead.

Maggie's been staring into space, holding her extra-dirty martini and remembering she's always in the market for new friends.

Looking around the room, she no longer sees playing cards. She sees interesting, complex, silly, and wonderful human beings. Each one has "superpower" in a different way, whether it's telling a terrific joke, writing a brilliant play, or bonding over shared experiences. What if they combined forces?

Because Maggie realizes she has a superpower, too—and she's ready to share it. In one fell swoop, she downs her martini, turns to her friend, and says, "Hey, thanks a lot for bringing me tonight. I owe you dinner, on me. In the meantime, wanna take another loop around?"

Creating Your Own Opportunities

Caroline is done waiting for someone to choose her. She knows that when actors create their own opportunities, they're choosing themselves—and telling the industry to pay attention. Whether it's producing a solo cabaret, recording an EP of original music, or gathering friends to read a play, making your own work sends a powerful message.

Caroline's inspired by famous actors who took initiative early in their careers. Leslie Rodriguez Kritzer impersonated Patti LuPone in a parody cabaret. Jay Armstrong Johnson donned drag as Winifred Sanderson in a hit Halloween show. Joshua Henry recorded original music. Alex Brightman wrote multiple musicals. And after Lindsay put up concerts of songs by Joni Mitchell and James Taylor, she formed a jazz duo with music director Marco Paguia. These artists, and so many more, still create their own work to feed their artistic souls.

Caroline has noticed that when she takes herself seriously, others do, too. Sometimes the industry just needs help seeing what sets an actor apart—and when she sets the terms, she creates the perfect fit. One day, she hopes to be picking the projects she wants, but realizes that those who don't wait for that day often find it arriving sooner.

Caroline's been thinking of doing her own cabaret . . . but as soon as she decides to pull the trigger, doubts creep in. What if no one comes? What if she bombs? What if she wastes thousands of dollars? She was excited—but now she's excited *and* scared.

But Caroline remembers: If she doesn't believe in herself, why should anyone else? She makes a list and sees she already has a strong base of family and friends who'll buy tickets. She remembers peers who produced break-even shows—and even one who made a profit. And as with her Hustle, she realizes that anyone who judges her for putting herself out there is probably just wishing they had the guts to do the same.

As for where to begin? In this chapter, we'll walk you through the process of creating your own work, step by step.

GOALS, MEDIUMS, AND STORIES

To lay the groundwork for the work you're going to make, identify what you're trying to accomplish, what story you're ready to tell, and what form is best to tell it.

Identify your goals

What does your artistic soul need right now? What do you hope this work will do for you? You might create this opportunity to:

- Showcase your strengths for the industry
- Sing the music you like
- Play the characters you want to play
- Build fans in person or on social media
- Get footage for your website and social media
- Have a show you can invite agents to
- Get your name out there
- Make money
- Collaborate with friends

- Build community
- Have something fun to do

While there may be crossover, it's nearly impossible to create work that successfully hits all of these goals. By knowing what you're *not* trying to do, you can alleviate the stress of taking on too much. If your solo cabaret is about getting footage, putting your name out there, and singing songs you love, then it doesn't really matter if the house is full or if you turn a profit. If the goal of creating a monthly reading series is about building community, collaborating with friends, and not breaking the bank, then you know there's no need to worry about promoting outside of your circle while keeping the budget to basically zero.

Determine your medium

Choose the proper format for your goals, budget, and resources. Certain formats are more costly to produce than others. Some cost a little but also bring in a profit. Some don't involve money at all.

Are you gunning to be the star, or are you excited to join a group? Are you stoked to splash this work all over the digital world, or focused more on the in-person experience? Based on where your friends and family live, do you have an audience?

Some mediums and their estimated budgets include:

- Cabaret ($400–$2,000 expense with $400–$2,000 income)
- EP of songs ($0–$10,000 expense, unlikely profit)
- Theatre group (almost $0)
- Putting on your own production of a licensed musical ($1,000+ in expenses with $1,000+ income)

Each of these mediums requires different levels of support and promotion, and results in equally different takeaways.

- Cabarets involve hiring musicians and inviting guest performers—unless you're playing and singing alone. Most venues include lighting and sound designers when you book their space. You'll have to focus on selling tickets, but you'll leave with tons of content to share.

- Writing an EP can be totally solo (you play, sing, record, mix, and master yourself) or could involve hiring others. You'll post about it after its release, but getting people to listen is mostly out of your hands. You get lovely recordings to distribute.
- Putting together a theatre group can cost nothing but time, but because of the insular nature, few people see the work unless it's posted on social media. It might not impress like other mediums, but building relationships is invaluable.
- Producing your own production of a licensable show (say, mounting your own *Bat Boy: The Musical*) can be expensive and time-consuming. But with smart producing, you can break even with ticket sales if people are excited to see you in familiar work. And what's better than being in a show you love?

Decide on your story

The more passionate you are about the story you're telling, the harder you'll work—and the more likely it is that your project will succeed. Whether it's a play, an EP, a cabaret, or a *Little Shop of Horrors* revival with your best friends, focus on what excites you. Don't worry too much (yet) about what will sell or what you think people want. Good art rarely starts that way.

Think about your strengths and what checks your boxes. Some create work drawn from personal experience or favorite genres, while others push themselves outside their comfort zone.

Whatever your choice, ask, "Why does the world need this?" If the answer is just vanity ("I want people to see me play Cathy in *The Last Five Years*"), it may turn people off. But if you dig deeper, you'll find the heart: Maybe your cabaret is hilarious, your theatre company fills a local need, or your play offers a vital new perspective. The reason can be big ("the world needs more trans stories") or small ("everyone loves great music"). As long as it matters to *you*, it will drive your project forward.

PRODUCING YOUR OWN CABARET

A cabaret is an evening of song and story held together by a theme. Because they're relatively easy to produce, cabarets are one of the most popular ways an actor spotlights themselves.

The major things to determine are the show concept, the set list, the venue, the budget, the personnel, promotion, performance, recording, and what to do after it's over.

The concept

Most actors putting on a cabaret start with a concept that is, well . . . themselves. They plan to put together a setlist of their favorite songs and tell bits of their life story as an actor in a big city. The show, they think, is created by them and therefore it should be about them. Most of the hundreds of cabarets put on every night are created this way.

Sadly, most cabarets are also terrible.

This is why putting on a cabaret can feel a little cringe. Imagine your friend tells you they're going to their roommate's cabaret. You're immediately sorry for their lost evening and may encourage them to drink a lot. But it doesn't have to be that way!

When an artist asks an audience to give their time and money to see them perform, it's not an excuse to hold them hostage with a spew of high-belted contemporary musical theatre ballads. Like any other form of entertainment, it's meant to be enjoyed by *both* the artist *and* their audience.

When planning a concept for a cabaret or solo show, answer this question: "What would my audience want to see?"

A cabaret should be a gift for your audience. Because of your show, they should leave having gained something for themselves. You could share a fascinating bit of your life story (your year studying abroad in Italy), tie songs together around a single relatable event (the loss of one's zany grandmother), center the evening around an entertaining fictional situation (you just won the lottery), or make use of a comedic bit (help, help, you've been kidnapped by the music director!).

Plus, you can perform solo, incorporate guests, or make it a small group affair featuring two or more performers equally.

Consider a cabaret that:

- **Makes them laugh,** full of silly characters, ridiculous stories, comedy songs, reinterpreted numbers in new and hysterical contexts, and skits with fellow jokers.
- **Makes them think,** exploring a genre of music, an artist the audience is unfamiliar with, or a relevant event. They leave knowing more than when they arrived, seeing their world in a new way.
- **Entertains them,** in a no-holds-barred onslaught of punchy numbers, dancing, variety acts, and surprise guests. It's a frenetic jamboree that says, "If you liked the last number, wait'll ya get a load of this one!"
- **Moves them,** exploring grief, uncertainty, or another powerful emotion. So long as you handle it with care and commit to discussing your concept in an insightful way, it's all right to invite people to something with gravity.

In part one, we told you that you were much more than a voice. Likewise, your cabaret should be much more than an evening of you singing. Test your concept with friends using a brief pitch of one or two sentences. Because this is also what you'll use to get people into seats, toss weak ideas aside until you find one that lands. If your friend is left with questions, trust us: Your audience will be, too.

The set list and banter

Filter a large set of songs you love through your concept so that they remain consistently on-theme. Reject material that is only there because you "really love the way your voice sounds on it."

Unless your show is focused on a decade of music or a musical genre, mix up your styles and—like your audition book—combine radio material with musical theatre.

Limit your ballads to a few, even if your show is about a heavier topic. In a high-energy cabaret space, too many slower-tempo songs will kill the energy and encourage phone-checking.

Most cabarets feature "patter" throughout, which is the spoken storytelling that outlines your dramatic journey. Be ruthless about delivering what you've promised your audience, whether it's laughter, spectacle, or tears.

Considering the length of your patter, plan twelve to fourteen tunes in a seventy-minute set (the usual time allotted by venues for a cabaret).

A useful template for a cabaret's structure is:

1. **An exciting, cold opening number** that tells the audience what they're going to get. "Cold" means you don't precede the song with anything—you simply start the show.
2. This may blend into **a second song** before applause to keep the energy up.
3. Break for a **spoken welcome.**
4. Around ten minutes in, **five to six songs dive into the concept**. A medium-tempo song or even a ballad is great here, and most songs are connected by a flash of patter.
5. About forty minutes in, **return to high-energy material, leading to a midpoint** that forms a turning point in your concept. If you're making them laugh, ridiculosity explodes. If you're dealing with an event, you *seem* to arrive at its conclusion. If you're focused on entertaining them, this is "end of Act One." For good storytelling,

arrive at the "obligatory ending" (the final "scene" we're anticipating) earlier than the audience suspects, so that you have room to explore what it all means.

6. Here on the **other side of a peak, the show relaxes to balance, taking a breath** through two or three songs before the final stretch. In comedy, you'll find some depth, and in deeper storytelling, take a surprising detour.
7. **Begin to wrap things up** with one or two songs that fully satisfy the theme. Many shows place ballads here.
8. You **reach the end,** encapsulating the experience of the evening in a grand finale. This might call back to something you discussed earlier in patter.
9. You *can* include an **encore,** but we think it's unnecessary. Better to include it in the regular set list and leave them wanting more.

This formula is a suggestion, but take note of what surprised you as you read the above. If you hadn't thought about it that way, most other actors probably hadn't either—which is why *your* cabaret won't be a drag . . . it'll be a delight!

The venue

Even in large markets, cabaret spaces are limited, which actually makes choosing easier. In New York, there are usually fewer than a dozen active venues; in smaller markets, you might have just two or three options.

Most venues don't charge a rental fee—they take a cut of your ticket sales, plus possibly extra fees. They typically provide staff for lights, sound, front of house, and wait staff. You'll get one to two hours of tech time, during which lights and sound are designed on the fly. You'll need to bring your own music director, singers, and musicians. While most venues have a piano, some also offer amps and drums. Others require musicians to bring gear, which can add \$50–\$100 in cartage fees per player who must lug their own instrument to the venue.

Decide on your ideal venue size by estimating your potential audience. Start with a list of close friends and family, then a second list of likely attendees, and a third of maybes. Include guests' guests and who your fellow performers might bring. Scroll through your text, email, and direct messages to spot regular contacts. The total is your target capacity. For most first-timers, this is between fifty and a hundred seats, which aligns with most small cabaret venues.

Next, explore typical ticket prices at the venues you're considering. Many also charge a food and drink minimum, which raises the cost for your guests. Choose a venue that fits your audience's budget.

Once you've picked your spot, find the venue's contact info online—or better yet, get introduced by someone who's performed there. Response times vary, and availability may not match what's listed. Some venues book you quickly; others ask for materials like a video, headshot, and assurance you can sell tickets.

If they're interested, you'll then choose a date and time from the options they offer.

The budget and personnel

Your cabaret can make a little money or a lose a lot. Luckily, smart producing helps you set yourself up for financial success.

Every venue's arrangement is different, but most will take around 50 percent of the ticket sales as payment. Sometimes they'll add a set fee (like a hundred dollars), a per-person fee (such as a dollar per audience member), or both. Most won't budge on their deal, so don't sour the relationship by trying to get them to. Negotiate additional comp tickets instead.

To identify a safe budget for your show, find 60 percent of the total number of seats in the house and multiply that by the ticket price, and then factor in the deal you've made with the venue. This number becomes our budget. We choose 60 percent because we're thinking that's a very safe bet on how many seats we'll sell, and that also means that any seats above 60 percent will be profit. If you like taking risks, you could move that as high as 80 percent. Don't bank on selling out or you can't make a profit—and will lose money if you fail.

Here's Caroline's example:

70-seat venue × 60 percent = 42 seats
42 seats × $22 ticket price = $924
Split in half with the venue = $462

Caroline's budget is $462. In order of priority, Caroline begins to outline her expenses.

- **Music director.** Caroline can't play for herself, so this is the first and most nonnegotiable expense. MDs can range from $150 to $400 or higher depending on the number of rehearsals needed and whether the MD is asked to make charts for musicians to play. In Caroline's case, she's only having the MD on piano, and has a talented friend from school who's willing to come aboard for $200. Lucky Caroline!
- **Promotion.** After your MD, you need an attractive image to get people to your show with the title, location, date, time, and where to get tickets. Caroline doesn't know the first thing about graphic design, so she'll need to get someone to help. Her roommate loves her and can do it, so she's not spending money there. You can get a reasonably great graphic for a couple hundred dollars, or much less—though with so many ways to do it yourself, save money where you can.
- **Videographer.** If an actor performs a cabaret and no one sees it online, did it really happen? The third most important expense is paying someone to record the show. Caroline's roommate's boyfriend will do it for $40 and a comp (though in other markets, a professional videographer can run well past $500 or more).
- **Special guests.** Inviting additional singers to join you for a duet or backing vocals can add variety to your show and help fill seats. Most guests are happy to perform out of support and enthusiasm,

but if compensation feels appropriate, offer a comp ticket, drink tickets, a share of any profits—or even $30. Caroline's two guests are being great sports and just asking for one comp each, though Caroline was very ready to pay them.

- **Extra musicians and rehearsal space.** Whatever money you have left over, you can spend it on musicians (like guitar, bass, drums, or a string player), a studio space to rehearse in, or paying for extra comps for industry guests. Note that while guitarists, bassists, and drummers can usually play off lead sheets or sheet music with chords on them, most other musicians need charts written out for them—probably by the MD, which can become expensive very quickly. With her $222 left, Caroline forgoes other musicians and splurges on studio space and buying additional comps beyond the two she was allotted.

Based on this budget, if Caroline sells her forty-two seats, she won't lose a dime. That's more than manageable, she thinks, and schemes to turn a tiny profit if she sells more.

There's no need to pour thousands of unnecessary dollars into your cabaret, no matter how much you enjoy setting money on fire. Don't pay for excessive band charts, high-priced photography, outrageous hospitality, too much rehearsal space, or anything else that would ultimately be a waste. People are only expecting a show that matches the ticket price they paid.

As for Caroline's show, a killer set list, a couple of guests, and a piano is exactly the kind of show her audience is expecting to see for $22. If Caroline went overboard and produced what was clearly a $3,000 cabaret, it could look desperate—and kill the scrappy excitement a low-budget cabaret is meant to be.

While your show should be well rehearsed, be mindful of your collaborators' time. Trust your MD to gauge how much rehearsal is needed with you, the band, and any guests. Don't overbook guests—listen to what they need to be ready for your show. Some may learn their part on their own and just come to a band rehearsal or sound check, which is normal for pros doing one or two songs.

Promotion

Some actors feel weird promoting their show, until they remember that no one is going to get people there except them—not the venue, not the musicians, and not the special guests.

Nearly every person in your first cabaret's audience will be someone YOU know.

Promote your show in a strategic, organized way. First announce your cabaret with your image and an appealing blurb on all your social media no less than a month ahead of time, but no more than two months, so that people feel some sense of urgency to buy a ticket.

Use an appealing picture or pictures in a collage (lifestyle shots are great for this), and be sure to include essential details like:

- Title of the cabaret, which can be as simple as your name and venue ("Caroline at Carrow's") or announcing your theme ("Caroline's Love Song Takedown").
- If your name isn't part of the title, make sure it's as big and bold as the title.
- If your theme isn't clear, you could note it ("A Goofy Cabaret About Grief").
- Date and time of the show.
- Venue name and address, noting any special instructions (upstairs, basement, etc.).
- Ticket price and any food or drink minimum.
- Names of your music director and any special guests.

Post to all accounts at the same time and tag everyone involved, then mass email all your nearest and dearest. Avoid pleading to get them to purchase tickets and instead be very direct about how terrific the show will be. People shouldn't come out of pity or obligation; they should attend because they're excited.

In the weeks leading up, check in with the venue weekly to ensure that tickets are moving, then every few days in the two weeks right before. They want to sell tickets as much as you do, so don't worry that you're nagging. After your initial announcement, the pace of your sales may slow, but should pick up two weeks out as people have a better idea of their schedule and if they plan to come.

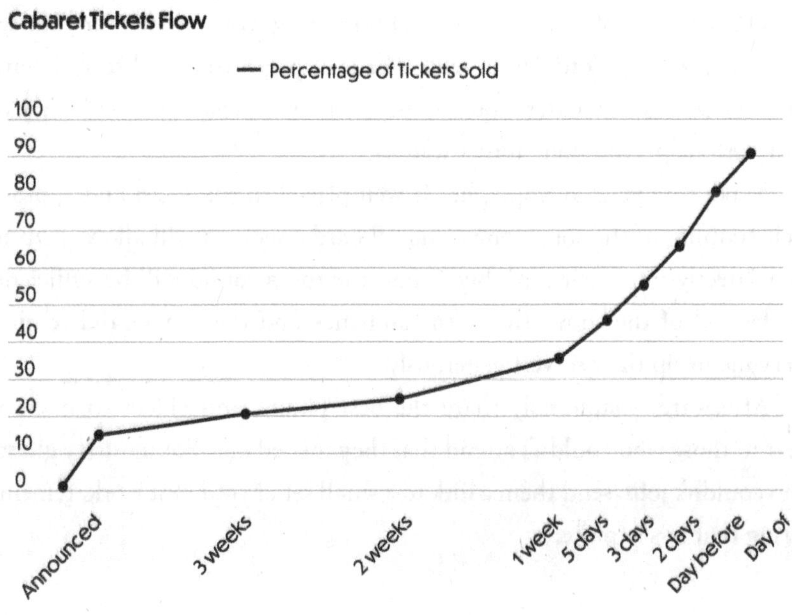

If your sales don't match your expectations, troubleshoot by:

- Texting friends to buy tickets. Ask something like, "Will I see you at my show on May 10?" Again, no pleading. State the facts about how awesome it will be.
- Message groups you're involved in, like your graduating class, a theatre group, and previous casts. People may be more interested to support you if they can reunite with old friends.
- Some venues will permit you to do a "flash sale" where you discount seats for a day or two.

Don't forget to set comp seats aside for your partner, representation, mentors, and any industry guests—but family* and friends can pay for their tickets. They're there to support you!

The night of

Get plenty of rest and hydrate in the days before your performance.

On the night of, if you're afraid of forgetting words, patter, or your set list, take the stage confidently with whatever pages you need to feel comfortable. The more cabarets you do, the less nervous you'll be, so it's okay to start with help. And don't forget water!

Make sure your videographer is well placed in the room and approve their framing of the stage. Some soundboard operators will allow them to plug directly into their feed, but if not, the room sound will be sufficient. At the end of the show, thank the audience and the venue, and remind everyone to tip their servers generously.

Afterward, shamelessly share the best photos and videos to make it clear to those who couldn't attend that they missed out. For industry guests who couldn't join, send them a link to a small set of your best work, remembering that less is more.

STARTING A THEATRE GROUP

If your goal is to build community, explore energizing material, and connect with other artists, consider creating a theatre group to host readings, concerts, or productions.

To get started, join an existing group to see how it works—or doesn't work, as you may discover. When you're ready to give it a go yourself, gather creative friends for a one-off reading. Whether classic or brand new, prep can be "cold" (everyone does the first read together), "lukewarm" (actors are asked to do one read-through prior), or "warm" (some light character work in advance).

* Except any family who invested money in the show—they're comped!

Team up to share the workload and host in a casual space like a home or community center. Share roles fairly—double up if there are too many parts, or split leads if there are too many people. Consider taking a smaller role to avoid giving off the vibe of a vanity project—or draw roles from a hat. Ask guests to bring food or drinks, and have everyone help clean up.

If the reading goes well, do one every four to six weeks to establish a regular group. See what kind of material your community enjoys and mix it up. As you work with more people, take note of those who show leadership and can take on greater responsibility. A small committee of five or more can run the group.

Some theatre groups grow into full companies, even registering as non-profit organizations to raise funds and mount larger projects. While a big commitment, it can be a rewarding way to create opportunities for yourself and your community.

Licensing a play or musical for an amateur production

Just as your high school and college put on shows, you can pay to license one and put up your own. A quick search will tell you which licensing house (such as Music Theatre International or Concord Theatricals) owns the rights to the show. Many of the tips on creating a theatre group and producing a cabaret apply to putting on an amateur production, just on a larger scale.

Though putting on a full production can be challenging, when done well it's an unforgettable experience (not to mention a wonderful new line on your résumé).

Here's how to get going mounting your own production:

- First, **determine the show** you want to do and figure out who'll be involved from the start (a director, additional producers). As with your theatre group, if you choose to direct, star, *and* produce, you may have difficulty getting others as excited as you are.
- **Create a loose budget** before you pursue getting the rights to the show to understand what the show will cost and identify *specifically*

how you will pay for it. You can find samples of production budgets online. Show your proposed budget to someone who's produced before and refine your numbers.*

- **Choose the right director** (if you haven't already) before you go further, because most directors want a say on the venue and who else is hired. They'll also suggest people they trust who'll work within your budget.
- **Find the right venue** to clarify realistic production costs. Some venues have equipment or rehearsal space to keep things economical, while others require you to rent from outside at a large additional expense. Be realistic about how many seats you can sell and for how many performances. Know that when you're the producer and you don't sell enough seats to meet your budget, *you're still on the hook for paying everyone*—out of pocket, if necessary.
- **Acquire the show's rights from the licensing house,** which can take a month or two. Licensing fees are calculated by the size of your proposal. A loose way to anticipate your fee is to multiply the number of performances by number of seats, by the highest ticket price, and take 10 percent of that number. So if you were doing three performances in a sixty-seat house for a $15 ticket, your licensing fee might be around $270. Better-known titles may cost more. Note that you'll have trouble getting the rights to shows that are already happening or touring near your city, or are currently on Broadway.
- **Decide compensation for your actors.** You can work with unpaid volunteers, non-Equity professionals, Equity actors, or a combination. If you employ Equity actors, you must obtain the correct contract through Actor's Equity Association and pay set rates to your actors. Pay can be different from actor to actor and can be

---

* If you plan to use your ticket sales to pay for the production, use the 60 percent model we learned for cabarets. (Multiply the proposed number of performances by proposed ticket price, by a rough estimate of the seats in the venue you'll obtain, and take 60 percent of that number as your budget.)

whatever your actors will agree to, but of course, at this stage, you may get what you pay (or don't pay) for.*

- **Finalize your budget.**
- **Finish hiring** the rest of the production team with your director, including your stage manager, designers, music director, and choreographer.
- **Cast the show** internally or hold open auditions. If you hold auditions yourself, get educated on best casting practices so that you don't sour the experience from the start. If you're opening it up to union members, learn all casting mandates and rehearsal procedures.
- **Outline a rehearsal schedule** with your director and stage manager. Carve out enough time but make sure you aren't asking too much of your cast (especially if they're working for free).
- **Strategize show promotion** and consider working with someone who has marketing experience, knowing that some is better than none. Use what you learned about promoting a cabaret here.

For more support on producing your own production, talk to mentors who've done it before and check out one of the many books available for first-time theatre producers.

......

Caroline learned a lot from her cabaret experience. She rediscovered how much her soul needed to get back onstage, and the feedback was very encouraging (note to self: fewer ballads next time). She realized she's more of a natural leader than she thought—and kind of enjoyed the planning and producing. She also faced how hard self-promotion can be, and impostor

---

* There's ongoing debate about whether all actors should be paid. In the past, low-budget shows often didn't pay their actors, attracting those willing to work for the credit. Today, some assume every producer is profiting while actors go unpaid—but that's rarely true, especially in community productions full of hobbyists doing it for fun. If an actor has moved beyond working for exposure, the opportunity simply isn't for them. Be clear about compensation in your casting breakdown.

syndrome crept in some days. It stung when people declined her invite—or didn't show up—but she stayed focused on those who did.

Most importantly, she learned the power of creating her own opportunities. Dozens of friends shared a pic of her program online, and supportive texts rolled in for days. Instead of stressing over the *Anything Goes* EPA, she's posting her jazz mash-up of "I Get a Kick Out of You" and "It's De-Lovely." She now has new materials to send to agents who asked to stay in the loop.

Caroline knows most people will scroll past her content—but it only takes the right few to notice. Someone might visit her profile, check her website, or simply remember her name for later. After all the effort she put in, she's already gained so much more than she could have ever imagined.

Time Management

After reading all of these information-packed chapters on doing the damn thing, Mikey's suddenly overwhelmed with everything he's got to do. (Sorry, Mikey, we're only trying to help!)

Where to begin? Strangely, now that he's on his own post-college, his days feel simultaneously jam-packed and somehow . . . kind of aimless? Most are structured around work shifts and time with his boyfriend. Though the rest are *technically* free, the sheer volume of work to do makes him want to quietly lie on the kitchen floor and not get up for a very long time.

Like Mikey, many actors live with a vague sense that there's a lot of adulting to do, but remain stuck in a mindset from their first twenty-one years. Isn't someone supposed to tell them where to be and when, dictating instructions on what they must do to "pass" the class?

But having learned that his career is in his control, Mikey realizes the first step is to master time management.

Successful professionals learn to maximize their productivity while carving out time to live a fulfilling life outside of their work.

Mikey knows he's his own boss. It's empowering to set his own schedule—deciding what gets done, when, and how. But he's also learned the downside: No one holds him accountable. No reminders, no encouragement through the daily, only the daunting adventure of doing it all.

But Mikey's about to discover the best part—once he takes control of his time, overwhelm turns into inspiration, and panic into excitement.

GOING TO THE ARTIST'S "OFFICE"

Carl Jung said, "You are what you do, not what you say you'll do." That makes you an actor, a best friend, a sibling, a business owner, a movie fan, and a pet parent—all at once. Stop doing one, and it fades from your identity. We learn to balance these roles based on the life we want to live.

When we get busy, the first thing we drop is whatever no one's watching—which is often our time spent pursuing our art. "Who cares if I skip learning this song or going to ballet today?" Well, *you* do, because being a singer and dancer are parts of who you are. You remain that person by making time for them.

Your competitive uncle says you're not a "professional" actor unless you get paid. As usual, competitive uncle is wrong.

> ***A professional is defined not by the money they make, but by the time spent working at their chosen profession.***

If your survival job takes up thirty or forty hours a week, it's up to you to be an artist at least part-time—finding ten to twenty hours outside of it. (This is why, as we saw in the money chapter, replacing your survival job with a Hustle is vital.) While your accountant cousin plays the latest *Legend of Zelda* after work, you're building your acting career in the five hours before your bar shift.

You can't view your acting career as something you'd "give more time to—if only I could." When you start treating it as your primary profession—which might be part-time for now—you suddenly recognize all the time that you're already at the artist's "office."

You are doing your job as an artist when you are
doing a musical,
seeing a play,
rehearsing callback sides,
waiting at an audition,
making a self-tape,
taking a lesson,
going to the gym,
submitting to an agency,
reading a director's biography,
watching a film for character research,
listening to new songs for your audition book,
getting coffee with a fellow dancer,
. . . and so much more.

Many professional artists would proudly tell you that they work more than sixty hours a week. Imagine if almost everything you did each day brought a sense of accomplishment, and any annoyance was just a small bump on the way to the next great hour. Some of us even get addicted to our rewarding, if busy, lives. Who wouldn't thrive while fulfilling their life's purpose?

Mikey realizes that he's been waiting for some unknown life change to invest necessary time in his career. His roommate isn't helping, telling him that being "busy for the sake of being busy" will damage his mental health. But there's so much that Mikey wants for his life, and with so little time on this planet, he sees that only by giving the maximum number of hours to his dreams *now* can he live the accomplished, selective, and relaxing life he dreams of later. (Plus, his roommate hasn't auditioned in eight months, and is generally pretty lazy, so there's that.)

Okay. Mikey's feeling motivated to master his time. He's also feeling . . . wow, a lot better now that he's seeing time in such a big, exciting way.

But first, Mikey, let's talk about tomorrow.

TAKING CONTROL OF YOUR TIME: PLANNING

Organizing your time requires three different systems working together:

- **A year-long calendar** that covers at least the next twelve months. Use it to track weddings, vacations, rehearsal processes, birthdays, holidays, and long-term deadlines. Your parents had a wall calendar—now it's an online calendar or a digital tool of your choice.
- **A weekly schedule** of fixed commitments: auditions, shifts, classes, meetings, therapy, and rehearsals. Some prefer a physical planner; others sync everything digitally.
- **A daily to-do list** with tasks like learning songs, sending emails, and running errands. It includes what must happen today, plus an ongoing list you pull from each day.

Having all three systems gives you peace of mind—you won't forget when *Godspell* closes next spring, the week your family is going to New Orleans, your niece's birthday, your updated voice lesson time, or that you need new tap shoes.

The savvy pro knows that the effort to maintain them is easily outweighed by the relief of running their business efficiently. Now, when they receive a heavy task, they think, "This isn't my problem—it's my planner's." When you're organized, you've got a loyal assistant managing your adventures, near and far.

In the digital age, it's easy to keep all three systems together. You've got the classics from Google and Apple, but also stylish options like Bullet Journal and the Happy Planner. Or you could go "full RSO" and track everything in a single, wildly customized Microsoft Word document (those who've seen it are a little terrified . . . and honestly, they should be).

Doing the damn thing . . . on time

Start with a comprehensive list of everything you've got to do for all aspects of your life. It will take time, but don't skip this step. Based on what you've learned so far, your list might look something like Mikey's:

Talk with my partner about my mission and vision, get feedback
Write my vision statement
Write my mission statement
Make a list of values
Commit to going to the gym four times a week (weights)
Buy three books on motivation and work ethic
Update my website with my new branding statement
Meditate five days a week for ten minutes
Identify my cost of living
Create my first budget
Get an app for personal budgeting
Brainstorm my dialect coaching hustle
Go part-time at Starbucks
Take first steps on my hustle (advertise, site)
Set my banking app to autosave 20% of all deposits
Make my IG profile public
Pin two singing videos to top of page
Simplify and improve my website
Upgrade to the paid version of Squarespace for my site
Get feedback on my website from mentor
Get on TikTok, post once a week
Reach out to summer stock MD
Reach out to Joe (mentor)
Reach out to Hannah (writer)
Talk to parents about $ assistance over the next year
Film seven cuts from my book and put on website/socials
Approach Ricky about producing a reading series at home
Plan a reading group with friends from class

Submit to two agencies
Update my Actor's Access
Prep for Friday's callback
Prep for the *Hair* EPA

Imagine if, in only a few months, you accomplished everything on your list. How much further would you feel on your path?

Spread the list over the next four months

We assign each item to weeks and months in the future. One handy technique is to use Roman numerals for each week of the month. "April I" is the first week, "November III" is the third. Some months may have a fifth week.

Here's how Mikey divided to conquer.

March I
Talk with my partner about my mission and vision, get feedback
Write my vision statement
Gym 4x this week
Update my website with my new branding statement
Make my IG profile public
Prep for Friday's callback
Prep for the *Hair* EPA

March II
Write my mission statement
Gym 4x this week
Buy three books on motivation and work ethic
Meditate 5x this week (10 minutes)

March III
Make a list of values
Gym 4x this week
Read Book 1
Meditate 5x this week (10 minutes)

March IV
Simplify and improve my website
Upgrade to the paid version of Squarespace for my site
Meditate 5x this week (10 minutes)
Gym 4x this week

April I
Reach out to Joe (mentor)
Pin two singing videos to top of page
Identify my cost of living
Create my first budget
Check in on gym and meditation routine
Read Book 2

April II
Get feedback on my website from mentor
Set my banking app to autosave 20% of all deposits
Get an app for personal budgeting
Brainstorm my dialect coaching hustle
Go part-time at Starbucks

April III
Reach out to Hannah (writer)
Reach out to summer stock MD

April IV
Talk to parents about $ assistance over the next year
Film seven cuts from my book and put on website/socials

May
Update my Actor's Access
Submit to two agencies
Take first steps on my hustle (advertise, site)
Read Book 3

June
Approach Ricky about producing a reading series at home
Plan a reading group with friends from class
Get on TikTok, post once a week

Mikey had a few thoughts as he organized his tasks. Some were urgent, like auditions this week. Others were quick wins—making his Instagram public and updating his site with a branding statement. He chose two starter projects: writing a vision statement and starting a gym routine to boost his energy.

He's spreading out his business plan over a few weeks to avoid rushing, and focusing on getting fresh creative input from the books he's buying. By month's end, he'll refresh his website. Next month, he plans to work on money management, develop his Hustle as a dialect coach, and reconnect with old contacts.

This month's "final boss" is filming cuts from his book, so in three months he can post them to his website, Actor's Access, and socials. Then he'll be ready to submit to agencies—and start a living room reading series with college friends (privately, Mikey hopes they'll be impressed and want to create a theatre group).

Organizing the week ahead

Fill in your weekly schedule with appointments already planned, like ongoing work shifts and lessons. Add any one-off events like dates, hangouts, meetings, and shows.

As you approach each of your projects, if anything feels too large to complete in two or three hours, break it down into more manageable chunks.

Now that Mikey has organized his tasks, he looks to the next seven days and places them throughout his schedule.

Monday
Gym
Update my website with my new branding statement
Make my IG profile public
Talk with James about my mission and vision, get feedback

Tuesday
Prep for Friday's callback
Gym
Write my vision statement (part 1)

Wednesday
(Work all day)

Thursday
Prep for the *Hair* EPA (part 1)
Gym
Write my vision statement (part 2)

Friday
ADDED: Buy three books on motivation and work ethic
Gym
Callback
Prep for the *Hair* EPA (part 2)

Saturday and Sunday
(Glamping with James)

Mikey plans to hit the ground running Monday with quick tasks (luckily, he's off from Starbucks) and sets aside the evening to dive into his career vision with his boyfriend, James, an organized paralegal and great sounding board. He's also starting his gym plan—if he skips Monday, he knows he'll keep putting it off. Tuesday, Thursday, and Friday nights are for audition prep, and he breaks a few larger projects into smaller chunks. Wednesday is packed with a double shift. Realizing Friday's open after work, he's moved his book hunt to then. His reward? A glamping weekend in the Catskills with James.

Take a moment to acknowledge the incredible work you're planning. Maybe you're seeing the untapped potential in your time. Mixing business with pleasure, obligation with stimulation, this is what a real professional's schedule looks like. Welcome to the club!

TAKING ON THE DAY: ACTION

Now to put your plan into action.

> ***The best way to organize your day is the way that* best fits your optimized lifestyle, accomplishing the most *while* bringing you the greatest satisfaction.**

Following our work on the macro, let's explore the micro by breaking down the artist's optimized day. Adapt this to whatever your life necessitates, whether you're still struggling to get rid of your survival job, if you need extra hours at the gym, or if you're a parent requiring ample time with your kids (and, oh yeah, your spouse—remember them?).

Discover your primetime (five hours)

Certain hours in our day are better than others for creativity and brain space.

> ***Our "primetime" is the five or so hours in our day when we are at our maximum energy. This is the time of the day we must do* our most important work.**

For many people these are the morning hours, but not everyone agrees. Our primitive ancestors broke up their tribes between those who would work all day and others who would keep watch at night. Some researchers believe that we've carried on this practice over several millennia, which explains why some of us are night owls and the others are early birds.

> ***Identify your individual primetime hours* and hold these hours sacred.**

That means prioritizing your creative energy, not choosing a survival job that conflicts with your primetime. If your best hours are in the morning and you have a nine-to-five office job, no wonder you have no energy to work on your art at night—because you gave it to someone else! Better to take a closing shift at a bookstore.

Your primetime is when you make important decisions and do your best work. It isn't a time for casual phone calls, errands, hangouts, or tedious tasks. And unless you want to be a professional chef or feel getting ripped is part of your actor brand, we wouldn't spend too much time in this zone meal prepping or working out, either.

Determining your primetime clarifies the other parts of your day.

Morning rituals (thirty to ninety minutes)

Morning rituals include making coffee, feeding pets, eating breakfast, taking vitamins, brushing your teeth, and showering, but it can also include more advanced habits like meditating, brain games, journaling, or exercise.

The most important ritual of all is organizing the tasks you've planned for the day, which should take five to fifteen minutes.

Be efficient and focused on your morning rituals so that they don't bleed into your workday. If your primetime is 10 AM to 3 PM, wake up around seven or eight. If you're a night owl and your best hours are 11 PM to 4 AM, then you might wake up closer to noon. Whenever you wake up, begin your morning with a routine that supports your lifestyle.

Business (one to two hours)

Business tasks grease the wheels of our artistic life and keep our activities moving at a pace. They include:

- Responding to emails (personal and professional)
- Errands
- Phone calls

- Texts
- Taking business-related meetings in person or on Zoom
- Noncreative tasks related to doing the damn thing, like:
  - Reviewing our business plans
  - Taking care of ourselves
  - Reconciling finances
  - Working for our Hustle
  - Connecting with our network
  - Keeping up with socials and updating our websites
  - Organizing self-made opportunities

We do these after our primetime, when our energy is reduced but we still have some "gas in the tank." We don't need to be at 100 percent to send a quick email, chat about cabaret specifics, or book a studio for the voice lessons we're going to give.

On weekends and days off, business time becomes home tasks and personal errands. It's a great time to plan our vacations, do our grocery shopping, and grab a new jacket for a party next week.

Survival job time, or "them-work" (six to eight hours)

The hours you spend at your survival job—or "them-work"—directly benefit someone else. For you, it's mostly lost time (even if it pays the rent). As we covered in the money chapter, you—the hyper-skilled theatre artist—have a purpose elsewhere. Save your best energy for that, not the bar, retail store, front desk, or restaurant.

"You mean I should show up to my job tired?" Yes—technically, that's the idea. Why not? If you give your nine-to-five your best energy, it'll drain you, leaving nothing for your real work. If you're making $22 an hour, give $22-an-hour energy.

If you don't take this approach, you risk getting *really* good at selling clothes or running someone else's spin class. Suddenly, there's better pay, promotions, and a tempting path pulling you into a career you never wanted. The longer you stay, the harder it is to return to your passion.

Them-work means fewer hours in the day for your creative business hours, which means you've got to work even harder to prioritize the time you do have—not to mention build the Hustle that will slowly let you exit the grind, shift by shift, for a life that's truly your own.

Evening rituals

Whether your evening begins at 8 PM or 2:30 AM, once your day is done you reflect on what you've accomplished and decompress through closing rituals—journaling, calming entertainment, catching up with your partner, or working out. No matter what else is happening (or not happening), you can say, "Today, I did everything I could do," and rest easy.

SORTING THE DAY

During your morning rituals, you sort all the day's tasks around appointments while protecting your primetime and maximizing productivity.

Give each task a proposed time limit. Do your best and don't overthink it, knowing that some tasks will take more or less time than you anticipate. If you notice you've taken on too much, simply move items to the next day and make them tomorrow's problem.

It would be amazing if you accomplished absolutely everything on your docket, but life comes at you quickly: an urgent discussion with your roommate, an important call from home, or six pages of unexpected callback sides due tomorrow. You won't always finish everything you set out to do each day. Be grateful for what you did accomplish, and roll over what you missed to tomorrow.

Organizing your day in practice: Mikey

Mikey's woken up on Monday with a few items on his agenda and a hefty list of to-dos. He crosses out the morning rituals he's completed, separates remaining tasks into categories, and times them out around his appointments. He makes sure to leave a bit of extra time throughout the day to buffer unexpected distractions.

MONDAY

8:30am First things first

~~Wake up~~

~~Coffee and breakfast~~

~~Read the news~~

~~Go through the day and schedule it all out~~

10:30am Gym

12:30pm Me-work!

Reset my password for my website since I've forgotten it (HA) (10m)

Review my branding statement and adjust (20m)

Send branding statement to two friends for last-minute feedback (20m)

Make list of things to address for the website for when I get to it (30m)

Update my website with my new branding statement (20m)

Change my IG name from "GoofBall5" to "MikeysaGoof" so my name's in there (20m)

All things Instagram (1h)

- Make my Instagram profile public
- Change my Instagram photo
- Add branding statement to my IG (and shorten it)

4:00pm Errands

Go to the grocery store because it's my night to make dinner

5:30pm Dinner

Make dinner for Jaaaaames

7:00pm "Meeting" (LOL) with James

Talk with James about my vision statement, get his feedback

After Hanging out

By ten thirty, it's time for Mikey to hit the gym. His day started on schedule—but of course, life laughs. During his primetime hours, a friend gives great feedback on his branding statement, so now he wants to tweak it and plans to update his site and Instagram tomorrow. He was *supposed* to grocery shop at four, but after the gym and a packed day, he's too wiped to cook. James won't mind if they just order pizza before their "meeting."

Day planning felt daunting at first, but after a few weeks, Mikey streamlines the process. Soon he wonders how he ever got anything done without it (the truth is, he didn't). Once, he waited around for something to change his life. Now, in a single day, he's done more than he had all month—on his own.

Today, he's not stressed about Friday's callback (that's tomorrow's problem), not dreading his café shift (because he's working on an exit), and he ends the day full of achievement, pride, and pizza—finally seeing what he's capable of.

Mikey is suddenly reminded of Newton's law of inertia—something that in school he thought he'd gladly forget—now takes on new relevance:

***An object in motion* stays in motion.**

And Mikey is a-movin'.

REVIEWING THE DAMN THING

Doing the damn thing propels both your life and career. As you improve, each becomes increasingly easier to maintain until forces come together to manage them *for you.* In the later stages of your thriving career:

- Your team of reps and creative contacts will offer you jobs, laying paths forward without you having to do anything *(and the business plan you made at the start will ensure you know which jobs to accept).*
- You'll be prepped to take on new artistic endeavors and have more free time to yourself *(and know how to navigate it all).*
- You will have more money at your fingertips *(and know where to put it).*
- Others will manage your digital life (an assistant), with your digital presence supplied for you from your active work *(and you won't be starting from scratch).*
- People will vie for your attention without you having to pursue them *(because relationships you invested in at the start will introduce you to new contacts).*
- You will have the resources to choose your own projects and create work from the ground up *(and your experience doing that at a smaller level will guide you).*

Building a business takes time and shouldn't be rushed. Piece by piece, you build it, and every day you're closer to your goals than you were before. When you realize your full potential, others can't help but realize it, too.

PART 3

BUILDING IT

Congratulations! (It's a Trap)

If you opened this book, ran your finger down the table of contents, spotted "Booking It," and thought, "Well, I've already 'built it,' so this is where I should start!"—congrats! You fell into our trap.

Most actors—especially those who've spent years training and weathering hectic, dismissive audition seasons—assume that if too many auditions go nowhere, they just haven't found the *real* ones yet. But the truth is, for most who've struggled too long, it's everything in parts one and two that they have yet to nail. Until they step back and focus on **building it** and **doing the damn thing**, confusion and burnout are all but inevitable.

For those still wondering why we waited this long to dive into booking work and fulfilling your purpose as an actor, the reasons are simple:

- Without a business plan, strong digital presence, and drive to create opportunities, it's tough to attract an agent.
- Without financial stability, great headshots are out of reach.
- Without knowing your specificity and target roles, you can't build a focused résumé.
- Without time management and a sustainable Hustle, auditioning regularly isn't realistic.

- Without a solid book, strong audition technique, and ongoing training, the auditions you do attend won't land.
- And without a grasp on "netwerqing"—which easily leads to roles and auditions without you even submitting—you'll be stuck hoping to be called in at all.

Once your artistic package is in place and you've made serious headway on doing the damn thing, *then* you have a real foundation to pursue your acting career with confidence. You don't need to have mastered everything in part two, but actively pursuing it will complement everything you take on in part three.

So, if you *did* skip to this page, be a good Von Trapp and start at the very beginning. It is—and this is true—a very good place to start.

But if you've read through and absorbed the essentials of the first two parts, congrats! You're ready to book it.

Headshots and Résumés

When the creative team is ready to confirm their cast, they gather around a table strewn with headshots and résumés. Role by role, they choose a tentative first pick until every slot is filled, asking, "Is this our cast?"

Someone suggests a swap, and a few photos are traded out. Suddenly, the director feels the cast is too "young," so they bring in a few seasoned pros. But now the dance ensemble looks fierce—and they've lost all their sopranos. Another swap, and the music director is happy. This back-and-forth continues until the team lands on a final cast, and offers are ready to go out. The headshots that didn't make the cut stay close—because someone is likely to decline, and a new offer will need to be made.

Your headshot and résumé represent you as an artist. Your headshot is a photo that looks like you at your everyday best. Your résumé sets expectations for the work you're right and ready for.

In this chapter, we'll explore what makes an excellent headshot and résumé; how to find the right photographer for you and everything you need to know before, after, and during the shoot; and the best ways to strategize the credits, training, and skills on your résumé.

THE SHOT YOU WANT

Your headshot should look like you at your everyday best—*no more, no less.*

When you go out for casual drinks with friends, you wear clothes that you feel great in and that suggest some effort—but not so much so that you've completely changed your style for one night.

If you don't have bangs usually, you wouldn't get bangs for drinks. If you're not the type who'd wear a white button down, you wouldn't go buy one for a date. You hope your friends will say, "You look nice!" but not "Oh . . . new hair!" or "Since when did you start wearing leather?" Approach your headshot the same way.

Your headshot matches the artist you bring into the room. If you have short spiky red hair in your headshot but now rock long blonde braids, the person in the headshot no longer represents the person they're seeing. When your headshot stands in for *you*, they must match.

Energy options

The standard headshot shows you with an active expression. Some photographers think of this as sharing a warm memory, a mysterious secret, or a flirtatious thought.

A full headshot shoot is broken down into several "looks" (individual, complete outfits showing different sides of yourself)—usually three to six, though not every look will be chosen when the time comes. All your looks should feature clothes you actually wear to auditions (which are, of course, clothes you'd wear at your everyday best).

Additional looks

Beyond your standard shot, many actors benefit from one or two additional looks that highlight different energies—joyful, serious, enigmatic, cute—and reflect their personal branding. Rather than overthinking what shots you *should* have, refer to the energy in your branding statement and make sure your headshots reflect that.

For example, if you describe your energy as a "bubbly badass," then you need a shot that sells "bubbly," another that sells "badass," or one that (somehow?) combines the two. Also:

- If you're often called in for a specific genre—like sketch comedy or film/TV drama—you should have a look tailored to that world. But unless your agent specifically requests it, don't get a shot just because you *want* to be called in for a particular genre.
- If your playable age spans a range, get shots that lean older or younger—but still feel like the same person.
- If you alternate between facial hair and clean-shaven, take one of each.
- If you regularly change hairstyles or dye your hair bold colors, pick a couple of favorites to capture—but you don't need a photo for every variation.

Avoid guessing what casting wants or chasing some idea of what you're "supposed" to have. You can't predict every ask that will come your way. What you *do* need are a few great shots that look like you and illustrate a few sides of who you are.

FINDING THE RIGHT PHOTOGRAPHER

While headshot quality varies, creatives can quickly tell if yours was taken by a professional. Your friend with a camera, a selfie, your mom in the backyard, or a teenager at a mall studio won't cut it. Think of headshots as a start-up cost for your business—composers need demos, musicians maintain instruments, dancers buy shoes.

Headshots can be pricey, and the phrase "you get what you pay for" applies . . . up to a point. Rates can range from $300 to over $2,000. While anything under $300 should make you nervous, once you pass $700, you're mostly paying for reputation, experience, and a streamlined process. Those things can be worth it, but if you're on a budget, a $500 photographer can still deliver high-quality results. A $2,000 photographer isn't "twice as good" as a $1,000 one.

Most rates include two or three fully edited shots, ready for printing or uploading. If you want more edits, you can usually purchase them à la carte.

Investigate the photographer's work on their website or Instagram page and take note of:

- Lighting (Is the face lit beautifully and clearly, or does the shot look overblown or dim?)
- Backgrounds (Do they have options, like outside, seamless, wall, or brick?)
- Hair and makeup (Do they supply a hair and makeup artist, or does the client have to bring their own? If they supply, how does their staff artist's work look?)
- If a client is tagged, check out the client's Instagram page to make sure they've posted it proudly, too. They may also offer a glowing review of their experience in the caption.

Trust your eyes and personal taste. If you love their work and the price is right, this photographer could be the one for you.

The shoot

Your professional photographer does this every day, so help them help you by following their instructions well ahead of time. They should send you a detailed list of information as well as what they'd like you to prepare, including:

- Reconfirming the day and time of the shoot
- The address of where you're shooting, best ways to get there, and any information about getting into the space (key code, elevator, etc.)

- Equipment on hand, like irons, clothing racks, steamers, and vanities
- Info on any hair and makeup person they're supplying
- Details on bringing a playlist to the shoot
- Verifying their cancellation or rescheduling policy

If your photographer doesn't send you this information, ask for it. You don't need to meet them in person or request a phone call unless everything's looking like a mess—but in that case, you're better off running elsewhere before you pay the deposit.

Hair and makeup

A hair and makeup artist (HMUA) is a key part of your shoot. They make sure you look your best *out* of camera while the photographer handles how you look *in* camera. They manage finishing touches, offer a trained eye, and fix issues as they arise. High-level photographers often require you to use their HMUA to ensure top results—and good ones. Unless stated otherwise, their fee is not included in the photographer's price.

If an HMUA isn't available through the photographer, definitely hire one yourself. Rates typically range from $75 to $300, depending on your location and needs. It's worth the investment.

Arrive at the shoot as close to hair-and-makeup-ready as possible, starting with your usual look. The HMUA is there to enhance your style, not change it. If they make adjustments that no longer look like *you*, speak up in the moment. If you don't, and the photos feel off later, you likely won't get a refund or reshoot.

Because your headshot should reflect your everyday best, you need to be able to recreate that hair and makeup look for auditions. In other words, it shouldn't look like you visited the Sephora counter and haven't been back since.

While we're on the topic of hair: If you decide to get a haircut before your shoot, make sure it's at least a week prior so that you aren't frozen in time with a fresh chop, since you'll rarely audition with one.

Take care of your skin

Hydrate extensively in the days before your shoot. Consider getting on a skincare regimen two weeks before you shoot, or at least start applying a high-quality moisturizer. Limit alcohol consumption and anything else that might dry your skin out, and get plenty of rest.

Playlists are awesome

The music that makes you dance is ideal to make your energy feel like you, so prepare a playlist for your shoot. Even better, tailor it to the roles you want, and the music *they* might dance to.

Prep clothing options

Bring at least twice as many options as you intend to wear at the shoot. Everything you bring should be a top choice for you, so that when the photographer gets excited about something, you're happy to wear it. (If you say "Oh, I don't want to wear that!" . . . why did you bring it?)

Wear items that make you feel fantastic, strong, sexy—or all of the above. Don't wear something brand new that you aren't positive that you like. Don't wear:

- Something that feels "new" on you
- Firetruck red (does not work well on camera due to its intensity)
- Solid white (catches too much light and can pull focus from your face)
- Busy patterns (can be distracting)
- Something that shows too much or too little skin for how you normally dress. Note that with the photo's crop, something like a halter top could read in the image like you are naked below the waist. Someone call security!

Other dos and don'ts

Do read and respect your photographer's policies. If they require three days' notice to reschedule, they mean it—even for illness or emergencies. Once you agree to the shoot, you're bound by their terms, even without a signed contract. (Emails and texts count as an agreement.)

Do be mindful of their schedule. Pros rarely have time to push things back or extend your session if you're late. So—**don't** be late. Arriving flustered won't help anyone.

Do relax and have fun with your team. The more open and playful you are, the more "you" will come through.

Don't chat nonstop during the shoot. They need enough shots with your mouth closed.

Don't bring a friend, parent, or agent—unless preapproved (and they probably won't approve it). This is your time to collaborate with a professional photographer, not take direction from Mom. Come alone!

Do trust your photographer. If you've done your homework and love their work, let them lead. They've got you.

AFTER THE SHOOT

After your shoot you will get a proof site of unedited photos to choose from. At this point the photographer has cut out unusable shots (blinking, making a funny face). Whatever the photographer sent you in the proof site are the photos that are usable, so don't ask to see "the others."

There's still a lot of editing for them to do once you make your choices, so don't stress if the images don't feel print ready. Trust the artist has captured more than you think.

Asking others for headshot feedback

Choosing the "right" shots from a huge proof gallery can feel overwhelming. Hold off on forming strong opinions until you've looked through the gallery a few times. Then follow these steps:

- Start by selecting your favorite twenty to thirty shots across all your looks. This gives others a focused batch to help you narrow down.
- Share that group with one or two close friends or a significant other—people who'll take the time and care. Don't tell them how *you* feel about the shots; it can skew their honesty. If you love one and they don't, they may hesitate to tell you what they really think. If you hate one and they love it, they might hold back, worried they're saying, "You really look like that!"
- Once you've narrowed it to about a dozen, ask for input from agents, mentors, or other trusted pros. Send an easy-to-access link—not a folder of giant files.
- Finally, based on the feedback, pick your top two to four shots for retouching. As stressful as it is, no one should make the final decision but you.

Retouching

Your photographer will tell you how many retouched shots are included (usually three to six) and how much extras cost—typically $25 to $75 each. You'll have about a month to send your selections. Miss the deadline and you may wait longer as they shift focus to new clients.

Most photographers don't allow use of unedited shots. Don't try to edit them yourself or post them online for opinions—you'll lose the benefit of professional retouching and risk damaging your relationship with the photographer (they really hate it).

Be clear with the photographer about what exactly you want retouched. You might want a more natural look or lots of editing, so be clear. It's appropriate to ask for:

- Skin cleared up, red patches lightened, acne smoothed or removed
- Hair cleaned up, unwanted frizzes or rogue strands removed
- Teeth whitening
- Eye brightening

It's less (or not) appropriate to ask for:

- Parts of your body to be altered to look smaller or bigger
- Editing features of your face so that you don't look like yourself
- Changing the color of your clothing
- Changing the color of the background
- Splicing different shots together to create a cute mutant

How often should you get new headshots?

As long as your shot still looks like you, it's up to date.

But when your look changes, get new ones. You should get new headshots if:

- You've gotten older, and feel it.
- Your hairstyle has changed significantly in color or length, and you plan to keep it that way for a while.
- You've gained or lost a significant amount of weight.
- The energy of the shot no longer matches yours. Maybe you feel it's too bright, dark, silly, or intense—it just doesn't feel like you anymore.

As a point of reference, our faces and bodies change more rapidly when we're younger and more slowly when we're older. Professional teenagers need new shots every year or two, actors in their twenties need them every two or three years, and actors in their thirties and beyond could probably update every four or five years.

A RÉSUMÉ IS A PICTURE IN WORDS

A résumé tells creatives how you might fit into their project.

Your résumé tells the creative team
how others see you by the roles you've been cast in,
how you see yourself by curating what you show them,
and where you've been via your experience.

Your job is to showcase the most useful, important, and impressive information clearly. Cut unnecessary details, outdated credits, and redundant training that is better saved for the early chapters of your memoir.

Some less-credited actors overcompensate with vague "filler" gigs to pad the page. But here's the good news if you're in or just out of college: No one expects you to have a packed résumé. If they're casting someone to play eighteen, they expect a newer actor. If you're older with fewer credits—maybe you started late or took a break—let your strong audition do the talking. If they're intrigued but unsure, they'll ask where you've been.

Some actors—*ruh-roh, Shaggy*—lie about their experience. Honesty isn't just ethical; it's protective. When casting takes a chance on someone without the listed experience, they're gambling on your ability to handle pressure at a new level. A small regional show is one thing; a multimillion-dollar Broadway juggernaut is another.

Each step in your career teaches you how the industry works—whether it's your first musical or your shift from school to professional theatre. Every new tier—tours, major regionals, Off-Broadway, Broadway—comes with new protocols and expectations. Whatever your path, there are smart, honest ways to frame your résumé. No need to fake it.

RÉSUMÉ FORMATTING AND SECTIONS

Like your website and headshot, don't overthink your résumé's design. There's a standard format for how it should look. To start, look at other professional actors' résumés (easily found on their websites) to get an idea. Here are two résumé examples to demonstrate formatting.

JOSEPH K. JONES

AEA

HEIGHT: 5'7" | **AUTHENTICITY**: Mexican-American & Queer

VOICE: Tenor | **CONTACT**: josephkjones@domain.com

NATIONAL TOURS

TOUR	CHARACTER	Tour producer (dir. Tour Director)
TOUR	CHARACTER	Tour producer (dir. Tour Director)

OFF-BROADWAY / NEW YORK THEATRE

PRODUCTION	MAJOR CHARACTER	Major NYC location (dir. Someone Great)
PRODUCTION	CHARACTER	Major NYC location (dir. Someone Great)
PRODUCTION	CHARACTER	Minor NYC location (dir. Someone Great)
PRODUCTION	CHARACTER	Minor NYC location

REGIONAL THEATRE

PRODUCTION	MAJOR CHARACTER	Big Regional Theatre (dir. Fancy Person)
PRODUCTION	CHARACTER	Regional Theatre (dir. Fancy Person)
PRODUCTION	CHARACTER	Regional Theatre (dir. Fancy Person)
PRODUCTION	CHARACTER	Regional Theatre
PRODUCTION	CHARACTER	Regional Theatre (dir. Someone Great)
PRODUCTION	CHARACTER	Regional Theatre
PRODUCTION	CHARACTER u/s (performed)	Regional Theatre
PRODUCTION	ENSEMBLE	Regional Theatre
PRODUCTION	ENSEMBLE	Regional Theatre

NYC READINGS/WORKSHOPS

READING NAME	CHARACTER NAME	Where and/or with whom
READING NAME	CHARACTER NAME	Where and/or with whom
READING NAME	ENSEMBLE	Where and/or with whom

FILM/TV

FILM	CHARACTER (supporting)	Film producer (dir. by Film Director) **Festival it was shown at*
STUDENT FILM	CHARACTER (leading)	Dir. by Film Director)

TRAINING

BFA in Theatre, COLLEGE
ACTOR THERAPY (Acting, Scene Study, & Audition Technique classes with Lindsay Mendez & Ryan Scott Oliver
OTHER PLACE Shakespeare Intensive (2 years) – Teacher, Teacher
DANCE (Intermediate)—Jazz/Theatre, Tap; experience with Ballet, Modern, African, Hip-hop

SPECIAL SKILLS

Basic Spanish, Dialects (IPA), Viewpoints, whistling, basic flute, sight-singing, stage combat, Driver's License, lots of hosting/MC experience, fully vaccinated for COVID-19

www.josephkjoneswebsite.com

AGENCY
YOUR UNION STATUS
123-456-7891
SAMUELRENALD@EXAMPLE.COM

SAMUEL RENALD

HEIGHT | EYE COLOR | HAIR COLOR | VOCAL RANGE

BROADWAY/TOURS

PRODUCTION	ROLE	PRODUCER | DIRECTOR
PRODUCTION	ROLE	PRODUCER | DIRECTOR

THEATRE

PRODUCTION	MAJOR ROLE	REGIONAL THEATRE | DIRECTOR
PRODUCTION	MAJOR ROLE	REGIONAL THEATRE | DIRECTOR
PRODUCTION	ROLE	REGIONAL THEATRE | DIRECTOR
PRODUCTION	ROLE	REGIONAL THEATRE | DIRECTOR
PRODUCTION	ROLE	REGIONAL THEATRE
PRODUCTION	ROLE	REGIONAL THEATRE
PRODUCTION	ROLE	REGIONAL THEATRE
PRODUCTION	ROLE *U/S ROLE (PERFORMED)*	REGIONAL THEATRE
PRODUCTION	ROLE	REGIONAL THEATRE
PRODUCTION	ROLE	REGIONAL THEATRE

READINGS + WORKSHOPS

NEW MUSICAL 1	LEAD	WORKSHOP | DIRECTOR
NEW MUSICAL 2	ENSEMBLE	WORKSHOP | DIRECTOR
NEW MUSICAL 3	LEAD	READING | DIRECTOR
NEW MUSICAL 4	LEAD	READING | DIRECTOR
BIG CONCERT	SOLOIST	DIRECTOR | MUSIC DIRECTOR
ANOTHER BIG CONCERT	ENSEMBLE	DIRECTOR | MUSIC DIRECTOR
ANOTHER BIG CONCERT	SOLOIST	DIRECTOR | MUSIC DIRECTOR

FILM/TV

FILM	ROLE	DIRECTOR
TV SHOW	ROLE	NETWORK | DIRECTOR
TV SHOW	ROLE	NETWORK | DIRECTOR

TRAINING

COLLEGE	MT BFA	GRADUATED
	ACTING	SAMPLE ACTING TEACHERS
	VOICE	SAMPLE VOICE TEACHERS
ACTOR THERAPY	CLASS	LINDSAY MENDEZ, RYAN SCOTT OLIVER
SELECT MASTERCLASSES	WITH ACTOR THERAPY	JESSIE HOOKER-BAILEY, KIRSTEN WYATT

SPECIAL SKILLS

A LIST
OF THINGS THAT I COULD DO
IF SOMEONE ASKED ME
AT ANY MOMENT
NOT A PLACE
TO MAKE THINGS UP

You can use a pop of color if you want, but otherwise text should be black. Use a basic serif font (Times New Roman, Garamond, Baskerville, etc.) or sans serif font (Helvetica, Arial, Calibri, etc.) and keep the font consistent throughout. To differentiate sections, use bold, capitals, underlines, or a combination for headings. Keep the rest of your résumé plaintext except for show titles, which should be italicized. Beyond this, don't get too cute with design because this paper shouldn't be a work of art—your performance should be.

Let's take it from the top

The elements at the top of your résumé should be as follows, but you can rearrange their order to suit your taste:

- Your name, big and bold: Keep it consistent with your headshot, website, and Equity name if you've registered one.
- Representation: You can use your manager or agent's logo, or not.
- Equity status (AEA or non-Equity): Be upfront with this information so no one is confused, since casting is often specifically looking for an actor who is in or out of the union.
- Physical stats are optional. You can include your hair and eye color and your height, but no need to include your weight.
- Voice range is also optional but can be useful. Tell them your voice type and/or vocal range using the exact same information you discovered in making your branding statement. You can include exact pitches. "Legit soprano," "folk-rock tenor to high B-flat," or "Bass-baritone with low D2" are great examples. Order can matter. "Belter with high mix" may indicate this person is first a belter but also has a strong mix, whereas the use of "and" in "belter and high mixer" might imply they're equally strong in both.
- No one can ask you about any additional authenticity, but if you *want* them to know about your gender identity, pronouns, queerness, ethnicity, nationality, faith, or neurodivergence, you can place it at the top below your stats—for example, "Proud autistic Nicaraguan American."
- Some actors include a secondary headshot inset at either upper corner if they want to present an alternative look. This isn't necessary (and some creatives find it distracting), but go for it if it floats your boat.

Now for your credits. This is where it gets complicated. You'll break them down into:

- Theatre
- Film/TV
- Readings, workshops, recordings, and concerts

In each category you have three columns:

Show in Italics	Role in plaintext	Performance venue (and any notable personnel in parentheses)

Theatre

If you have eight or fewer total theatre credits, you can put them all together under one "theatre" section, placing your educational theatre experience at the bottom.

If you have more, you can further break the theatre section into other categories as they apply, from top to bottom:

- Broadway
- Tour
- Off-Broadway
- Regional Theatre
- Off-Off-Broadway
- TYA (Theatre for Young Audiences)
- Educational Theatre

If certain categories have only one credit, you can combine with others to streamline. Some combine Off- and Off-Off-Broadway with TYA theatre as "New York theatre."

If you understudied a lead role, be sure to include it. "Grantaire (Javert u/s)"

If you performed as an understudy, say so. "Norma (Chris u/s—performed)"

If you were dance captain, fight captain, or a featured ensemble member, mention it: "'Seasons of Love' soloist."

In the third column, attach to the venue any notable personnel that may catch the creative team's eye. This includes Broadway or television and film names, but also active directors, music directors, choreographers, or writers with whom the table might be familiar.

Film and television

All film, TV, and streaming credits can go in one place, including student films at the bottom. If you have extensive experience here, you can separate "film," "television," and "commercials" accordingly—but if your résumé is overrun with film/TV credits compared to theatre, you'd be better off truncating your list with "more film/TV credits upon request."

Remember that this is a theatre résumé. For a film/TV résumé, you'd lead with film/TV credits and similarly truncate your theatre experience.

Readings, recordings, concerts, and workshops

These credits can go under one umbrella (if you only have a few) or be separated based on the experience you have. These are all relatively lightweight credits, so don't list every cabaret you've ever been a part of if it leaves your production experience looking specious. Better to keep this list brief.

For readings and workshops, use the same formatting as productions (show, role, venue).

For recordings and concerts, if you played a role, use production format, but if you were a backup singer or sang a specific song, include that: *54 Below Sings Taylor Swift* is the show title and your role was "'I Can See You' singer."

Opera

Some actors coming from the classical world may have opera* credits to include. Like an extensively experienced film/TV actor, remember this is your theatre résumé. You can include an additional section for opera but keep it to three or four credits and say, "additional opera experience on request," and reverse it for your opera résumé.

Don't add an opera section simply to tell them you're trained classically. In that case, include opera credits under professional or educational theatre as needed.

Training

In the training section, start with your highest level of education and work down from there.

- Master's degree in acting, musical theatre, music, or dance
- Bachelor's degree in musical theatre, acting, music, or dance
- Any other degrees or post–high school training, including well-known intensives or certificate programs (like Actor Therapy's New York or Bust)
- Established theatre camps or other training programs (like Stage Door, French Woods, or Broadway Evolved)
- If you went to an esteemed performing arts high school, you could include it; otherwise, high school is unnecessary.

As we discussed in part two, don't worry that where you went to school will dramatically impact your audition. Regardless of where you graduated from (or if you graduated at all), the best person for the role wins.

---

* Because of the many cultural and artistic differences between the theatre and opera communities, some creative team members casting a musical may have questions about your training and experience if it's all in the classical world—in the same way someone going to an opera audition with few opera credits but tons of musical theatre might give that team pause. We aren't saying you can't be both; we're saying that you might create questions that your résumé—or your audition—will have to answer.

If you have a degree that isn't in the arts (like, say, communications or microbiology), you can omit it if you don't want to cause confusion ("Soooo . . . why have you given up your career as a rocket scientist for this regional production of *Amelie*?"). Some actors in that scenario simply put the school's name and leave it there. It's not a lie!

You don't need to include the year you graduated, will graduate, or if you graduated at all. And if you're currently in school, be sure that you're willing to leave school for the job . . . or otherwise risk annoying the creative team whose time you've wasted when they cast you.

Master classes and teachers

Listing master classes and teachers shouldn't be a who's-who of everyone you've ever breathed the same airspace with. When you include a name, you're saying, "This person shaped my training and would vouch for me if you contact them."

This section acts as your references. If the creative team couldn't realistically text or email someone you've listed and get a strong endorsement, leave them off. And yes—they *do* reach out. (We get contacted all the time.)

Include names of teachers in acting, voice, and dance. If you're currently studying with them, note it with *(current)*. As for master classes—if you only had five minutes with a celebrity who likely won't remember you, skip it. But if you had a real exchange with a teaching master? Go ahead and include them.

Special skills

You'll put all your interesting, impressive, bizarre, and *useful* skills at the bottom of your résumé in a paragraph list. The keyword here is "useful," and you should filter all the skills you're thinking of including through the question of "When would this matter to a creative team?"

Special skills come in handy when a role requires that the actor has already learned something *before* the first rehearsal. This is usually a skill that's integral to the character. Typical examples include:

- **Foreign languages:** Use qualifiers to tell the team your level. Tell them you're fluent and whether you're a native speaker or if it's your second language. If you learned the language later, tell them at what level—and be conservative. Use the CEFR system (A1, A2, etc.) or indicate intermediate, advanced, or proficient. If you're just excited about your new Duolingo subscription, it's not worth including.
- **Accents and dialects:** Only mastery applies here, and you should get confirmation of your skill level from a dialect coach so you're not overselling a skill that many actors claim to have.
- **Specialized vocal styles or abilities:** Beyond what your audition book can tell them, add anything that would inform or surprise the team. Rapping, beatboxing, a cappella singing, countertenor range, whistle tone, scatting, or the like applies. Be mindful that being an enthusiastic "jazz singer" isn't the same as having been the lead vocalist of a jazz band for six years. If your rapping wouldn't pass for a pro rapper, for example, we wouldn't include it.
- **Musical instruments and abilities:** Like the above, include any instrument you play and at what level you play it. Unlike the above, and in consideration of the number of shows requiring that actors play instruments, basic skills can work. If you're a songwriter, an arranger, or someone who is adept at sight-singing, holding complex harmony, or improvising music, let the team know here.
- **Dance styles:** Mention any nontraditional dance style you haven't covered in your training and indicate your level: "professional Irish dancer."
- **Uncommon athletic abilities:** Include skills like stage combat, gymnastics, tumbling, fencing, martial arts, or cheerleading. Qualify, if it will impress ("State champion").

- **Other authenticity:** If you didn't want to include your authenticity (as part of your specificity) at the top, or would like to elaborate on it, you could include more information here.
- **Driver's license:** This is usually useful for shows that may require an actor to drive other actors to and from rehearsal, as with children's touring shows where the actors are asked to drive city to city, but occasionally it comes up elsewhere.

Double-check your list and remove any extraneous skills that you don't think are at a level that would impress. For example, most actors think they have a terrific British accent, but most are quite amateur.* If you don't have complete confidence in yours, remove it from your skills or take the time to work with a dialect coach. It's better to put "British accents and dialects (certified): Yorkshire, Cockney, R.P., West Country" than just the accent alone.

The team can ask you to demonstrate any of your skills at any time for any reason, so be prepared.

Special skills are great conversation starters but avoid personality traits ("Type-A Virgo," "Low-maintenance"), quirks ("double-jointed," "plays the kazoo"), and hobbies ("love to cook," "Disney adult").

Many actors love to include impressions they can do, which also happen to be the special skills creative teams ask to see most frequently—often for their own entertainment. We'd shy away from common ones (Liza Minelli, Jennifer Coolidge, Moira Rose), but one or two brilliant, party-stopping impressions can be delightful ("Jennifer Aniston paying her taxes," "dolphin on LSD," "Bjork eating a sandwich"—you're welcome).

STRATEGIZING YOUR RÉSUMÉ

Now that you have the basics down of building your résumé, let's talk strategy.

---

* Oh, crumpet, we've *all* got a smashing British accent if there's work, haven't we?

Less is more

Creatives are likely skimming your résumé—during your audition or while reviewing submissions. Like your material and website, it should deliver the most important information *quickly* and *impactfully*. Cut anything extra.

More credits don't equal more talent, and it's better to have ten strong credits than thirty forgettable ones that bury the lede.

The currency of a credit

Each credit on your résumé has a value based on where, who, and what it says about your specificity and experience. Elements of a credit include:

- **Tier:** Broadway followed by Broadway tours, Off-Broadway, Off-Off-Broadway, major regional, educational, community theatre.
- **Show:** A major, recent show that has yet to conquer the regional circuit suggests some exclusivity in casting (*Wicked*, *Hamilton*), followed by shows recently released to amateur markets (*Waitress*, *Beautiful*), original shows at major theatres, shows that can be licensed anywhere (*Gypsy*, *Next to Normal*), well-known works in the public domain (*As You Like It*, *Pirates of Penzance*), and finally, shows that no one's heard of. Shows might carry more weight if they demand a certain skill level—a heavy dance show like *A Chorus Line* or *Cats*, playing an instrument in *Once*—as long as you indicate "original Broadway choreography" or "actor-musician."
- **Role:** A principal role carries more weight on a résumé than an ensemble track, but indicating you are an understudy or dance captain elevates smaller credits.
- **Venue:** Prestigious, major market venues followed by lesser-known regional ones, university venues, and then theatres the creative team has probably never heard of.
- **Personnel:** A big director or star lifts an otherwise small credit into a bigger one. If a well-known writer worked on the show with you, mention that.

- **Initial outings:** If your production was the world premiere, first regional production, West Coast premiere, it boosts impact.
- **Awards and nominations:** If you were nominated or won an award in your market for the role, include that with an asterisk.

Who? In what? And where?

If a credit is an unknown role from an unknown show at an unknown theatre, ask what you're trying to tell the creative team. If your credit is "Sam" in *Pick a Pocket or Three* at Pacoima Community Center—a production that could be real or something we've just made up—it tells us nothing except that you've done a show somewhere. Sam could have had one line or the last bow, the show could be a twenty-minute disaster or a complex southern Gothic masterpiece, and Pacoima isn't known for being a particularly competitive market (sorry, Pacoima).

If you have plenty of others, credits like these can be left off. On the other hand, if you're hurting for lines to fill on your résumé, they're useful to acknowledge that you do have production experience.

Organizing your theatre credits

The best way to strategize your credits within their sections is to place them according to value, from top to bottom. You don't need to order them chronologically.

Weigh each credit according to the system above and move higher-value credits to the top. If your lowest-value credits aren't adding much to your résumé, let them go.

Let's help Bryce with his résumé. Here are nine credits he needs to order under theatre on his résumé. Though we've made up some of these shows, theatres, and people, it will give you the experience of seeing an unhelpful credit.

1. *Legally Blonde*–Ensemble/Emmett u/s–The Muny (D. Sarah Jenkins)
2. *Spring Awakening*–Moritz–Point Park University
3. *Rent*–Roger–Papermill Playhouse
4. *Tethered*–Jim–Theatre Atlanta (World premiere)
5. *Robert's Last Letters*–Jordan*–New World Stages (D. Marshall Pailet)
   *Theatre World Award Nomination
6. *Jesus Christ Superstar*–ensemble–Point Park University
7. *And So It Goes by the Wayside*–Green Soldier–Jones Auditorium (Pittsburgh, PA)
8. *Fiddler on the Roof*–Motel–La Mirada Theatre (D. Rick Sanchez)
9. *Sheer Madness*–swing–La Habra Playhouse (starring Ricki Lake)

Let's suppose that the (entirely fictitious) *Robert's Last Letters* was a smash Off-Broadway hit last season at the (real and prestigious) New World Stages, directed by the (real and award-winning) Marshall Pailet. Bryce got great notices for playing Jordan. Since it's his only Off-Broadway credit, it won't get its own section, but he'll list it at the top.

Next, the biggest standouts are the venues—namely, the Muny and Papermill Playhouse. Nothing carries more weight than those, so they go next. In *Rent*, he played the lead; in *Legally Blonde*, he was ensemble and an understudy—so *Rent* goes higher. Even though the (fictitious) Sarah Jenkins is a rising director, her name doesn't elevate the credit.

Then comes the (real) La Mirada Theatre, paired with a solid role—Motel in *Fiddler on the Roof*—which beats being a swing in *Sheer Madness*, even if Ricki Lake was a guest star (we love you, Ricki).

Tethered (fictitious) is a credit Bryce debated cutting, but "world premiere" and Theatre Atlanta help show range. The show only ran one weekend and was a disaster, but it adds just enough to stay—at the bottom.

The final three credits are from Bryce's time as a BFA musical theatre major at Point Park University. Since the shows are well known, he lists the roles over ensemble tracks. Even though he did *Superstar* his senior year and *Spring Awakening* sophomore year, timeline doesn't matter here.

Finally, *And So It Goes by the Wayside* (and its mystery venue, Jones Auditorium) carries no real weight. It could be real or totally made up. Either way, it adds nothing his other credits don't—so it goes by the wayside.

Off-Broadway/Regional Theatre

Robert's Last Letters	Jordan*	New World Stages (D. Marshall Pailet)
Rent	Roger	Papermill Playhouse
Legally Blonde	Ensemble/Emmett u/s	The Muny (D. Sarah Jenkins)
Fiddler on the Roof	Motel	La Mirada Theatre (D. Rick Sanchez)
Sheer Madness	swing	La Habra Playhouse (starring Ricki Lake)
Tethered	Jim	Theatre Atlanta (World premiere)

Educational Theatre

Spring Awakening	Moritz	Point Park University
Jesus Christ Superstar	ensemble	Point Park University

*Theatre World Award Nomination

High school credits

Most high school credits don't belong on a professional résumé—but not just because they're from high school. Teens book real work, too.

The issue is that high school roles are often misaligned with your age (a sixteen-year-old Baker's Wife), gender (a cis girl playing Nathan Detroit), ethnicity (don't get us started on mostly white schools doing *Once on This Island*), or brand (you're an Ariel who got cast as Ursula). These credits might be fun memories, but they're not résumé material.

That said, some high schoolers *do* play roles they'll soon be ready to do professionally. We see little difference between Hodel in *Fiddler* as a high school senior and as a college sophomore—just tweak "Franklin High School Auditorium" to "Franklin Auditorium." Where's the lie?

Auditions

When first navigating the world of auditions, casting, and contracts, the sheer amount of information is overwhelming. We'll cover the most important elements here, but our focus in this chapter is on audition navigation and strategy, including:

- Key insights into Actor's Equity Association, including when (and when not) to join
- Types of contracts and opportunities
- Where to find and how to understand audition breakdowns
- The timeline of the audition day and the callback process
- The confusing world of self-tapes
- Tools for combating audition anxiety

UNDERSTANDING EQUITY

To understand the landscape of professional auditions, we have to start with the actor's union. Actor's Equity Association—AEA, or simply "Equity"—has protected performers and stage managers for over a century.

All Broadway theatres hire exclusively Equity actors. Most major tours, Off-Broadway shows, and top regional theatres do as well, though some include occasional non-Equity contracts. The rest of US theatres vary, with a mix of union and nonunion work. Some venues—like theme parks, arena shows, and certain tours—are entirely non-Equity, and many cruise ships fall outside Equity's jurisdiction, though some operate under union agreements.

We know—it's complicated.

In general, Equity shows pay more, operate on a bigger budget, and employ more experienced actors working in more competitive environments. Still, with the rise of strong non-Equity tours using Broadway sets, costumes, and orchestrations, audiences often can't tell the difference—hence the "Ask if it's Equity" movement.

Benefits of Equity membership

As a labor union, Equity requires that producers agree to payment minimums, overtime compensation, pension, and more. The union provides legal advice, career coaching, and "muscle" when an actor is mistreated by their employer. Working actors enroll in union health insurance based on the number of "health weeks" they accrue on Equity contracts.

At auditions for union shows, Equity actors get seen before nonunion actors (who may never be seen, even after waiting all day) and can even sign up for an audition time. Because of the ease with which Equity actors are seen compared to the rest, many early-career actors feel that this is the most important benefit of joining the union.

Joining Equity

Since AEA instituted the Open Access program in 2021, any actor can join Equity after participating in one or more professional (paid) productions.

For any actor joining Equity, the initiation fee is currently $2,200, payable over three years. This is almost always paid by the actor, but occasionally a producer covers the fee while promoting the actor to the union. After that, actors pay about $100 in union dues every six months, plus 2.5 percent of every paycheck.

Of note, Equity actors are forbidden to work in theatre outside the union. Working in film, television, radio, and voice-over falls under a separate (sister) union, SAG-AFTRA.

Being non-Equity

Many actors accrue a solid handful of nonunion credits to build their résumé, experience, and skill before joining the union. Whether they consider it a rite of passage or a period of paying their dues, their time being "non-Eq" is a wild and wonderful start to their career.

While we'd like to believe every employer treats their team fairly, many don't—especially without a union holding them accountable. Producers and creative teams can exploit nonunion actors: asking for unpaid overtime, offering few breaks, not covering injuries, assigning unsafe tasks, or creating toxic environments. Actors often feel stuck in these productions: either endure it or quit. Taking legal action is rare due to the time, cost, and fear of retaliation.

Producers are also allowed—and expected—to pay nonunion actors significantly less than union actors doing the same job. If a producer hires only nonunion talent, it often signals a desire to avoid union policies and pay lower rates, regardless of ticket prices, which are often the same. Not great!

Nonunion tours are often grueling, with back-to-back one-night stops and little rest. While touring is tough for everyone, union contracts ensure guaranteed breaks and regulated travel.

Still, many actors build solid careers as non-Equity performers, believing they'll book more consistently outside the union—for now. Usually they plan to join later, but see this as the best strategy in the short term.

WHEN TO JOIN EQUITY

With Equity's Open Access program, joining Equity is no longer out of your control. Today, it's a decision you can make for yourself . . . when the time is right. But:

> ***Staying non-Equity too long means* working at an unlivable wage . . .**
> ***but joining Equity too soon can* stall an otherwise advancing career.**

To remain competitive at the union level, you need both the training *and* the credits to support an established career.

> ***Join the union when your considerable skill meets your considerable experience.***

The wrong reason to join the union

The most common rationale we hear to join the union too early comes from actors who struggle to be seen at Equity auditions. "At this rate, I'll never be on Broadway," they say. "If I join Equity now, I'll get seen—and I know if I can just get seen, I'll get cast."

> ***Joining the union because you can't get seen at major auditions* is a professionally hazardous *reason to join the union.***

Guilty actors raise their bar too early—refusing low-paying or unpaid gigs, skipping nonunion calls, and only aiming for shows their mom has heard of. They grow impatient waiting for their Broadway dream to materialize. It's one of the most common mistakes an actor can make.

When your résumé is starved for professional credits, it's crucial to pursue work that matches where you are. If unpaid work is what's available at the start, take it. Then gradually raise your bar—first aiming for low-paying gigs, then increasing your minimum rate as you gain traction. Note what you're offered, try everything once, and use each experience to guide your next step.

The perks of being nonunion

While you're non-Equity, take full advantage of the benefits of remaining nonunion:

- The talent pool is less competitive.
- You stand a greater chance of booking leading roles.
- You meet hungry creative team members who will rise with you.
- Some performers have little training or training they don't know how to use. If you put into practice our advice (especially in part one), you will immediately rise to the top, so finding work will be—for you—easier.

There's another advantage for younger actors who read older. If you're twenty-six but could pass for thirty-six, you're in high demand to fill mature roles in non-Equity productions since most older actors will have already joined the union. This is why so many twenty-somethings play thirties (and even forties) in non-Equity productions. Casting understands that you're not marketing yourself decades older, but rather making the non-Equity system work for you.

Join Equity when your résumé is stacked . . .

Once you've gotten everything you can from nonunion life, it's time to make the switch.

Another way to think about it is that if you could snag a non-Equity job without breaking a sweat (because, perhaps, you have a relationship with a theatre, or a director is often excited to cast you), it's time to upgrade your status.

. . . Or when you have nothing to lose

Another (sort of grim) reason to join Equity is because you've stopped seeing traction as a nonunion actor. That is, you attend all the nonunion calls but rarely book, you're receiving none of the benefits of being nonunion, and you think that if things don't change soon, you'll probably quit the biz altogether. In this dire circumstance, you've got nothing to lose by joining Equity since being nonunion isn't serving you.

AUDITION BASICS

Let's break down the kinds of auditions out there.

Non-Equity open call

At a nonunion open call, anyone can show up. There's little consistency to the process of seeing actors without union oversight, and many would describe the process as "chaotic." Some calls are better organized than others, and most who show up are seen if there's time.

Equity Principal Audition (EPA)

Every Equity production is required to do an EPA, specifically looking for actors to fill leading roles. Long-running shows are required to hold EPAs every six months—even if there are no open roles.

You sign up on the Equity website once auditions go live—usually at noon several days before. Each twenty-minute slot allows four or five actors to sign up. The breakdown tells you what to sing.

These calls are the most competitive. Equity actors who didn't reserve a slot can show up on the day, and they'll be seen if there's space (there usually is). If, after all Equity actors have been seen, there's still time to spare (there usually isn't), casting will see non-Equity actors—but much of the time, nonunion actors who show up wait for hours and hours only to be turned away.

Equity Chorus Call (ECC): Singers and dancers

Also required by Equity, these calls are for ensemble tracks. ECCs are almost always separated into singers (who sing from their book) and dancers (who learn a group combination). These calls are frequently gendered.

If an actor moves forward, they'll be called back to sing if they danced, or to dance if they sang. Note that actors who attend ECCs can be called back for principal tracks, and some use the ECC as a clever way to skirt the crowd at an EPA.

Appointments

At an appointment, casting requests to see specific actors they think might fit their show. Usually, you're given material from the show but bring your book just in case.

These are considered more "serious" auditions because they aren't mandated by Equity. They're given out directly by casting either to actors they're familiar with or following an agent submission. If casting allows it, you can submit yourself.

Self-tapes / Online submissions

A self-tape is a step beyond an open call but one behind an in-person appointment. When casting requests a self-tape, you submit material (either from your book or from the show) on video to the casting team.

An "Eco Cast" is a self-tape requested through Actors Access (more on that in a moment). A live Eco Cast is a real-time audition (usually for television and film).

WHAT YOU MAY BE ASKED FOR AT AN INITIAL AUDITION

Casting specifies what they need to see from you, which could include:

- **Thirty-two bars (sixty seconds) or sixteen bars (thirty seconds)** from your book in a specific genre.
- **Eight bars (fifteen seconds)** for large open calls where casting wants to meet a lot of people quickly. Think of this as a rapid "swipe right," "swipe left."
- **A monologue** for plays. They'll usually specify if the monologue should be comedic or dramatic, classic or contemporary. Actors who frequently audition for plays should have four monologues: comedic classic, comedic contemporary, dramatic classic, and dramatic contemporary. Though rare for musical theatre auditions, it's better to be safe than sorry.
- **An audition packet** with character-specific scenes or songs at an appointment or callback ("sides"). Some EPAs for plays will allow you to choose sides for a character of your choosing in lieu of a monologue.
- **A song on which you can accompany yourself** to see how well you play an instrument. They can specify the instrument (usually guitar or piano) or leave it up to you. Don't accompany yourself unless they ask you to. If you're able to choose your own song, it's better to nail something easier than try to impress with something more advanced. You'll be more nervous than you think!
- **Singing a cappella,** because an accompanist isn't provided. Some major open calls rush actors in for eight bars a cappella. Otherwise, if a longer cut is requested a cappella, it suggests the team couldn't afford an accompanist—and we're left to wonder what

else the team can't afford. Choose a tune without modulations or key changes and use a piano app to get your starting pitch.

- **Something unusual.** When Lindsay auditioned for the Broadway revival of *Godspell*, she was asked to prepare a parable from the Bible as performance art. The good news is that if they're asking for something that most actors don't already have prepared, only the most interested will audition. If the ask is "up your alley," this is the call for you.

When you're called back from your initial audition, you're given **callback sides**, material from the show that includes a song (or several songs) and a scene (or several scenes). Callback sides can be daunting, but they'll often include a "plunk" of the melody and a track to learn new material. At your callback, you might not show everything they gave you—but be prepared anyway.

KINDS OF CONTRACTS

Audition breakdowns outline the contract offered upfront, including:

- Pay
- Rehearsal timeline
- Production run
- If applicable: housing, travel, and per diem included

Here's what you need to know about the most common contracts. Note that the industry is constantly changing rules and rates, but this is accurate as of this book's printing.

Production contracts

All actors performing in the forty-one Broadway theatres must be members of AEA. If someone is hired who isn't, they must join the union.*

* There are complicated exceptions to this, but if a Broadway actor doesn't join the union, they have to pay the union from their paycheck anyway.

Actor contracts are divided into "pink contracts" for ensemble members and "white contracts" for principals.

Chorus contracts start at the base minimum required by Equity and are almost always open-ended for the duration of the production, whether that's two months or twenty years. Pay increases if you fulfill other duties like understudying, swinging, or dance captaining. Ensemble members are usually required to sign on for a six-month or one-year commitment, but afterward they have a four-week "out" to leave the contract whenever.

Principal contracts start at a higher rate. For original casts, they too are locked in for a year. For long-running shows, replacements are usually offered a nine-month term, after which the producer can offer an extension.

Off-Broadway contracts

While many shows in Manhattan that aren't on Broadway call themselves "Off-Broadway," a production with the *official* "Off-Broadway contract" is governed by Equity and features exclusively Equity actors. Minimums vary based on house size, starting at about $600 and rising just past $1,000 per week.

Other theatres in New York City not using the Off-Broadway contract can employ nonunion actors and pay significantly less.

Off-Off-Broadway contracts and showcase code agreements

Still other New York City theatres work with Equity on a "showcase code" production, which allows them a mix of union and nonunion actors. For these, the cash is limited—basically a couple of bucks and a Snickers—but enough to offset a performer's participation cost (travel, etc.). Actors take these contracts to build their résumés or work on a piece they hope will progress from this lower tier to a bigger production.

Major tours (Equity and non-Equity)

Equity tours are contracted on levels going from one through seven. The highest level (one) pays close to Broadway minimum. Lower levels pay a base fee (going incrementally downward from Broadway chorus minimum) and incentivize additional compensation depending on how well the show sells in each city ("overages").

Non-Equity tours make their own ungoverned agreements. High-level nonunion tours can pay comparably to a lower-tiered Equity contract, but they lack union protection.

Work sessions

Development opportunities beyond readings are called "work sessions"—previously called "labs" and "workshops"—and their compensation can vary. They start around $600 a week and rise to over $1,000 at the top, but give union actors health weeks to maintain their insurance.

In days past, actors were offered the right of refusal (or they had to be bought out by the producer for a large sum), but no longer. Today, actors receive a tiny percentage share (called a "point") in the overall profit of the show—after it recoups its initial investment, which most do not.

Nonunion development agreements are paid nominally and can be too time-intensive for experienced actors to take on (working out to well below minimum wage), but are fantastic for those looking for experience and to build their résumé.

Regional contracts

The League of Resident Theatres (LORT) governs most major regional theatres, like the Fifth Avenue Theatre in Seattle, the Old Globe and La Jolla Playhouse in San Diego, the Guthrie in Minneapolis, and the Goodman in Chicago. Theatres are categorized by letter, from D to A+ (which is the highest), based on seating capacity and gross box office receipts.

These theatres have agreements with Equity for a certain number of union contracts, with the rest hired nonunion. Smaller regional theatres may work on smaller union agreements or none at all.

Summer stocks

The term "summer stock theatre" covers a wide range. Some, like the Muny, Theatre Under the Stars, and the Hollywood Bowl, are technically summer stocks but operate more like major regional theatres. Rehearsal periods can be brief, but contracts are often lucrative. Though the pressure is high, the pay and prestige make these gigs appealing to both new actors and seasoned pros.

At smaller summer stocks, actors may rehearse one show during the day and perform another at night—or rotate productions in rep: *Carousel* on Tuesday, *Rocky Horror* on Wednesday, *The Full Monty* on Thursday. Pay is usually very modest, but early-career actors take these jobs to build résumés and make connections. Housing can be rustic, like adult summer camp, and most performers are nonunion.

Some dinner theatres and Theatre for Young Audiences (TYA) follow similar models. For touring TYA shows, nonunion actors may also be responsible for driving, setup, and teardown.

OTHER KINDS OF CONTRACTS

Here are a few other types of contracts worth knowing:

> **Industrials** are musicals created for corporate events or conventions (a bank's holiday party, an investor meeting, etc.). The pay is often shockingly high for a fast-paced rehearsal process leading to a single performance. Creative teams typically cast by direct offer, without holding auditions.
>
> **Cruise ship contracts** pay well and include room, board, and a built-in international artist community. The schedule can be intense—multiple daily performances plus ship duties—with few true days off. Some

actors find the experience life-changing, but others struggle with isolation. Ship rules can be strict, but many return home with strong savings. Auditions resemble traditional stage calls and often ask for radio songs.

Disney World has an Equity agreement. Base pay is just above Florida's minimum wage, but stunts, features, and long-term contracts increase earnings—along with paid time off and great health benefits. Rehearsals are short (about a week), with frequent, short performances six days a week.

Disneyland and **Universal Studios Hollywood** operate under the American Guild of Variety Artists (AGVA). Other theme parks, while non-Equity, offer similar terms to stay competitive.

Twenty-nine-hour readings under Equity limit actors to (you guessed it) twenty-nine total hours, including performance(s). Producers are only required to cover a performer's travel expenses—typically between $100 and $500. Nonunion actors may receive less (or nothing), and there are no hourly restrictions. Auditions are rare, with the team making direct offers to dependable colleagues.

Concerts and non-cast recordings often skip contracts and auditions. Payment is typically outlined via email or text (which—don't forget—is legally binding). Always confirm the amount of time needed and the payment terms *before* agreeing to the job. If you're building your network, low or no pay may be fine. Just know what you're agreeing to upfront.

WHERE TO FIND AUDITIONS

There are several places to find audition opportunities.

Playbill.com is the most widely used site for finding EPAs, ECCs, and other open calls. These auditions are usually packed. Some listings request headshots, résumés, or video submissions. However, exclusive or invite-only auditions rarely appear here, and many Equity calls listed are mandatory—meaning they're not actively casting.

ActorsAccess.com is currently the most robust platform for serious audition opportunities. Unlike Playbill, producers aren't required to post EPAs or ECCs here—so if they do, it usually means they're actively casting. The site separates agent and performer accounts. Agents receive exclusive breakdowns for their clients, while performers create profiles to submit directly to public breakdowns. Creating a profile is free, but uploading video clips costs a one-time fee (currently $22 per minute). Submitting to a breakdown also costs a small fee unless you have an annual subscription. Many actors link the same videos from their personal website to their Actors Access profile. If casting is interested, they'll reach out for an in-person appointment or request an Eco Cast.

Backstage.com also posts casting notices but places them behind a paywall. Most listings can also be found for free on Playbill or Actors Access.

Individual theatre websites occasionally post audition notices in the months leading up to a production—worth checking if you're eager to work at a specific venue.

CLIMBING THE AUDITION LADDER

When you first arrive in a big city, conventional wisdom says you should go to every audition you can and get your feet wet. If, after a year or so, this doesn't yield results, many actors burn out. Soon they think, "Why bother?"—until months or even years pass without going to an audition, and . . . well, you know the rest.

To avoid this, you must choose your auditions strategically by understanding how the casting ladder works.

Work begets work

At any given moment, all artists exist on a ladder of accomplishment that informs both the work they pursue and the money they can demand. At the bottom of the ladder are the beginners just starting out. At the top, experienced veterans climb the ladder until it disappears into the heavens. With every achievement, the artist climbs another rung. Setbacks and dry spells lower them down.

Right now, you exist somewhere on this ladder based on your résumé, reputation, and demonstrable skill. While a tiny, rare few fly upward with one big break, the vast majority of artists climb one or two rungs at a time, season after season. Being aware about where you're at in your career means simultaneously knowing your worth *and* being flexible to take work as it comes—even if it means momentarily stepping down to lower rungs (to get a better grip, let's say).

Lindsay's climb

Lindsay began her career in New York City close to the bottom of the ladder.

Her first major gig was a German tour of *Grease*, where the scenes were in German and songs were in English (climb up one rung). The pay was fine for a first gig and the experience had its highs and lows,* but it helped set her up for her next major gig in the Broadway revival of *Grease*.† By twenty-four, she had raised her "stock" considerably (climb five rungs).

After her Broadway debut, she pivoted Off-Broadway as a replacement in *The Marvelous Wonderettes* (if you're keeping score, that's four straight years stuck in the 1950s and '60s—descend one rung). During this time, she focused on collaborating with emerging writers, singing in their concerts for free. Some days she worried she was just spinning her wheels, but she knew building relationships was key to moving forward.

Her growing reputation helped land her next Broadway contracts: first as a backup singer for Sherie Rene Scott in *Everyday Rapture* (thanks to a

---

* *You* try getting four emergency root canals from a German dentist.

† Actually, it almost derailed her booking *Grease* on Broadway. They were looking for "fresh eyes on the material," so she actually took the tour *off* her résumé.

recommendation from her friend Sierra Boggess), then in *Godspell* (though she was second choice). Meanwhile, her work with new writers hit a high when she played Woman 2 in RSO's *35mm: A Musical Exhibition*. "Bless the Lord" in the former and "The Ballad of Sara Berry" in the latter made Lindsay a fan favorite. She'd upped her street cred (climb three rungs).

With two supporting Broadway roles behind her, it was time to lead. That opportunity came Off-Broadway with *Dogfight* (climb two rungs), which earned her industry-wide recognition and set her up to lead *Wicked*'s tenth anniversary cast (climb two more).

But it's hard to move laterally from Elphaba. Lindsay doubled down on proving herself as a serious actor, returning Off-Broadway in a supporting role in *Significant Other*. After that, she joined Broadway's *Nerds*—only for it to be canceled in rehearsals (one rung down).

It took over a year for *Significant Other* to transfer to Broadway, and Lindsay felt her momentum stall (some rungs down, some up). Auditioning for Carrie Pipperidge in the 2018 *Carousel* revival, she hoped to shift the narrative and prove she wasn't "just" a belter—but she didn't book it (one rung down). Months later, the original actress dropped out. After a tough audition process, Lindsay got the part (climb one rung)—and won a Tony (climb ten more).

With her Tony still warm, it was time to tackle film and TV. But the ladder was new, and the high rung she'd reached in theatre didn't translate as well as she hoped in Hollywood. For six months, she struggled to gain traction (two rungs down). Then came a supporting role on the network series *All Rise* (climb five)—which quickly hit the pandemic and was canceled twice (three rungs down). Anxious to return to her roots, she joined the acclaimed revival of *Merrily We Roll Along* alongside Daniel Radcliffe and Jonathan Groff, earning her second Tony nomination (six rungs up).

And so, her climb continues. Some years up, some down—but Lindsay never loses sight of where she is.

To outsiders, it may look like a smooth leap from rung to rung. But Lindsay started nonunion, uncredited, agentless, and alone—like every actor starts—and climbed patiently, one step at a time.

AUDITION STRATEGY FOR NONUNION ACTORS

The best strategy for nonunion performers is to focus on accruing credits and building relationships with casting and creatives.

Gather roles in nonunion theatre

Your number one priority is to pursue nonunion productions both regionally and outside of Broadway. These are the easiest to snag ("easiest" is a relative term here) and will help you build the credits you need to climb ahead.

A good rule of thumb is to do everything at least once—twice, if it's fun. Do your best to climb upward when you can, but if time passes and the best move is returning to a similar gig or *even* stepping backward, trust your gut and stay open to whatever comes.

Get your name (and face) out there

Connect with writers, directors, and emerging producers by getting involved in nonunion readings and concerts. If the relationships feel genuine and you (mostly) enjoy the work, these can be excellent opportunities.

Be bold about introducing yourself—to those ahead of you and those coming up behind. Share your website and socials the way people once handed out business cards. Don't fear being "too much" or "that girl." In fact, *be* that girl—the one who knows the rising talent and becomes one herself. Just be sure to follow the tips in the netwerqing chapter!

Go to concerts featuring new talent like you and stick around after. Engage with others' work on social media. Offer your help often—and get people familiar with what you bring to the table.

Create your own opportunities and crow about your work shamelessly. If it's your thing, utilize social media by posting work you're proud of: performances, comedy, clever thoughts on life, or just singing around your apartment. If people respond, listen.

The point here is that you want people to hear about and see you as often as possible. Don't worry about wearing out your welcome through overexposure. It's a miracle to be seen once. If they see you a second, third, fifth, or tenth time, it's probably because you travel in the same circles or because the algorithm senses they want to.

It's not about the money (yet)

During this time, it's normal not to make your full living doing theatre. Whether you're moonlighting in a survival job or building up your Hustle, most of your income will be outside of the contracts you book.

Introduce yourself at EPAs and ECCs

Attend EPAs and ECCs to understand how they work, but don't take rejection at these open calls seriously (whether you're not seen or don't get a callback). The point is to meet casting. If you *do* get seen, most casting directors don't care whether or not you're Equity—they're interested in every audition equally.

Still, expect that most of these jobs will go to Equity performers with more credits (as you will expect for yourself when *you* are Equity). If you can get your big break as a nonunion performer, congratulations! But if that isn't your journey, once you're satisfied you've met enough casting teams through these calls, deprioritize EPAs and ECCs and double down on nonunion auditions.

This isn't the time to be picky

Most early-career actors are too selective about the auditions they attend—especially as the years pass and the city wears them down. They focus on major, well-paying productions where they're unlikely to be seen (perhaps both literally and spiritually), or they've raised their minimum standards for work without yet building the résumé to justify them.

It's not that they're delusional—they often know how tough it will be to land those big jobs. But instead of going after work they're more likely to book, they chase long shots and overlook realistic opportunities. Like Buddy in *Follies*, they want what they can't have and ignore what's right in front of them.

We get it. Everyone wants to protect their time. Like Cathy in *The Last Five Years*, after a summer in Ohio, no one's eager to return. But until a bigger market calls, your résumé may still need a little more Ohio before New York is ready for you.

In your first few years, every audition is a win. Staying home is almost always a loss—even if you're not right for *this* show, casting may remember you for the next one.

AUDITION STRATEGY FOR EQUITY ACTORS

Once the time is right to join the actor's union, your strategy changes.

Take stock of where you're at in (this new, exciting) line

At this stage (newly Equity and still building your résumé), remember that you're arriving late to someone else's party when it comes to major "big box" musicals—like *Wicked* and *Hamilton*—or those newly licensed for large regional markets. For years, someone just like you has already made it to final callbacks for Elphaba multiple times, and she's more top-of-mind to casting than you are. At this level, seniority matters—and one day, you'll want it to matter for you. It doesn't mean that casting is operating with a "she was here first, so it's only fair" mentality—rather, they've built a kind of trust with an actor they've seen five times, versus a new one they're only just meeting. So if you're choosing between a *Wicked* EPA and a singers' call for a regional *Oklahoma!*, the latter is more likely your next step up the, well, ladder.

This still (probably) isn't the time to be (too) picky

Union performers can be just as hyper-selective as those who are nonunion. Some will only go to auditions for familiar roles in major titles, reasoning their bright line is "If booking this contract wouldn't make my roommate a little jealous, it's not worth it."

Go to auditions for shows you've never heard of. Equity will protect your bottom line, so keep your mind open to new works and opportunities that may simply be gaining health insurance weeks and another line on your résumé. And above all, don't predetermine whether doing a show is worth it until you've *actually* booked the show.

Casting directors: Collect them all

A good tip as you decide which Equity auditions to attend is to prioritize casting teams less familiar with you. The goal is that, after seeing your work at six or seven open calls, they get to know what you do and will call you in for an appointment (skipping the EPA), solidifying your "relationship" with them.

If you've met a casting director more than seven times and have yet to get an appointment through them, it's possible that they aren't responding to your work. If you're faced with two auditions and one is with a seemingly disinterested casting director and another is with one you don't know well, attend the second.

And until you've booked a few Equity principals, don't sleep on the ECCs. Sometimes attending an ECC over an EPA may be to your advantage. Don't forget that you can be called back for a principal through an ECC.

The netwerqing never ends

Similarly, continue fostering relationships with writers and music directors in concerts and directors in AEA readings. If you know someone on a creative team at an audition you're attending later in the day, it's totally appropriate to contact them (email, direct message, or text if you have their number) to let them know you're "excited to sing for them today."

WHAT THEY WANT YOU TO KNOW

There's a lot that the folks behind the table wish you knew.

What casting wants you to know

Casting is on your side. They want you to perform well, showing how confident, prepared, and grounded you are in your material. They want you to care, but not so much that this audition feels make-or-break. They're hoping to see how *you* see yourself fitting into *their* cast.

Sometimes they may seem distracted. It's not personal—they could be reading your résumé, taking notes, or texting with an absent team member. Occasionally, they may be ordering lunch or messaging their spouse. If they've checked out, it likely means they've already seen what they need. You won't know why, and it's not your job to figure it out. Your job is to tell the story you've prepared for today, professionally and expertly.

Remember, casting isn't watching you like they're in the audience of a theatre; they're working. They may cut you off early, either because they want to see more or know you're not right for this gig. Warm goodbyes can mean nothing, and cold ones might lead to a callback. Don't read into it—and don't take it personally.

What directors want you to know

Directors are trying to solve a puzzle. They have ideas about what they're looking for, but aren't set on anything in particular. Otherwise, they wouldn't be attending the audition.

Don't do their jobs for them. Regardless of how it was cast on Broadway, how this director cast it last time, or who else you see auditioning, you can't be sure of what they want—because *they* aren't precisely sure of what they want. (If they were, they would have made an offer.) Use the breakdown and your best judgment.

Be open to their direction and willing to try a different take, demonstrating options and ideas. It's easier to tell someone to pull back than to push them to give more, so show them what they're working with from the get.

Some of it's just a vibe test. The director will be spending weeks or more with you and the rest of the cast. Beyond your skill and preparation, they're looking for warmth, imagination, perspective, a sense of humor, and a willingness to collaborate.

What writers want you to know

Writers play a unique role in casting, often as a minority voice in the final decision. When involved, they're presenting new work to strangers on both sides of the table—and understandably feel self-conscious about how it's received. They hope every actor walks in and delivers their vision perfectly. The bad news? You don't know what that vision is. The good news? That means all you *can* be is yourself.

If you're working with sides, aim for accuracy. Writers have spent a lot of time getting to this draft—so read the lines as written and sing the notes on the page. Show you understand the genre and demonstrate the musicality you bring to the table.

If possible, read the full script in advance. Asking a thoughtful question or two shows curiosity and helps them see how well you "get" the material—which is useful if they're still writing or revising around the actors.

THE INITIAL AUDITION PROCESS

Understanding the audition schedule helps you manage your time before and after.

Wear "you at your everyday best"

Approach audition attire the same way you approached your headshots, wearing something suitable for a low-key first date or a high-key night out with friends.

If you're into this kind of thing, you can subtly choose clothing that suggests the time period or role you're after. For example, if you're auditioning for *Hair*, a contemporary '70s throwback could be a nice touch. If you want Orin Scrivello in *Little Shop of Horrors*, you might bring out that leather jacket you love. Coming in for *A Gentleman's Guide to Love and Murder?* A dress is more useful than jeans.

Never wear anything that feels like a costume. Don't go in for Evan Hansen in a blue striped polo, or to a *Wicked* open call in Elphaba green or Glinda pink.

Arriving: Monitors

All Equity open calls are required to have a monitor to receive you on arrival, check your Equity card, confirm your appointment time, or let you know when (or if) you may be seen. The monitor handles traffic between the actors waiting their turn and the casting team. Some nonunion calls will have a monitor, but they don't have to.

For appointments and callbacks, there likely won't be a monitor and the ins and outs are handled by the casting director or their associate.

Holding rooms

Most open calls provide a holding room for actors to wait in and leave their belongings—but not all. If they don't, take your things into the audition room and gently place them by the door to grab as you exit.

Share the space. Don't warm up loudly (a lip trill or light hum is okay) or practice your material full-out. You need to get into the right headspace, so if you want to be left alone, wear headphones, review your material, or read a book.

How to make the most of the day if you aren't seen

As you wait to be seen, bring a book you love, learn something new, work on your Hustle, or enjoy a hobby. If casting decides there isn't time to see you, making sure you've done something with your day dulls the annoyance of wasted time.

After the holding room

As your number draws near, you'll take your place in a line leading to the audition-room door. This is the time to focus on what you're about to do, calm your nerves, and remind yourself of your story—especially the moment before, your location, and the person to whom you're singing. If you've been gabbing with someone else in line, this is the time (for everyone) to get centered.

TROUBLESHOOTING WHAT TO SING

No matter how many times they've been advised what to put into their book, some actors still get stumped on what to sing at an audition. Usually, though, the answer is clearer than they think.

- **Follow directions.** Bring in whatever the breakdown asks for. If they ask for a folk song, bring in a folk song. If they ask for a Sondheim song, it's a Sondheim song. If they ask for a song that "shows range," show your range. Don't surprise them with something else that suggests you know better.
- **If you can't follow the directions** because the directions are unusually specific—asking for, say, a disco song, or a song by Michael John LaChiusa—you can take a risk and learn something last minute. In this (annoying) case it might be okay, because you probably won't be the only one. Alternatively, you can tactfully sidestep the directions with whatever you have that is closest. You also might consider that if they're asking for a certain style you don't already have, it could be a hint that this audition isn't for you, as those who've invested in the style—niche as it may be—already have an advantage.

- **Always start with an up-tempo over a ballad (if you have a choice).** What a weird feeling of déjà vu—it's like we've said that a few times before . . . Anyway, we mean it.
- **Don't learn a brand-new song for *one* character in the cast.** The song you have in the genre specified will already point your voice and energy to the character you fit in the show (and if it doesn't, you may have chosen the wrong song for your book). You *never* need a song specifically for *one* character. If you feel you're a Fantine in *Les Misérables*, your contemporary legit song shouldn't be soprano and point to Cosette. If you're a soprano everywhere else, but Fantine is the only place you're high belting in the genre, a "Fantine song" will only confuse you and the casting office, who is trying to understand who you are outside of this one audition.
- **When you're confused about "the style of the show,"** do more research. Sometimes it appears in the title's subheading (*Hair: The American Tribal Love-Rock Musical*). If it doesn't, scour press and reviews about the show to learn how the score is described. Shows can live between styles, so if the team has been vague, sing your preference. Also:
  - Radio music isn't contemporary musical theatre and vice versa. Don't confuse them.
  - Rock and pop are technically different, and most rock scores will require more edge than a typical pop score. But if your radio up-tempo is solidly pop and you don't have a harder rock song, it's probably okay to sing.
  - Check the time period the show is set in. Is the score meant to sound authentic to the early twentieth century (which defines it as classic)? Does it sound kind of vaguely legit while not being totally authentic to a past time and place (which probably makes it contemporary legit)? Does it sound original, yet mimics the radio music of the last fifty years (which probably makes it contemporary musical theatre)?

By paying close attention to the breakdown, relying on the brilliant material in your book, and using critical thinking, you can solve any "what should I sing?" dilemma. If you're still stumped, others will probably be, too. When in doubt, sing something you love and let the chips fall.

DO THE ASSIGNMENT, NOT EXTRA CREDIT

If your high school English teacher asked for a critical analysis of Poe's "The Tell-Tale Heart," you wouldn't turn in a paper titled "Poe's Influence on Stephen King," right? Yet every day, talented actors do the equivalent in auditions—ignoring the assignment in favor of extra credit. They veer off course, showing something that wasn't asked for that leaves casting confused or, worse, put off.

They're not trying to be difficult—they just assume the basics are obvious. "*Of course* I can sing a thirty-two-bar cut in the style of the show! But did you know I can screlt a B-flat and riff down?" They fear the material we recommended in part one won't be "enough" to show off their talent. So they sing higher, riff harder, push more—and sabotage themselves. As cool as it looks, doing tricks on a motorcycle doesn't pass a driving test.

When casting doesn't know you (and at an open call, they probably don't), they've never heard you sing, seen you act, or spent time with you. They don't know if you're kind, professional, or capable of doing what they've asked. You have to show all that *first—before* you show them everything else you can do.

The assignment is simple

Bring a well-cut song (almost always an up-tempo "nice-to-meet you" song) in the requested style. Tell a clear story, show your technique, and let your voice sit in its sweet spot. Be warm on your entrance, kind to the room, and leave with confidence. If you're fun and intriguing, they'll see it—either in your song or the way you carry yourself.

Skipping the assignment suggests you think you know better than the team. That's an automatic "no" and raises the bar for your next audition.

Some of us have extremely exuberant personalities. We've been told we're a little bit "extra," and because we can do more, we think we *should*. Isn't musical theatre about "giving it all you've got"? But growth means learning your own strength. Some learn to turn it up; others learn to turn it down.

If someone asks you to "dial it back," listen. They're not trying to dim your fire. You wouldn't shout in a library, show up naked to temple, or sit on a stranger's lap on the subway—no matter how expressive, confident, or fun you are. Every space has limits. The creative team is already taking up most of it. Your job is to fill what's left—no less, and no more. The good news? That's still a lot of space.

......

You're prepared now to step into the room and audition—which we covered thoroughly in part one. But what happens after?

CALLBACKS

If you're called back for a show, casting will give you sides for the role (or roles) they're considering you for. Sometimes they'll give you the callback before you leave the room. Other times the callback will come that night, next week, or even months later as casting evolves.

Sides can be extensive, but casting is expecting you to be familiar with whatever they give you when they see you next. Even if they tell you to focus on one part of the side or another, learn everything if you can.

Learn (and, if possible, coach) the material

If the casting team has sent you the full script, read the show completely—because others will. If it's a well-known show and there's a video or cast recording, watch and listen. You're not there to recreate someone else's performance, but getting familiar with the show is informative.

If casting specifies that they'd like to hear a certain dialect, it's wise to pay for coaching if you're not already a pro.

Speaking of coaching: If you have the time and resources, coach both songs and scenes with someone knowledgeable who can guide you through the material, scope out your interpretation, and offer feedback. When you're starting out, it's better to use every resource you have.

You will probably sing first

When you're given both songs and scenes, casting will usually have you sing first (unless the scene leads into the song). This is a bit of trickery, because directors and their associates tend to get attached to actors if they see their scene work first . . . and make excuses if their vocal performance is lacking. If they first see that the actor is unable to sing the part, it simplifies the decision. (So if you're given the option, you could use this to your advantage and suggest doing the scenes first.)

Have a "take"

One of the most important things to bring to the callback is a strong idea for the character, or a "take." Forget about what you *think* they want or what it "should be." Once you've gotten to know the show and callback material, focus instead on *your version* of the character. Deliver the essentials given by the text but discover what only you could bring to the story.

Most directors appreciate an actor who brings a sense of play to their callback, so get creative. Even if it doesn't work, it will show them you're a resource of imagination.

Memorize the sides, but hold the paper

At an initial callback, get as close to memorized as you can *but* hold the sides to under-promise and over-deliver. If you run out of time, be familiar enough that you aren't glancing too often at the pages.

Show growth as you advance

If they seemed receptive to your take and asked to see you again, something is working. Continue in that direction and find out where else you can grow. If they gave you notes, spend time implementing them into your performance.

The larger the production, the more rounds of callbacks there might be. As you get further along, don't be surprised if the director gives you a bold adjustment to guide you closer to their vision. Doing so is critical to booking the job, so stay flexible. The worst thing you can do is change nothing at all.

If your callback doesn't include sides

When you're called back to sing again from your book, it's okay to sing what you sang before. After all, it got you the callback, and likely they're introducing you to more (serious) members of the team. They will probably want to hear something else, so be prepared with a second or third idea.

AFTER THE AUDITION

Post-audition—regardless of the outcome—reflect on your experience and move on.

You did your best

After every audition, Lindsay reminds herself, "I did my best. If I could have done better, I would have."

"Of course I could have done better—I cracked!" the confused actor thinks. They forget that every audition is different. They didn't crack before because they were practicing in their room, singing with their voice teacher, or at some other, totally unrelated audition. They hadn't been in *this* environment on *this* day. However you did was your best for today.

In the event you simply forgot a word, had trouble finding a pitch, or lost your breath on the big final note, don't stress that you've ruined your shot with this casting director. Unless you threw up mid-song, slipped in it, and left screaming, they aren't likely to hold it against you. (And even then, they—and you—will have a fantastic story to tell.)

Audition log

Keep a detailed record of every audition you attend. Notice patterns and learn about what works and what doesn't.

Whether it's in a hardcopy journal or a spreadsheet, input all the details from the breakdown, including who was there, what they asked for, what you sang, where the call was, and how things went. How were your nerves? Were you "checked in"? How did they respond?

Later on you can reference your history with individual material and personnel. You'll discover which songs are serving you over time, and which can be replaced. You'll learn to be clearer about that tempo or that that one casting director loves when you sing your comedy song. Even if you bomb, you save yourself from making the same mistake again by putting down the details of *why* it didn't go well.

If, after a dozen auditions of presenting your solid go-tos, there's *still* no callback, it's time to regroup. But instead of blaming the casting team, the weather, or the songs you've worked long and hard to master, focus inward. Head back to class or return to a trusted coach and check in on your work—because a quick tune-up is likely to reveal what the problem is.

Preparing for what happens after

Every actor is anxious to know the results of their audition.

AuditionUpdate.com allows fellow actors to report if they got a call-back or learn who booked the job.

If you have representation, you can ask for an update after a week has passed—though we think that if you booked, someone would be sure to let you know. If you haven't heard anything, it's because no decision has been made or it's not one in your favor. You're better off moving on to the next audition. You can only control your own actions at this point, because if casting needed any more information from you, they'd request it.

When to ask for feedback

If you were in final callbacks, gave a lot of your time, and ultimately didn't book, the casting team might offer you or your representation a reason: "This wasn't your time," "We went a different direction," "next one," or even "too young" or "too tall." In rare situations they could be prescriptive: "Needs to work on tone," "Needs to brush up dance." When you get feedback like this, take it seriously—but as with any note, if the feedback doesn't serve you, it's your job to let it go.

SELF-TAPES

Thanks to the pandemic, self-tapes are an easy way to show teams your work in a lower-stress environment.

A self-tape can be a recorded sample of something from your book for your website, social media, or Actors Access page. When the time calls for it, you submit it for the appropriate project.

Casting can also request a self-tape of material from the show they're casting, which skips the EPA and ECC and is, in its way, a kind of appointment.

When making a self-tape, you're a storyteller, not a filmmaker. Don't worry too much about whether you have a fancy backdrop, high-tech camera, top editing software, ring light, or expensive microphone. Focus on your performance and work with whatever fits your budget.

Dos and don'ts of self-tapes

Just like an in-person audition, there are certain conventions to follow while self-taping so that you don't stand out for the wrong reason.

- **Camera:** Using your phone camera is totally fine, but if you want to use a proper camera, that works, too.
- **Framing:** The bottom of your frame hits just above your navel; the top leaves a few inches of space above your head. You have some room to move or gesture left and right.
- **Background:** Some actors swear by a blue backdrop, but others wing it without setting one up. So long as nothing is distracting in the background (a roommate walking around, a busy bookshelf, a curious decoration), use whatever is easiest.
- **Lighting:** Light the room well, naturally (sunlight) or artificially (lamps). If the frame is still too dark, turn on another light source.
- **Sound:** The mic on your phone or camera is probably good enough. If it's not crystal clear and you can afford it, use an external mic clipped to your shirt. You'll record to a track played out loud or through a headphone in one ear.

If your home doesn't work to film your tape, rent a rehearsal space. Many studios have designated self-tape rooms with equipment you can use.

There's no need to do it a thousand times

Actors often film too many takes thinking eventually they'll make a "perfect" one.

On one hand, everyone can send in their best take, so don't send one in with obvious mistakes, forgotten lyrics, or noticeable pitch problems. On the other, once you've done the material accurately a few times, the difference between take three and take fifteen is negligible—we promise.

Instead, spend more time on your preparation. The longer you work on your storytelling and vocal approach off-camera, the better your first few takes will be. Choose the best from only a few and move on. If you want feedback, send your top pick to someone you trust—but don't make the mistake of sending three virtually identical takes ("I like my little giggle a few seconds in on the first take, but I love my eye focus on measure sixty in the second one").

How casting directors watch your videos

Actors tend to overthink what happens to their self-tape once it's been submitted. Here's some insight from several of our casting director friends:

- Many offices download all video submissions to a protected server to keep them on file (in case the actor takes their video down before they've watched it). This means that when they watch it, you won't know . . . so don't reload your video page obsessively to see if the view counter has changed.
- Most say they watch every video that comes in. Seriously! But most also don't watch *all* of every video.
- Some start at the top of each video and watch thirty seconds to decide whether they want to know more. Others start right at the "good stuff" and work backward. For those starting at the top, they'd like to hear the tone and quality of your voice immediately, rather than sit through something more talky, so as with making any cut, start in the middle part of your voice—unless you're filming sides, in which case, do the cut given.
- Many report that they don't separate Equity from non-Equity, and watch them in the order they arrive. If there is a high volume of submissions, the team may divvy them up.
- It's true that sometimes they don't get to your video. If so, they've already found the person they were looking for. That's out of your control, and like an in-person audition, your job is to move on to what's next.

MANAGING YOUR NERVES

Audition anxiety comes in many forms. Sweating, shaking, blanking on lyrics or story, panic attacks . . . the mind can be a remarkable place. Here are useful tips for addressing your heebie-jeebies.

- Recognize that nerves are normal—they mean you care.

- Reframe your nerves as excitement, which is easier to do when you've prepared your story expertly and are eager to share it.
- If adrenaline spikes before you go in, press firmly against a wall or pull firmly upward from the bottom of your chair, as though trying to lift your whole body off the ground. This channels excess energy.
- Steady your heart rate with slow, focused breathing.
- Close your eyes and imagine stepping into the world of your song. It may feel silly, but disassociating from the pressure and grounding in your character's world helps focus your thoughts.
- Don't bring a freshly learned song into an initial audition. Choose a go-to piece you've coached and performed many times, so the words flow like the Pledge of Allegiance and the notes feel as natural as singing "Happy Birthday." This frees you to stay fully present in the story.
- Avoid super rangy material. When you're nervous, your voice is likely to surprise you—and not always in a good way.

Above all, don't see your anxiety as a personal failing you have to "fix." Think of it as a thorny bramble you're slowly working through. Every time you survive an audition, you cut away a bit more. Little by little, the path clears.

You've been nervous plenty of times before. Terrified of a flu shot? Shaking during that oral report? Petrified to ask someone out? Those moments once felt huge, but now they might make you laugh. With perspective comes clarity.

Future You will look back at this anxiety and wish she could tell you, "It's going to be okay." Channel a little of her next time your brain tries to take over.

Further anxiety troubles

For many actors, anxiety naturally sheds as they get older and more comfortable in the room. For others, the anxiety gets worse over time as new, larger fears arise.

- “Maybe I’m losing my touch? I haven’t been called back in a while.”
- “My best friend just booked big. Why wasn’t it me?”
- “My folks are pressuring me to rethink this career. They’re disappointed in me.”

When anxiety becomes debilitating, your nerves are telling you they aren’t coming from a place of excitement, but of unpreparedness or self-doubt. At this point, take a step back and look to the root cause more deeply.

- If you’re worried about your voice or that you’ll forget the words, it means you need to spend more hours preparing your story rather than rehearsing the song. Return to the text and your story questions.
- Work with your vocal coach or voice teacher to gather encouragement. Sometimes a mentor who knows you can help you regain your confidence.
- Sing your audition cuts in a safe classroom setting. Simulate the audition experience and practice singing to someone behind a table. Be transparent with your teachers about what you’re working on emotionally.
- About thirty minutes before your audition, try calling (or texting) a loved one who you know will give you emergency TLC. Sometimes we just need to hear, “You’re not crazy, you got this. You’re going to nail it. I love you.”
- Get creative. If you’re superstitious, make a centering routine. If you’re squirrely, play a crossword. If you’re spiritual, pray.

Non-performance-related anxiety

Still others arrive at a realization that their nerves have nothing to do with auditioning. Instead, their anxiety is signaling a physical condition that needs to be addressed. Talk to a professional about what you’re going through. They’re likely to provide answers you can’t otherwise get.

EVERY AUDITION MATTERS

An audition is valuable even if you don't book. The late Philip Seymour Hoffman emphasized the value of auditions, even if they don't go your way: "If you're given a chance to act, take those words and bring them alive."

No matter what the result, you still made an impression. It's also a chance to get another rep in on the material—not to mention meet new casting associates, creative team members, and fellow actors. Maybe even a new friend.

An audition is a message in a bottle, a lottery ticket, a penny in the well, a challenge to the universe. Though it can feel like diminishing returns, the more you audition, the greater your odds of success . . . and that's a fact.

Representation

An agent is a valuable part of your team. They help you access rooms you might not reach alone, negotiate contracts, secure better deals, and ensure you're not being taken advantage of. When big decisions come up, they offer insight.

Because of these advantages, many early-career actors believe their career is stuck without one. They stop auditioning, convinced the roles that matter are locked behind agent-kept gates. Once they land an agent, they imagine the doors will swing open, their career will take off, and the industry will finally take them seriously.

But for most early-career actors, that belief—that someone powerful is out there who could save them—is what *actually* holds them back.

An agent isn't your hero, they're your teammate.

In this chapter, we'll bust common myths around representation and explore what agents really do, how (and when) to find the right one, and how to navigate the relationship once you're in it. We'll also cover the role of managers in a young actor's career (insert clenched teeth emoji).

HOW AN AGENT WORKS (FOR YOU)

It's true that part of an agent's work is to connect their clients with exclusive auditions. Casting offices regularly send breakdowns to agencies to elevate the talent pool they see. Agents want to find you work—not only so that you both make money, but also so they rise within their agency and increase their own salaries. And yet:

An agent's primary job is to negotiate contracts on your behalf. **Finding you auditions is secondary.**

Most working actors with an agent will tell you that they're still responsible for finding most of their work. We asked two hundred working actors with agents to tell us what they credited most for the auditions they get and jobs they book.

- ***Just 12 percent*** **credited their agent or manager**
- ***29 percent credited themselves for attending an audition without an appointment***
- ***A whopping 59 percent credited*** **their personal relationships with casting and creatives**

Too many actors rely solely on their agent to get auditions. That's why so many complain about how little their reps are doing for them. Eventually, one side cuts ties, and the actor starts the agent hunt again . . . believing a new agent will do more and fix everything, instead of realizing that, usually, the person who needs to work harder is themselves.

This mindset isn't just problematic—it's illogical. Agents get you into bigger rooms for bigger projects looking for more competitive talent. So if an actor is struggling to book in *less* competitive spaces (like the ones they already have access to), why should they assume the solution is to enter *more* competitive ones?

While an agent can open doors, so can a writer, director, music director, choreographer—even a fellow actor. In fact, that second group can carry more weight. Agents submit out of mutual professional interest; peers and creatives recommend you simply because they believe in your work. When an agent submits a group of actors to casting, casting picks and chooses who they want to see. When a peer vouches for you, casting may be more inspired to pay attention . . . out of respect for the relationship, even if it's simply doing their peer a favor.

You know yourself, but your agent knows the industry

When your agent signs you, they have a clear idea of how to "sell" you to casting. They know the projects they'll submit you for and the roles you're likely to book. In a dream world, their vision matches yours—but it rarely does.

You may see yourself as Dot in *Sunday in the Park with George* (because, let's be real, you'd crush it). But your agent sees you as Sophie in *Mamma Mia!* at a Colorado summer stock. Maybe you're craving Marius in *Les Miz*, but they're eyeing a slot in the *42nd Street* ensemble. Why? Because they know a stronger résumé leads to bigger roles. Without trust and a track record, it's a leap for casting to go from "Who are you?" to "Here's the lead in our $500,000 *Grease*."

Some gigs are dreams, some are disasters, but most are about the paycheck—and the true value lands somewhere in between. It's not just about paying dues; it's about moving with the industry's current. You're one of thousands of talented actors, and dozens who are right for the role. Some got here first and earned trust. They deserve to be ahead of you—and when it's your time, you'll deserve it, too.

You work together as a team

Some say your agent works for you because you pay them. You're in the "power" position and your agent should be working diligently for you. But if they are a kind of employee, when you don't pay them, they can quit. So . . . if you're not paying them much and they're still working for you, then it's the agent—not you—who is in the "power" position.

But any healthy relationship is strongest when it's a collaborative team. Now that we're clear on how the relationship works at its best, let's figure out how (and when) you should get one.

COLLEGE AGENT SHOWCASES

One of the earliest ways an actor acquires an agent is through their college showcase. It's a special circumstance that's similar to when an actor signs with an agent sometime after college, with some notable differences.

An agent who attends a senior showcase expects to see young talent with mostly school and summer stock credits, still-maturing voices, and skillsets continuing to grow. They're searching for promising actors with a clear idea of their marketability at twenty-one years old, who demonstrate sharp savvy that will serve them moving forward.

At a college showcase, the agent is taking a chance on an unseasoned artist. If years go by and the actor doesn't book, or the agent doesn't come through as the actor hoped, one side decides the experiment was not a success and ends it. The actor regroups and finds a new agent once they've gained experience and both sides feel confident in the relationship.

With this in mind, most actors will pursue an agent outside of college at some point in their careers.

PURSUING AN AGENT

There are many steps to securing an agent outside of a college showcase.

Make sure you're ready to work with an agent

Once we take "I'm not booking work, so I must need an agent" off the table, we realize how crucial timing is in signing with one.

An agent needs a client they can sell. If no one else has ever hired you, it's a challenge for an agent to explain why this casting director should be the first. An agent is most interested when they know you have the work ethic, knowledge, and contacts to help yourself. By demonstrating your own acumen, you create a team an agent wants to join.

Be intentional about your search

Do extensive research on potential agents and agencies, because not every agency is looking for someone like you, and you won't be happy with just any agent.

First investigate the agency's client roster. Do you notice a theme? Are there a lot of leggy model types? A dearth of dancers? A plethora of pop singers? Are they low on Latinas, or busting with Black actors? Are they quite into queer performers, or in negative numbers of nonbinary actors? Rosters with a lot of actors like you may specialize in actors of your specificity. It could also mean they are full up and looking to expand with other types of clients. Make a list of agencies with rosters you'd be proud to join.

If you can, talk to a client repped by the agency. Ideally, it's someone you already know, but it's perfectly acceptable to contact a client on social media or through a mutual friend. Don't be surprised if they're anxious to share their experience with you . . . for better or worse. They may even help put you in contact and offer a good word.

Note that if you and your contact share similar specificity, you're asking them to invite more competition. Better to find someone different.

Beware the scam agencies

Some agencies are glorified scams. No legitimate agency should require you to enroll in special classes or to get brand-new headshots from a certain photographer—likely, the "agency" is taking a cut. A serious agent may suggest further training or an update to your materials, but they shouldn't demand you go to one specific place.

You can trust most agencies that've been around for a few years, but if you spot an agency that's new, has no client you recognize or share a mutual friend with, or has little online to back them up, this agency may be a trap.

Submitting to agencies

Believe it or not, every agency looks at *all* the submissions they receive. What they do with them is another story.

Agencies taking on new clients will tell you how to submit your materials. If there's no clear request for submissions but a general contact email is provided, that's usually an acceptable avenue through which you can submit. If they say they aren't currently seeking new clients, they mean it.

From your search, whittle your choices down to a handful.

You must make your cover letter specific to the agency

When an agency receives a cover letter that's clearly a form letter meant for any agency, it goes to the bottom of the pile (or the trash). Treat every agency as individually as you want them to treat you. Here's a good structure for an agency cover letter:

> To the Very Specific Agent at the Very Specific Agency I Researched,
>
> I am starting with an opening hook. Impressive, funny, or bold, it's a short opening paragraph introducing myself via my branding statement. I end stating that I'm seeking representation.
>
> I continue with a paragraph explaining "Why you, agent?" Using my research (including referencing your clients and the wonderful feedback about your agency I've received), this is a two-to-four-sentence paragraph detailing why your agency is the right home for me. I can name a specific agent if one is of particular interest, or else I can speak to the culture that the agency fosters via their client focus, roster, and scope of work.
>
> Next, here's a short paragraph answering, "Why me, agent?" I explain why I'm right for you by referencing my past work (without detailing my

entire attached résumé) and how it relates to the clients you've taken on. I lead with any major credits I have, especially recently.

As a sweetener, I mention industry contacts I'm close to, casting directors who frequently call me in, and any notable collaborators I work with. I could also list recent major callbacks—and especially any that saw me to finals.

To close, I outline what else I've included in my submission and that I'm available to meet if you're interested.

I sign off,
My Full Professional Name

If this is an email, your subject heading can grab attention. Rather than "Seeking an agent," adapt your branding statement in the subject line. Be bold ("Award-winning soprano just in from Chicago") or even cheeky ("Looking for a 6'2" rock tenor?"), but don't be pushy ("Trust me—you want me") or desperate ("I need an agent!").

As with your website, you don't need a paragraph telling them extensive background information that isn't already in your branding statement or featured on your résumé. You absolutely don't need to offer generalities about your "compassion and natural warmth," how "professional and organized" you are, or how life-changing seeing *Maybe Happy Ending* was. At most, tell them your hometown, offer any additional authenticity, or share a fun fact.

Once you've drafted, proofread, and trimmed, get sharp outside eyes on it and adjust accordingly.

Materials to include

If the agency has specified what they'd like you to submit, send only that. If they've left it open, send along:

- Headshot and résumé
- Link to your website
- If you have a vocal reel, you can send that or up to four video links—don't send bulky files

- If you have them, send links to acting, dance, or film/TV reels. (Use your research. An agency that doesn't work on film and television will wonder why you sent a student film.)

After submitting, trust it was received and don't follow up. If they're interested, they'll reach out, though it may take weeks or months.

You can submit to multiple agencies at once, as long as each cover letter is personalized.

Other showcases

Many non-university training programs offer agency showcases for a fee paid by participants. Unlike college showcases, you're essentially paying to rise to the top of the submission pile—and they're getting paid to put you there. Some of these showcases offer written or verbal feedback.

Before pulling out your credit card, speak to someone who's participated recently. Make sure you can choose your material and that you're allowed to present at least two pieces—like two song cuts, or a song and a monologue. Avoid any showcase where an unfamiliar instructor decides what you perform after only a class or two.

THE AGENT MEETING

Before you're asked to sign, you'll usually take an official meeting at the agency's office to discuss sealing the deal. If you've sent out multiple submissions, you may receive multiple meetings—and because you did your homework and selected each with care, it's wise to take all of them so that you may compare options.

Other colleagues may also attend. While the agency has had hundreds of these meetings and streamlined their process, it's likely to be one of only a few you'll ever have. Find out exactly who will be in your meeting and learn about them from their website, information online, and social media.

If you're asked to sing for the team and you've already performed for one of them, sing the song again unless they specify otherwise. If your book is in great shape, bring it. If you're still putting it together, bring only what's ready.

You are who you are

Show the agency who you are by referencing your branding statement (but not reciting it).

If a potential agent questions core aspects of your brand, dig into what's behind their hesitation. Maybe it's your voice type, your opera background, or identifying as a dancer first. If their perspective offers a compelling shift that aligns with your values, it could mark the start of a new chapter. But if it feels like they're dismissing something central to your identity, it's a red flag. Stay open and curious—but if your agent doesn't see you the way you see yourself, they won't submit you for the work you want.

Share your dreams

Bring a list of dream roles and shows—both leads and ensemble—that perfectly match your voice type, physicality (including playable age), your energy, and your authenticity if applicable. This isn't the time to bend the essence of a role, look ten years into the future, or generalize your skill. You're saying, "Put me in, coach, and I'll win the game."

Include roles currently on Broadway, on tour, and in recently released licensed musicals (the ones every regional theatre is doing), and cover as many genres as possible.

Come with questions

The agency should sell themselves to you as much as they hope that you'll sell yourself to them. Get the answers to all the questions below—except those covered by their website.

- Do they have multiple offices in New York City, Los Angeles, London, elsewhere? Do these offices work together?

- In addition to theatre, does the agency at large also handle voice-over, dance, modeling, film and television, and literary (writing)? How does crossover work for clients who do more than one thing?
- Will you be assigned to one agent, or a team? If one agent, should yours go on temporary leave, who will take over representing you?
- Can you go to—and submit for—auditions you find on your own, or does the agency require that you only go to what they approve? (If they do require exclusivity, see below.)
- What level of communication should the client expect from their agency, and how frequent? Do they prefer email, phone, or text?
- Vice versa: How often would the agency like to get updates from their clients?
- What do they wish that their clients understood about the work they do?
- What's their biggest advice for their clients in the first year of working together?
- While you'd never expect feedback after every audition you go to, how does the agent feel about asking for it on a case-by-case basis?

One question NOT to ask is how many clients they represent. It's a bit like asking how much they weigh or any other personal measurement. Instead, you might ask, "Do you currently represent a lot of people my type, or would I be a bit more rare on your roster?"

Agent-splaining

We know of many situations where a smart actor walked into an agent meeting and left turned upside-down and shaken. Sometimes the actor hadn't prepared enough or gained a basic understanding of how the industry works . . . but in others, it was a case of "agent-splaining."

Many an agent will monologue about their view of the industry and how they see you inside of it—especially if they think you have no idea what you're talking about. If they're completely disinterested in your perspective, it's likely to get worse over time. If you leave feeling like a bad kid in trouble, this isn't the right agent for you.

Everybody wants to be on TV

Before asking about film and television audition access, make sure this agency offers that.

It's worth noting that taking the step into TV and film from theatre is a leap. Just like your theatre auditions, your agent alone can't bridge the gap for you. Explore on-camera classes, accrue contacts, and build a résumé of training and low-budget films before asking an agent to sell you in a brand-new arena.

Beware audition exclusivity

Some agents forbid their clients from auditioning or submitting for things unless the agency says it's okay. This is acceptable if they're bringing you one or two appointments per week and you're satisfied, but you won't know if that's the case until after they've signed you and you've agreed to audition exclusivity. This ties your hands, and we ultimately think this is a situation to be avoided.

Materials checklist

Make sure to bring your book of audition-ready material. Also bring enough copies for everyone you're meeting with (plus yourself) of the following:

- Headshot and résumé
- A list of songs in your book broken down by genre
- A list of dream roles perfect for you today, including leads and ensemble, from recent Broadway smashes all the way back to the classics

Mentally prepare your branding statement, but no need to print it.

SIGNING AND BEYOND

Within a few weeks after your meeting, the agency will let you know if they'd like to officially sign you, freelance with you, stay in touch, or if the relationship isn't a fit.

Signing

If the agency offers to sign you (congrats!), there's still time to ask final questions. Don't fear "looking a gift horse in the mouth," because at this point, you're as much a "gift" as they are.

With a formal contract, you agree to pay the agency 10 percent of *all* acting work you take on, whether they negotiate the contract for you or not. Some actors think that if there's no contract for the show (perhaps a casual letter of agreement by email), or the agent doesn't "do anything" for the contract, they aren't entitled to compensation—but your signed contract with the agency says otherwise. Sometimes an agent will let a tiny gig of a hundred dollars or so slide, but that's up to the agent.

Your contract will specify a length of one to three years, at the end of which both parties can decide to renew (or not). There should be a clause that allows you to leave if they don't bring you an audition appointment in a certain number of months, and vice versa if you're not bringing them enough work.

Freelancing

Going freelance with an agent means you have access to representation while decreasing the benefits, commitment, and exclusivity of both sides.

For the actor, it means you don't have to automatically give 10 percent for contracts you get on your own unless you ask your freelance agent to negotiate it. It also means you can submit to other agencies who'll consider an official signing while still having some representation . . . but you also aren't at the top of their list when they're submitting clients to casting.

Staying in touch

If the agency isn't ready to sign you but remains interested, take them at their word. Email them about the work you're doing to increase their interest. It also means the door is open if you need a contract negotiated as a one-off.

AGENT TROUBLESHOOTING

With so much at stake, complications easily arise working with your agent.

"My agent isn't doing enough for me"

The most common concern among agented actors is that their rep is holding them back by not getting them enough appointments. First, remember that an agent should only be doing *part* of the work to get you seen . . . like, say, 10 percent, which is what they get paid. That may be an exaggeration, but you see our point.

You must do the rest—and you should, attending or submitting to at least two auditions for each appointment your agent gets you.

But if you're still left doing all the work, here are three possibilities of what's going on:

- Your agent may be submitting you all the time but they're not getting bites. This is usually the truth because they're submitting you for higher-level gigs that your résumé can't always unlock. Keep building credits and amp up how many auditions you go to yourself.
- Or . . . you and your agent are due for a conversation about expectations. It could be that you're expecting too much from your agent, or that your agent is not making good on the promises they made to you in your initial interview. Ask for a meeting (in-person or by phone), and if they put you off, it may be a signal that things are going south.

- Or . . . it's possible you're right, and despite what your agent tells you, for one reason or another, they are prioritizing other clients ahead of you or not submitting you much at all. If this is the case, per your contract's escape clause, you have the right to leave.

"We hardly communicate, and I don't know what's up"

Ideally, you and your agent are touching base every few weeks. But if every time you contact them, you're harping on them for updates and demanding to know where your appointments are, you're not doing your part. Remember that communication works both ways. In addition to bringing them audition notices and asking them to submit you:

- Update the agent on auditions you've gone to and how they went.
- Tell the agent about meetings and classes you're taking.
- Send along self-tapes and videos of recent performances they missed.
- Now and again, brainstorm larger projects and goals with your agent, like getting new headshots, planning a cabaret, and a list of contacts to reconnect with.

If it comes time to discuss your working relationship, ask your agent what you can do to help them help you. Collaborate on ideas and be open to what they have to say. Afterward, decide if you agree. The agent isn't likely to change their mind about what they think at this stage, so either accept that you aren't on the same page or decide you're better off elsewhere.

Your agent may be protecting you

Your agent is human. This means they care about you and don't want to needlessly hurt your feelings. For this reason, your agent isn't going to immediately tell you every casting director they submitted you to who declined to see you. "Hey, three casting directors saw your headshot and résumé and didn't care" isn't an email they want or need to send.

It also means that they don't want to give you the impression they aren't good at their job. Some actors believe that if they don't get seen, their agent is responsible: "If only they pushed for me" or "If only they were more important, I would get seen." For absolutely any reason—which includes those that are, and are not, about you—if casting declines to see you, it's a waste of energy guessing why.

"Can I see a submission list?"

Some actors request to see a list of all the jobs their agent has sent them out for, which can easily send the message that you don't trust them. Understandably, this can create tension. It isn't precisely the same thing as asking to check your partner's texts, but it certainly won't create *more* enthusiasm on either side without a larger conversation. Best to ask for a submission list only if you feel you have nothing to lose.

"I'm afraid of getting dropped"

It's a real fear and it does happen. If it does, you'll recover—we swear. You got this agent, and you'll get another one when the time is right.

You can't live in fear of your agent any more than you would advise a friend to stay in an unhealthy relationship. Constantly worrying if they're going to drop you puts both parties at a disadvantage—and rarely yields positive results. Better to ask how to improve your relationship and see if you can make progress. You don't have to be silent out of fear.

"Whoops, I got dropped"

Some agents who drop you are jerks who can't see genius when they have it.

But most will be transparent about why they need to part ways. Perhaps you aren't booking enough work, or maybe your perspectives aren't aligned on your marketability. At this point, the agent no longer sees how they can help you book work. If the agent's reason for dropping you is one you can address for the future, take the note and try to move on.

Breaking your contract and switching agents

The cleanest way to switch agencies is to end your contract with your current agent *before* meeting with a new one. But many actors hesitate, afraid to jump without a soft place to land—leading to messy mistakes. The key is to be honest with the new agent and, no matter what, don't bad-mouth your old one. Stay professional, because agents often know each other and may talk.

Be transparent with your current agent about considering a change, even if it speeds up the breakup. Like any important relationship, if you're unhappy enough to leave, it's unethical to date around behind their back just because you're afraid to be single.

When it's time to part ways, there will be an official correspondence (as little as an email, or as much as a letter) ending the relationship. This creates clarity as to when your representation ends and who gets the commission when you book.

NEGOTIATING WITHOUT AN AGENT

If you're hired for a job without an agent, you can sign the offer as is or negotiate it yourself.

Alternatively, if an agent isn't ready to seal the deal long-term, many fantastic agents will agree to handle a contract as a one-off, because you're effectively handing them money—especially if it's a major, lucrative contract. If it's under a thousand dollars a week, you may be better off just negotiating it yourself.

Bargaining power

Each side in a negotiation holds power based on who needs the other more. At the start, sadly, you need the agent much more than they need you. Still, since you'll be working closely together, both parties have an incentive to reach a fair agreement.

The other side has more power when they're taking a chance on you—especially if the credit they're offering could boost your future prospects, which may affect their offer.

You hold more power if you are hard to replace, filling a special niche, playing the lead, have done the role before, or don't *need* the contract because you're so in demand.

Be honest with yourself about how the scale tips. Negotiations usually fall apart when one side doesn't see the reality and makes unreasonable demands.

When to negotiate for more

The initial offer is usually fairly set—so don't expect to double your pay or upgrade to a private dressing room. Other actors in your position are likely getting similar offers.

Still, there are always a few areas where you can advocate for yourself, and it's smart to try. Assume the best of the other side and treat negotiation as a conversation, not a battle. No need to plead your case unless they say no and you need to push back.

Companies rarely show all their cards up front, maintaining room to negotiate. Unless the offer is marked "final," they anticipate that you may ask for more, so don't fret that it will hurt how they see you. Depending on their budget, some requests will be a hard no, while others may get a "we can make that work" or "let me investigate." You won't know unless you ask . . .

. . . Or unless a friend is also negotiating. Sharing intel might feel sneaky, but it helps both parties get a fairer deal. If you're joining a long-running show, reach out to past or current cast members—they could know which areas have wiggle room.

Negotiating money

Pushing for more pay is one of the trickiest areas of a contract. The moment they budge on one actor, others may come forward as well. Many contracts have set minimums mandated by Equity that management is sticking to. The good news about these union contracts is that the starting pay is a "fair wage," and the bad is that it's also difficult to get it increased.

But there's no harm in asking. Start with a figure 20 percent higher than the initial offer. If you're lucky, they'll meet you in the middle at 10 percent more. If your bargaining power feels higher, you could start with a 50 percent increase. When asking for a pay bump, best to also ask for at least one other thing. This allows the company to weigh which is easiest to give you—which could be more money.

Note that in a "favored nations" contract, all actors agree to be paid the same, including the stars. No budging.

Negotiating complimentary tickets

Comp tickets for guests can be simple to work into your contract (especially if the company is already stressed about ticket sales). Ask for four more comps than you're offered in the hopes you'll land on an extra two.

If you know your guests aren't coming opening night, barter with your opening night seats. Instead of two comps for opening, ask for six comps usable at other performances.

If you're a principal track in the show, there are other areas you can explore negotiating—and at this stage it's wise to seriously weigh whether keeping an agent's 10 percent is worth the headache of negotiating yourself.

Negotiating outs

"Outs" allow you flexibility to leave for all or part of the rehearsal schedule, performance schedule, or run of the show. Outs can be tricky to get and the company may be more inclined to give you a pay bump than let you leave.

If you have known personal conflicts during the run (your sister is getting married, or you have a high-paying concert gig), get those days cleared first.

Dressing rooms

Ask about the logistics of your dressing room. If you're a lead of the show and there are private or two-person dressing rooms to be assigned, request them—usually the squeaky wheel gets the room. Don't wait to arrive at the theatre and realize you've been shafted.

When to accept the terms or walk away

If the answer to your requests is "no," don't worry that they're upset with you for asking. It's your job to advocate for yourself.

In this scenario, be honest with yourself about whether the deal is sufficient for you—not forgetting what the credit will do for your résumé. Consider if you already have a similar credit and taking the job will ultimately cost you money (because of taking time off from a better-paying day job).

MANAGERS

A great manager serves numerous functions. They collaborate on career strategy, network on your behalf, assist with audition prep, and help keep your schedule organized (on both the micro and the macro levels). Nearly every chapter in part two of this book is supported by a manager.

Managers can also help get you into audition rooms and offer contract advice if you don't have an agent—but they can't legally negotiate for you unless they happen to have a license as a theatre agent or are a lawyer.

Some take the view that agents find you work and negotiate on your behalf, while managers handle everything else. And whereas an agent takes 10 percent, most managers take 15 percent for their hands-on approach to their client's professional affairs. An actor with both an agent and a manager usually pays 25 percent for dual representation.

Many early-career actors get a manager before (or in lieu of) an agent. These actors also frequently find themselves in bad situations. While there are many terrific, useful, and even powerful managers out there, there are even more bad ones who will do very little and take very much from their client. To become a talent agent, you need a license and you generally join or form a regulated agency. To become a manager . . . you just need to say you're a manager.

An actor needs a manager when they have a busy, thriving career to manage. They don't replace an agent.

That is, when an actor is so busy that their schedule of appointments and auditions and rehearsal and filming and script reading and project picking and personal errands is so packed that they need someone to handle it for them . . . it could be time to get a manager. A manager takes a big cut of your income, so they need to have plenty to do.

When a manager takes on a young, uncredited actor and promises to help them, we wonder what they're actually doing for them. Unless the manager is very well-known and influential, how exactly are they selling their client—and to whom? Knowing that this actor may end up doing most of the work, not-so-good managers can cash in on clients who are desperate to say they have representation.

Experienced members of your industry already know all of this. When we hear that a young actor—with a lightweight résumé, mostly empty schedule, and crickets in film and television—has a manager* but not an agent, we're not particularly impressed . . . but we *are* a little nervous.

Once you've built a strong foundation of credits and relationships, an agent is your next step. As your career elevates, your thriving business may

* If you already have a manager you love, congrats to you: You've a good one! If you have a manager and reading our warnings makes you feel like you're watching *Dateline* and the sketch of the killer on television bears a striking resemblance to the other person sitting in the room . . . well, maybe consider making a run for it.

need another teammate. At that point, an experienced manager could be the right next step for you.

If, despite our warnings, you're still considering signing with a manager (perhaps you tripped on 8th Avenue and ran into one) before an agent, consult with one of their existing *and* former clients to see what they have to say. If you can't identify any of their clients (hmmm . . .), ask for a client reference. If they can't produce one for you: abort, abort, abort!

CONCLUSION: REJECTING REJECTION

There are forty-one Broadway houses, about 150 Off-Broadway houses, and about eighty major regional theatres. There are only so many shows in each of those spaces and only so many people in each cast. There are an estimated *seventy thousand* professional actors in the United States. You don't have to do the math to see that there aren't enough jobs for everyone at the same time. Many will apply and, audition to audition, few will win.

Rejection isn't just a normal part of being an artist. It's by design.

This isn't meant to make you despair. Every major profession—not just acting—relies on scarcity (that is, extremely limited availability of opportunities) to make sure only the best-suited to the project rise to the top. When casting selects one actor out of dozens of serious contenders (who themselves were selected from hundreds or thousands who applied), the ticket-buying audience (now paying well over $150 for an orchestra seat) can trust they're seeing the person the creative team thought was best for the role. Sometimes you'll be that person and everybody else won't be. Other times—most of the time—someone else's number will be up, and you'll live to audition another day.

Absolutely everyone gets rejected at some point, and the vast majority gets rejected far more than they are chosen.

As an actor books bigger roles, their audition-to-booking ratio doesn't change as much as you'd expect. With every new achievement, they set their sights on newer, greater ones—ensuring they will always be fighting to break into the next higher tier. Sure, they *could* stay put in the comfort zone they've conquered, book similar jobs, and see their success rate soar . . . but instead they *actively* chase bigger challenges—and pursue inevitably more rejection.

People are funny, huh?

Rejection challenges us to level up. When someone tells us "no" and someone else "yes," it's human to wonder why we weren't picked. In most cases, it isn't a failing on our part, but sometimes it reveals areas in which we can improve.

When the "no's" pile up, though, it's natural to start feeling silly. "Maybe I was crazy for going into this field, and everyone back home knows it?" "What if my father was right and I wasted all their money on majoring in theatre?" "Is my voice actually bad?" To make matters worse, most rejections in acting jobs are delivered implicitly: "Thank you," they say, and you leave.

"Maybe they're giving out callbacks later?" you hope. Sometimes they are—but most of the time a week passes and you're still refreshing your email just in case. Feedback is rare, which leaves you wondering if it was your height, or what you were wearing, or the song you picked, or your résumé, or your voice, or your personality, or your name, or your birth chart, or your existence . . .

Yes, too much rejection makes you feel insane. But aren't we all basically sociopaths for going into this art-making business? It takes a certain level of cuckoo to think that we have the winning lottery ticket. It's a belief we hold so tightly that we wager tens or hundreds of thousands of dollars training for it. On the other hand . . .

Even against all odds, someone has to believe they're bound to win. Why shouldn't it be you?

If you've chosen this path and come this far, it's all right to accept that you—and everyone else in this business—might be bonkers. Take the latest disaster on Broadway. The writers, producers, investors, and actors all hoped it was good enough to run—at least a little while (they wagered $20 million on that hope, in fact)—and yet audiences and critics alike declared it was not, shaking the reality of those involved.

Even the greatest writer of our artform, Stephen Sondheim, felt lots and lots of rejection. His earliest works were lambasted by his mentor Oscar Hammerstein II (albeit constructively). His first would-be Broadway musical, *Saturday Night*, fell apart after the producer died. For his first full score (*A Funny Thing Happened on the Way to the Forum*), he wasn't nominated or even acknowledged by his collaborators in their Tony speeches. *Anyone Can Whistle*, his next show, was an explosive flop. Even after he'd won four Tonys (three of them back-to-back) over ten years of constant success, he basically went into hiding in 1981 when *Merrily We Roll Along* bombed and ended his long collaboration with Harold Prince. It took a couple of years for him to start again with a new collaborator—James Lapine—and write *Sunday in the Park with George* and *Into the Woods*.

Lindsay wasn't the first choice for her track in *Godspell*. They wanted a star, and only once that star turned it down was she cast. She was also the second choice for Rose Fenny in *Dogfight*, and in fact it was a battle behind the scenes to cast her. And—if you can believe it—she wasn't even the first choice for *Carousel*, which won her a Tony Award.

RSO had an inverted experience with rejection. He found career wins left and right as soon as he began (like your college classmate, perhaps, who booked an original Broadway cast during her senior year), winning the coveted Richard Rodgers Award and Jonathan Larson Grant in his first three years of writing. He quickly joined a well-known group of contemporary musical theatre writers and got hired by studios like Disney and Universal.

Everything was going to plan . . . until at around twenty-eight years old, his luck flipped, and all that failure and rejection he thought he'd avoided came piling down like an avalanche. He got fired from a major job, his big new musical got universally panned, awards became elusive, and opportunities appeared to dry up. Suddenly the song "What Did I Have That I Don't Have Now?" seemed to be written about him. Throughout his thirties, he frequently contemplated quitting. But after ten whole years of feeling like a failure, things—seemingly out of nowhere—turned the page again. He won the prestigious Kleban Award, was offered more projects than he could take on, and felt industry eyes taking him seriously once again . . . and still he wondered why things got better just the way he wondered why things got worse. Even today, he hasn't figured out the answers. All he knows is that he's glad he didn't quit in the face of all that rejection.

Biographies of artists are littered with stories like these, and what they all have in common is just how pervasive rejection is in any career. As they say, them's the breaks. Another thing they have in common is that hard work pays off.

> ***There is an absolute correlation between***
> **increased effort and increased results.**
> ***Work begets work.***

We aren't claiming that every story ends happily ever after. We *do* believe that when things get bad, if you stick with it and work hard enough, circumstances will improve. And we *also* believe that when things get better, they will probably get bad again. And then better. Schedules get busy, and then suddenly, inexplicably slow. You win big and wait a decade for a reprise. No career ascends smoothly without incident, and few plummet without occasional reprieve.

All you can control is the effort you put into it. No matter how many times you don't get a callback, it doesn't mean you're not talented. Losing the job after the final work session doesn't mean you aren't good enough. Being turned down by an agent doesn't mean you'll never be signed. You aren't devastated when you don't win the Powerball any more than you're disappointed when, playing party games with a group of ten friends, you don't draw the "fun" card. "Those are just the odds," you say, and move on—sure that your next prize is just around the corner.

None of these are reasons to quit. After all, you fell off your bike *a lot* before you learned to ride. You probably had some pretty crappy friends and lovers before you found better ones. And pro bike riders still fall off their wheels. "Perfect" marriages enter rough patches, and some even fall apart without warning. Hope for the best and prepare for the worst.

That isn't to say that there isn't a right time to quit. It's true that, for some, quitting musical theatre becomes the best decision they ever make.

> *The time to quit is when the*
> *pain of the pursuit* hurts too much . . .

. . . When carrying the weight of this career becomes impossible, and letting go becomes the only option; when the wound of hopelessness opens so wide it can't seem to heal; when dreaming of being on Broadway batters our mental health so much that it empties out our life, bleeding resentment into our home and our relationships.

We all have bad days. Sometimes we have a bad year—or two, or ten. You'll know when the streak of bad luck has gone too far. Everything inside you will say, "I physically do not think I can take one step further on this path, or I will crumble."

But while it's important to note where the exit signs are in the theatre of your life, recognize that they are much further away than you think. Don't start staring at them just because it's been a few hard seasons and you're afraid. Look for them when only their promise fills your future with hope.

Some weary actors at the breaking point find solace in making a plan, rather than stewing over their situation. They decide that in a year or two, on an established date, they'll reassess and reflect on their progress, taking stock of how things have changed since they last saw rock bottom. This mindset helps push away the daily doubts: "I don't need to deal with feeling inadequate today—that's a problem for next January. Today the focus is simply attending the next audition."

For many, this ignites a new fire—one that successful actors often later recall: "I almost quit, but I didn't. And look at me now."

But it's true that for others, next January arrives not a moment too soon. For them, on that cold January date they set, they sit with their reality, figure that they tried their best, and accept that things didn't work out.

Leaving the business won't mean you failed. It will mean you got everything you needed from this time in your life and you're ready to move on, like moving out of a beloved first apartment or amicably ending a long relationship that had run its course. A precious few things last forever. No matter what you choose to do, at some point you plan to retire. So you'll retire from this now, and take on a new adventure.

But you're not going to quit—not yet, because you made it this far in this book. Right now, it's time to reject rejection. Remember:

When no one is choosing you, you have to choose yourself.

Sit down for a "career regroup": a one-person small business meeting.* It's time once again to revisit the damn thing.

- Check in with your business plan. When you feel stuck, first look at your mission. Are you holding yourself accountable to the practice you've set? Have you let things slide—and need to recommit (or adjust) to get back on track? Is it time to revise your vision? Have you stayed true to your values?
- Think about exploring a new class, working with a new coach, or changing voice teachers—it could be the start of a new chapter.
- Can you take better care of yourself? In a rut, is it time to try a new approach to protect your mental health? Are you missing the

* RSO likes to imagine a boardroom inside his head, full of twelve people who all look like him dressed in cozy black turtlenecks: the board of directors of RSO, Inc.

boost that comes from moving your body? Drinking too much? Not sleeping enough? Lacking time with those who inspire you?

- How much of your stress is financial? Are you stuck in a draining survival job? Have you neglected your Hustle?
- How's your website? Are your social media accounts updated with fresh performances—even if they're just you in a studio? If someone searches for you, what do they find—and does it reflect who you are now?
- Take stock of your team and make a list of ten people to reconnect with. One good coffee with someone you trust can spark your fire anew.
- And if no one's putting you onstage, put yourself there. Create your own opportunity. At the very least, it will remind you what you're doing this for.

Remember, you aren't stuck in a time loop. Just because you were told no yesterday doesn't mean you'll be told no again tomorrow. When you go to work, you believe that the subway will run on schedule, even though trains get delayed all the time. In your romantic relationship, you believe it will last forever, even though statistically most fail. You're sure your sweet doggo will outlive all the others, even though whenever *it* happens it will always be too soon.

You're pretty loony for thinking these things, but we're glad that you do. (We think them, too.)

What else can we do in a world as dark and crazy as our own but be a little crazy—and outrageously optimistic? So go on, you crazy kid. It's you against the world.

The funny thing is, though . . . the world is rooting for your success.

We are, too.

NOW FOR THE MEGAMIX

Cue the click track, call cast to stage, and let's sing the greatest hits together!!!

With everything you've now learned, you're able to transform red flags into green flags. Collect them all!

In the package...

- Your specificity *proudly* defines your voice, look, energy, and authenticity, and forms a branding statement when these qualities are combined.
- Discover what makes you singular and don't worry about being generally good at everything. The best thing you can be is the most of who you already are.
- Build a book of genres, so you can follow directions with the material you're asked for.
- Double-check that every song in your book is a perfect match for your specificity and help casting see which roles you're right for.
- Keep all the songs in your book well prepared and don't bring in anything you've just learned—unless they're callback sides.

In the performance...

- In most every initial audition, sing a positive "nice-to-meet you" song in the requested genre to showcase your amazing personality and voice . . .
- . . . And don't lead with a ballad—positive or negative—if you can help it, mmmkay?
- Don't forget that a great cut starts at the middle part of your voice, ascends to an exciting climax, and leaves them wanting (a little) more.
- Prepare a masterful story for *every* song in your book.
- Focus on your action and tactics, always asking, "What am I *doing* right now?" Never "feel your way" through a song by over-rehearsing the vocal performance.
- Musical theatre demands the highest stakes possible, while radio music wants a low-stakes story that allows you to vibe with the music.
- Make sure you aren't focusing on how you sound, so that your hands move naturally.
- Memorize the material, not the performance. Leave your song unchoreographed.
- Practice alternative takes—changing the answers to your story questions, so you're free to take direction.

In the profession...

- Keep eyes on your business plan, review your vision, and check in with your values. Your mission ensures you're keeping up with the standards you've set.
- Regularly revisit your training and remain tuned in to your mental and physical health. Change up your routines, exercise, and classes to stay stimulated and growing.
- Track your finances, budget your cost of living, save 10 percent, stay out of debt, and nurture a Hustle to support your artistic life.

- Nurture relationships with peers, mentors, co-workers, and your "investor group" of family and friends. The people who can help you the most are the ones you already know!
- If you're ready to work, you're ready to create a website and put material on social media—so that when others go looking for you, you know what they'll find.
- Fill your site's video page with mostly single-song videos rather than reels, and work toward filming every cut in your book so you're ready to submit anything.
- If no one is putting you onstage, create your own opportunities via a cabaret, a theatre group, or whatever else scratches your artistic itch.
- Manage your time effectively, stay organized and productive, and carve out necessary "you time."

In the pursuit . . .

- Make sure your headshot always looks like you *today* and gives off the energy you specified in your branding statement.
- Strategize your résumé to let casting know the work you're right and ready for.
- Remember, an agent is your teammate, not your hero. You'll always be the one finding most of your work, and you can find your next job without one.
- As a non-Equity performer, prioritize non-Equity work to build your credits.
- Join the union when your considerable talent meets your considerable experience.
- Wherever you're at, start there and move forward. When you don't know where to start, you can start anywhere.

Break a leg out there. You got this!
Lindsay and RSO

ACKNOWLEDGMENTS

RSO would like to thank his extraordinary support system: Sherry Oliver; Matthew Murphy (who fulfilled his husbandly duty and read every draft); Ethan Carlson; Joshua Zecher-Ross; Kirsten Guenther; Kerstin Anderson; Daniel and Araceli Oliver; Scott Oliver; and Linda, Michael, and Carson Murphy.

Lindsay would like to thank her beloved family and friends: J. Alex Brinson, Lucille Rosalind Wakefield, Ruby Beck Brinson, Michael Mendez, Lauren Hernandez, Mike Mendez, Jonathan Groff, Dan Radcliffe, and Katie Rose Clarke.

Thanks to our reps who helped make this book a reality, especially agent Michael Johnston at CAA, who helped spearhead our idea, as well as RSO's agent, Diana Glazer (CAA), and Lindsay's manager, Craig Gartner.

Thanks to our publishing team led by Leah Wilson and Sarah Modlin, plus Kim Broderick, Morgan Carr, Kellie Doherty, Adrienne Lang, Susan Welte, Alicia Kania, Madeline Grigg, the rest of the BenBella team, and our copy editor, Amy Handy.

We are grateful to the many people who gave us permission to use lyrics and sheet music in this book—above all, the unbelievably generous Rick Pappas for the Sondheim estate. Thanks also to Michelle Ritter at Alfred Music, Michael Kerker at ASCAP, Brad Ross, and Ellen Greenfield.

We'd also like to thank the many brilliant artists on the staff and faculty of Actor Therapy who've sustained and inspired our company since 2012.

First and foremost, Mathieu Whitman, Emily Foley, and Miranda Luze, as well as Chelsea Moss, Adam Chanler-Berat, Afra Hines, AMDA Studios, Anne L. Nathan, Craig Manzino, Gilbert L. Bailey II, Heath Saunders, Jason Wetzel, Jessie Hooker-Bailey, Joe Hornberger, Jonathan Mushock, Kamilah Marshall, Kirsten Wyatt, Lera Zamaraeva, Matt Lowy, Open Jar Studios, Peter Duchan, Stephen Sposito, Sydney Noller, and William Stull.

We thank the many Actor Therapy alums who served as models (both literally and figuratively) for the examples we've used, including Caitlin Doak, Amanda Domb, Holly Marie Dunn, Charlie Fusari, Lillie Langston, Kim Onah, Matthew Moròn, Jack B. Murphy, Nathan David Smith, Minami Yoshimura, and Kayla Zanakis, plus additional photo subjects Sarah Bowden, Jay Armstrong Johnson, Pearl Sun, and Bruno Vida.

We received a lot of help researching this book, and thank Lindsay Levine, Andrew Fem, Todd Buonopane, Bobby Hall, Joshua Doss, and Catherine Shook.

Thanks to MurphyMade Photography, Green Otter Design, Evan Zimmerman, and Alex Michaels for our photography.

Of special note, we thank the teachers and friends who laid the groundwork for our love of musical theatre; we probably wouldn't be in this business without them: Gayle Bluemel, Emily Clark, Stephanie Vlahos, John Hall, Jan Ritschel, David Green, Stevi Meredith, Laurie Younkin Mason, Patrice Barakat, Tim Rosser, and Joe Mantello.

Finally, we owe our biggest debt to all the students we've had the joy of teaching over these past two decades. Without you, this book wouldn't exist. Thank you for trusting your growth with us, sharing your powerful experiences, and asking your insightful questions. Above all, to the students, past, present, and future at Actor Therapy, we have learned more from you than you will ever know.

INDEX OF REFERENCED MUSICALS

The 25th Annual Putnam County Spelling Bee (2005)
Conceived by Rebecca Feldman, Additional Material by Jay Reiss, Music and Lyrics by William Finn

35MM: A Musical Exhibition (2012)
Music and Lyrics by Ryan Scott Oliver

9 to 5 (2008)
Book by Patricia Resnick, Music and Lyrics by Dolly Parton

The Addams Family (2010)
Book by Marshall Brickman and Rick Elice, Music and Lyrics by Andrew Lippa

Aida (2000)
Book by Linda Woolverton, Music by Elton John, Lyrics by Tim Rice

Aladdin (2011)
Book by Chad Beguelin, Music by Alan Menken, Lyrics by Howard Ashman, Tim Rice, and Chad Beguelin

Amélie (2015)
Book by Craig Lucas, Music by Daniel Messé, Lyrics by Nathan Tysen and Daniel Messé

American Idiot (2010)

Book by Billie Joe Armstrong and Michael Mayer, Music by Green Day, Lyrics by Green Day

Annie, Get Your Gun (1946)

Music and Lyrics by Irving Berlin, Book by Herbert and Dorothy Fields

Assassins (1990)

Book by John Weidman, Music and Lyrics by Stephen Sondheim

Avenue Q (2003)

Book by Jeff Whitty, Music and Lyrics by Robert Lopez and Jeff Marx

Bandstand (2015)

Book and Lyrics by Richard Oberacker and Robert Taylor, Music by Richard Oberacker

Bat Boy (1997)

Story and Book by Keythe Farley and Brian Flemming, Music and Lyrics by Laurence O'Keefe

Be More Chill (2015)

Book by Joe Tracz, Music and Lyrics by Joe Iconis

Bells Are Ringing (1956)

Book and Lyrics by Betty Comden and Adolph Green, Music by Jule Styne

Bullets Over Broadway (2014)

Book by Woody Allen, Music and Lyrics by various (adapted by Glen Kelly)

Candide (1956)

Music by Leonard Bernstein, Lyrics by Richard Wilbur and others

Caroline, or Change (2003)

Book and Lyrics by Tony Kushner, Music by Jeanine Tesori

Chess (1986)

Book by Richard Nelson, Music by Benny Andersson and Björn Ulvaeus, Lyrics by Tim Rice

A Chorus Line (1975)
Book by James Kirkwood Jr. and Nicholas Dante, Music by Marvin Hamlisch, Lyrics by Edward Kleban

Daddy Long Legs (2009)
Book by John Caird, Music and Lyrics by Paul Gordon

Damn Yankees (1955)
Book by George Abbott and Douglass Wallop, Music and Lyrics by Richard Adler and Jerry Ross

Dogfight (2012)
Book by Peter Duchan, Music and Lyrics by Benj Pasek and Justin Paul

Dreamgirls (1981)
Book and Lyrics by Tom Eyen, Music by Henry Krieger

The Drowsy Chaperone (2006)
Book by Bob Martin and Don McKellar, Music and Lyrics by Lisa Lambert and Greg Morrison

Edges (2005)
Music and Lyrics by Benj Pasek and Justin Paul

Elegies: A Song Cycle (2003)
Music and Lyrics by William Finn

Everyday Rapture (2009)
Book by Sherie Rene Scott and Dick Scanlan, Music and Lyrics by Various

Falsettos (1992)
Book by William Finn and James Lapine, Music and Lyrics by William Finn

Fiddler on the Roof (1964)
Book by Joseph Stein, Music by Jerry Bock, Lyrics by Sheldon Harnick

First Date (2013)
Book by Austin Winsberg, Music and Lyrics by Alan Zachary and Michael Weiner

Floyd Collins (1996)

Book by Tina Landau, Music and Lyrics by Adam Guettel

Follies (1971)

Book by James Goldman, Music and Lyrics by Stephen Sondheim

Footloose (1998)

Stage Adaptation by Dean Pitchford and Walter Bobbie, Music by Tom Snow, Lyrics by Dean Pitchford

Funny Girl (1964)

Book by Isobel Lennart, Music by Jule Styne, Lyrics by Bob Merrill

A Funny Thing Happened on the Way to the Forum (1962)

Book by Burt Shevelove and Larry Gelbart, Music and Lyrics by Stephen Sondheim

Gentlemen Prefer Blondes (1949)

Book by Joseph Fields and Anita Loos, Music by Jule Styne, Lyrics by Leo Robin

Ghost (2011)

Book and Lyrics by Bruce Joel Rubin, Music and Lyrics by Dave Stewart and Glen Ballard

Godspell (1971)

Conceived by John-Michael Tebelak, Music and Lyrics by Stephen Schwartz

Great Comet (2012)

Book, Music, and Lyrics by Dave Malloy

Guys and Dolls (1950)

Book by Jo Swerling and Abe Burrows, Music and Lyrics by Frank Loesser

Hadestown (2016)

Book, Music, and Lyrics by Anaïs Mitchell

Heathers (2010)

Book, Music, and Lyrics by Laurence O'Keefe and Kevin Murphy

Hercules (2023)

Book by Kwame Kwei-Armah and Robert Horn, Music by Alan Menken, Lyrics by David Zippel

High School Musical (2007)

Book by David Simpatico, Songs by Matthew Gerrard, Robbie Nevil, and others

Hunchback of Notre Dame (2014)

Book by Peter Parnell, Music by Alan Menken, Lyrics by Stephen Schwartz

If/Then (2014)

Book and Lyrics by Brian Yorkey, Music by Tom Kitt

Jagged Little Pill (2018)

Book by Diablo Cody, Music and Lyrics by Alanis Morissette

Jerry Springer: The Opera (2003)

Book and Lyrics by Stewart Lee and Richard Thomas, Music by Richard Thomas

Jersey Boys (2005)

Book by Marshall Brickman and Rick Elice, Music by Bob Gaudio, Lyrics by Bob Crewe

The Last Five Years (2001)

Book, Music, and Lyrics by Jason Robert Brown

The Light in the Piazza (2005)

Book by Craig Lucas, Music and Lyrics by Adam Guettel

Little by Little (1999)

Book and Lyrics by Ellen Greenfield and Hal Hackady, Music by Brad Ross

The Little Mermaid (2007)

Book by Doug Wright, Music by Alan Menken, Lyrics by Howard Ashman and Glenn Slater

Mack and Mabel (1974)

Book by Michael Stewart, Music and Lyrics by Jerry Herman

The Marvelous Wonderettes (2006)

Written and Created by Roger Bean, Music by Various

Maybe Happy Ending (2016)

Book and Lyrics by Hue Park, Music by Will Aronson

Mean Girls (2017)

Book by Tina Fey, Music by Jeff Richmond, Lyrics by Nell Benjamin

The Most Happy Fella (1956)

Book, Music, and Lyrics by Frank Loesser

Moulin Rouge! (2018)

Book by John Logan, Music by Various

Mrs. Sharp (2008)

Book by Kirsten A. Guenther, Music and Lyrics by Ryan Scott Oliver

The Music Man (1957)

Book, Music, and Lyrics by Meredith Willson

Nerds (2005)

Book and Lyrics by Jordan Allen-Dutton and Erik Weiner, Music by Hal Goldberg

Next to Normal (2008)

Book and Lyrics by Brian Yorkey, Music by Tom Kitt

Nine (1982)

Book by Arthur Kopit, Music and Lyrics by Maury Yeston

On the Town (1944)

Book and Lyrics by Betty Comden and Adolph Green, Music by Leonard Bernstein

Once (2011)

Book by Enda Walsh, Music and Lyrics by Glen Hansard and Markéta Irglová

Once on This Island (1990)

Book and Lyrics by Lynn Ahrens, Music by Stephen Flaherty

Pippin (1972)

Book by Roger O. Hirson, Music and Lyrics by Stephen Schwartz

Pirate Queen (2007)

Book by Alain Boublil and Claude-Michel Schönberg, Music by Claude-Michel Schönberg, Lyrics by Alain Boublil and Richard Maltby Jr.

The Prince of Egypt (2017)

Book by Philip LaZebnik, Music and Lyrics by Stephen Schwartz

Rent (1996)

Book, Music, and Lyrics by Jonathan Larson

Road Show (2008)

Book by John Weidman, Music and Lyrics by Stephen Sondheim

Rocky Horror Show (1973)

Book, Music, and Lyrics by Richard O'Brien

Saturday Night (1955)

Book by Julius J. Epstein and Philip G. Epstein, Music and Lyrics by Stephen Sondheim

The Secret Garden (1991)

Book and Lyrics by Marsha Norman, Music by Lucy Simon

She Loves Me (1963)

Book by Joe Masteroff, Music by Jerry Bock, Lyrics by Sheldon Harnick

Show Boat (1927)

Book and Lyrics by Oscar Hammerstein II, Music by Jerome Kern

Shrek the Musical (2008)

Book and Lyrics by David Lindsay-Abaire, Music by Jeanine Tesori

Singin' in the Rain (1983)

Screenplay by Betty Comden and Adolph Green, Songs by Nacio Herb Brown and Arthur Freed

Something Rotten! (2015)

Book by Karey Kirkpatrick and John O'Farrell, Music and Lyrics by Wayne Kirkpatrick and Karey Kirkpatrick

Songs for a New World (1995)

Music and Lyrics by Jason Robert Brown

The Sound of Music (1959)

Book by Howard Lindsay and Russel Crouse, Music by Richard Rodgers, Lyrics by Oscar Hammerstein II

South Pacific (1949)

Book by Oscar Hammerstein II and Joshua Logan, Music by Richard Rodgers, Lyrics by Oscar Hammerstein II

Sunday in the Park with George (1984)

Book by James Lapine, Music and Lyrics by Stephen Sondheim

Sunset Boulevard (1993)

Book and Lyrics by Don Black and Christopher Hampton, Music by Andrew Lloyd Webber

Waitress (2015)

Book by Jessie Nelson, Music and Lyrics by Sara Bareilles

West Side Story (1957)

Book by Arthur Laurents, Music by Leonard Bernstein, Lyrics by Stephen Sondheim

White Christmas (2004)

Book by David Ives and Paul Blake, Music and Lyrics by Irving Berlin

Woman on the Verge of a Nervous Breakdown (2010)

Book by Jeffrey Lane, Music and Lyrics by David Yazbek

Young Frankenstein (2007)

Book by Mel Brooks and Thomas Meehan, Music and Lyrics by Mel Brooks

CREDITS

All music and lyrics of Stephen Sondheim reprinted courtesy of the Stephen J. Sondheim Trust. All rights reserved.

"I'm Not" from the musical *Little by Little.* Music by Brad Ross, lyrics by Ellen Greenfield.

All photography courtesy of Matthew Murphy

Lillie Langston landing page (233) courtesy of Lillie Langston

Jack B. Murphy landing page (233) courtesy of Jack B. Murphy

Emily Foley landing page (234) and video page (235, top) courtesy of Emily Foley

Kim Onah video page (235, bottom) courtesy of Kim Onah

ABOUT THE AUTHORS

LINDSAY MENDEZ is a 2024 Tony Award nominee for her portrayal of Mary Flynn in the Broadway production of *Merrily We Roll Along.* For the Off-Broadway run at New York Theatre Workshop, she earned the Outer Critics Circle Award as well as Drama Desk and Lortel nominations. Mendez won the Tony, Drama Desk, and OCC awards for *Carousel.* Other Broadway: *Significant Other, Wicked, Godspell, Everyday Rapture, Grease.* Off-Broadway/regional: *The Golden Apple, Dogfight* (Drama Desk, Drama League, OCC nominations), *The Rose Tattoo, 35mm: A Musical Exhibition, The Winter's Tale.* On television, Miss Mendez most recently starred in FX's *American Sports Story: Aaron Hernandez* from Executive Producer Ryan Murphy, and previously starred in *All Rise* (CBS/OWN). Other TV and film credits include *Elsbeth, These Little Ones Perish, Station 19, Elementary, Modern Family, Murphy Brown, Smash, The Grotto.* Debut album: *This Time.*

RYAN SCOTT OLIVER is a Kleban Prize, Rodgers, and Larson Award–winning composer and lyricist. He was called "the future of Broadway . . . a major new voice in musical theatre" (*Entertainment Weekly*) and is "shaking up musical theatre with his dark, twisted and genius work . . . [Oliver] could very well be musical theatre's answer to an auteur filmmaker or a gothic novelist" (*Huffington Post*). He wrote the music and lyrics for *35mm: A Musical Exhibition*; *Jasper in Deadland*; *Tomorrow, the Island Dies*; *Mrs. Sharp*; *We Foxes*; and many more. He is also the winner of New Musicals Awards from Weston Playhouse and Pace University, and the recipient of numerous fellowships, residencies, and ASCAP awards, as well as commissions from Disney Theatricals, Universal Theatricals, Broadway Across America, and others. Follow his morbidly optimistic musings @ryanscottoliver on all platforms and listen to his music everywhere you stream music.